D1498224

SEAMUS HEANEY

a reference guide

A
Reference
Guide
to
Literature

Ronald Gottesman,
Editor

Seamus Heaney

a reference guide

MICHAEL J. DURKAN and RAND BRANDES

G. K. Hall & Co.
An Imprint of Simon & Schuster Macmillan
New York

Prentice Hall International
London   Mexico City   New Delhi   Singapore   Sydney   Toronto

G. K. Hall & Co.
Simon & Schuster Macmillan
1633 Broadway
New York, NY 10019

Library of Congress Catalog Card Number: 96-15049

Printed in the United States of America

Printing Number

1   2   3   4   5   6   7   8   9   10

Library of Congress Cataloging-in-Publication Data

Durkan, Michael J.
    Seamus Heaney : a reference guide / Michael J. Durkan and Rand
Brandes.
    p.   cm. — (Reference guide to literature)
Includes bibliographical references and index.
ISBN 0-8161-7389-3 (alk. paper)
1. Heaney, Seamus—Criticism and interpretation—Bibliography.
2. Northern Ireland—In literature—Bibliography. I. Brandes,
Rand. II. Title. III. Series
Z8393.6.D87   1996
[PR6058.E2)
821'.914—dc20   96-15049
                                                           CIP

This paper meets the requirements of ANSI/NISO Z39.48-1992 (Permanence of Paper).

For
Maeve, Virginia, and Jennifer

Beth and Blake

Contents

Introduction

"Shakespeare takes second place to Seamus Heaney as the writer whose name appears most in English Literature courses at polytechnics and colleges of higher education [in Britain]," announces a 1992 *Guardian International* article. Toppling Shakespeare on his home turf is no small task. While it may be more to the point to ask which institutions did not teach the Bard, Heaney's preeminence on syllabi across the imperial isle signifies the phenomenal international appeal of the Irish poet. Readers of contemporary poetry written in English should not be surprised that Seamus Heaney is one of the most often taught (contemporary) writers in England and perhaps in the English-speaking world, notably in America. Heaney's institutional and canonical stature is matched by the immense international scholarly reception of his work and by the almost fanatical media coverage of his professional life in Ireland and England. More critical and media attention has been focused on Heaney and his work than on any other contemporary Irish poet and perhaps any other living poet in the English-speaking world outside of America in the last thirty years.

Between the first reviews of his 1965 publication, *Eleven Poems*, and the recent publication of *The Midnight Verdict* (Gallery Press, 1993), more than twenty full-length studies (books, pamphlets, and collections of essays) of Heaney's writing have appeared, along with over fifty dissertations in which he is a major figure; dozens of interviews; hundreds of articles; and even more reviews, profiles, and notices. These relative figures do not include the myriad articles, collections of essays, and books on Heaney circulating or going to press or the endless number of conference papers presented on his work around the world. The debate still continues as to whether Heaney's international reputation has opened or closed doors for other Irish poets. Whatever the conclusion, this exposure has not been without its professional and private costs, as Heaney comments in a 1991 interview (1991:35): "Too late did I realize that everything like this [the interview] is in a way stealing from me, comme artiste . . . so it's a condition of complete self-destruction [he laughs]." The extreme condition of the poet's self-deconstruction is seen in a 1990 interview (1990:4) in which he says that he had been interviewed so many times that "I don't even believe I was born on a farm in Derry anymore."

If Heaney feels that he has been buried alive under paper after having been strung up in classrooms around the world and then x-rayed by the critics, he has good reason. *Seamus Heaney: A Reference Guide* contains approximately 2,000 entries, which include citations not only from scholarly studies, but also from reviews, interviews, newspaper articles, notices, and profiles. These secondary Heaney materials, when taken together, do have theoretical implications, especially in terms of literary production, cultural reproductions, and canonical constructions—issues beyond the scope of this introduction but worth mentioning in passing.

The immense critical focus on Heaney's poetry, beyond any inherent quality/value of the poetry itself, is certainly affected by market forces in the publishing world, audience expectations regarding subject matter and form, and the institutionalization of the work itself. In some ways the extensive critical reception of Heaney's work is a historical phenomenon related to changes in the academy, technology, and publishing. Who, why, where, how, when, and what one writes on Heaney is more than a matter of interest in the poetry. Each critical response bears the imprint of its occasion and its history. The projected audience, for example, will affect the writing; thus, critics writing in Ireland for a mostly Irish audience work from a different set of assumptions than, for example, American critics for American audiences.

Whether one critical perspective has advantages over another is a complicated issue. Certainly, critics writing in different countries have access to different primary materials as well as secondary sources. Thus a bibliography attached to a book on Heaney published in England or Ireland may not include references that an American critic would consider essential for a thorough understanding of a particular critical issue or vice versa. Consequently, while some Irish critics may complain (but rarely in print) that American critics (or even English critics) have missed the point and have not done their homework when writing on Heaney, often the reverse charge could be made. This is not to privilege one cultural perspective and framework over another, but to emphasize the difficulty in discussing the diverse international response to Heaney's work and the need for a comprehensive bibliography of Heaney criticism.

Even though Heaney himself initially rejected the notion that the vast international interest in contemporary Irish poetry is related to the Troubles, he has more recently agreed with those who argue that many (international) critics are attracted to Irish poetry because of the eroticism of the politics in the North and the post-colonial buzz. "But we cannot be unaware, at this stage of our lives, of the link between the political glamour of the place (Ulster), the sex-appeal of violence, and the prominence accorded to the poets. There was certainly some journalistic help there" (Tom Adair, "Calling the Tune," *Linen Hall Review*, 6, 2 [Autumn 1989]: 5). In particular, critics are attracted to the cultural politics of contemporary Irish poetry because of its unresolved condition. Ireland appears as a never-never land where dreams can come true or where nightmares can be explored with the horrified pleasure of the voyeur. In addition, discussions around contemporary Irish poetry often focus upon women's writing and class politics, topics of great international concern. Interest in Heaney's writing is directly related to the broader framework of Irish poetry and culture, even if this culture is ignored or simplified. The more recent studies of Heaney's work have attempted to come to terms with the complex cultural constructs informing the poetry, especially in terms of post-colonial forces. These highly theoretical studies are a far cry from the initial 1960s reviews of Heaney's poetry which described the poems' subject matter and points of view or speculated on the poet's potential.

From the beginning the reaction to his poetry was positive. As successive volumes appeared he was hailed as "the greatest Irish poet since Yeats," a comparison that Heaney himself rejects. Not all the criticism has been so positive. There is much debate on Heaney's "place" in modern poetry. *Wintering Out* (1972) was accused of keeping too much to the subject matter of *Death of a Naturalist* (1966) and *Door into the Dark* (1969). In *North* (1975) he was accused of sectarianism. In the past ten years some very fine book-length studies have been published in England and the United States. No other contemporary Irish writer has received such full, and on the whole, competent attention. Special issues of journals (e.g., *Salmagundi* and *Agenda*) have been devoted to his work. Bibliographies have been less apparent; the two most important are those by Henry Pearson in *American Book Collector* 3 (March/April 1982), and by Michael J. Durkan in *Irish University Review* 16, 1 (Spring 1986). The annual cumulations in *PMLA*, in *Irish University Review*, and elsewhere are helpful and point to the increasing interest in his work.

Here we attempt to present a comprehensive listing of criticism in the English language since 1965. We have omitted items written in a language other than English, unless printed in readily available publications; we have also omitted brief and fragmentary items that amount to little more than a listing of the work. We have included newspaper articles and profiles because they often offer significant information usually taken from Heaney's own formal and informal comments. This information will be of use to all readers of Heaney's poetry who want a thorough understanding of the poetry, the poet, and the culture. We have also documented and annotated interviews with Heaney in the belief that they are crucial to the entire body of Heaney criticism. Beyond our attempt at being comprehensive, we have included numerous student interviews because we believe that while they are occasionally reductive, they are also of extreme interest as a result of their youthful directness. These interviews often bring an issue to light that "mature" interviews would avoid.

The items are listed chronologically by year of publication. Within each year the arrangement is alphabetical by author or title. Each entry is accompanied by a summary annotation. The entries include:

Books

Doctoral dissertations

Essays in books

Journal articles and reviews

Newspaper articles, stories, and reviews

Interviews

The *Reference Guide* includes material published through 1993, presenting some 29 years of Heaney criticism.

As with all similar compilations this one is incomplete. Many trivial, unscholarly items were excluded. While we have tried to be otherwise all-inclusive, items are bound to escape listing, because of questionable relevance or simple over-sight. We have attempted to verify each citation as fully as possible. We accept full blame for all errors.

Dr. Brandes and G. K. Hall regret the death of Michael J. Durkan while this book was in the final phase of production.

Acknowledgments

Jonathan Allison, James J. Blake, the late Dennis Clarke, Lester Conner, Pat Donlon, Thomas Geraghty, Florence Goff, Seamus Heaney, John Hildebidle, Bill Hubbard, Conor Kenny, Des Kenny, Stephen Lehmann, Lucy McDiarmid, Ronald Marken, F. C. Molloy, James J. Murphy, P. Murray, Thomas O'Grady, H. O'Sullivan (Cork City Library), and Maureen Waters.

At Lenoir-Rhyne College: Hank Cathey, Barbara Herman, Burl McCuiston, Jennifer Roupe, and Robert Spuller.

At Swarthmore College: Libby Amann, Nat Anderson, Nancy Bech, Ann Blackburn, Kate Cleland, Ed Fuller, Amy Graham, Minda Hart, Teresa Heinrichs, Alison Masterpasqua, Julie Miran, and Steven Sowards. We also gratefully acknowledge the assistance of Lenoir-Rhyne College, Swarthmore College, and the National Endowment for the Humanities.

To these and others too numerous to mention, our heartfelt thanks. They have been helpful beyond measure and bear no responsibility for any errors.

Chronology

1939	Born April 13, Mossbawn, Tamniarn, Co. Derry, Northern Ireland.
1945–51	Attends local Anahorish School.
1951–57	Attends St. Columb's College, Derry.
1953	Family moves to The Wood.
1957–61	Queen's University, Belfast. Graduates with first-class honors degree in English language and literature.
1961–62	St. Joseph's College of Education, Andersonstown, Belfast. Postgraduate teacher's diploma.
1962	St. Thomas Intermediate School, Ballymurphy, Belfast. Teacher. *Belfast Telegraph* publishes his first poem, "Tractors."
1963	St. Joseph's College. Lecturer in English. Philip Hobsbaum's "Group" in Belfast.
1965	Marriage to Marie Devlin (August). *Eleven Poems.*
1966	*Death of a Naturalist.* Geoffrey Faber Prize. Gregory Award. Somerset Maugham Award. Son, Michael, born (July). Queen's University. Lecturer in English.
1968	Son, Christopher, born (February).
1969	*Door into the Dark.*
1970	Provisional IRA officially formed in Dublin.
1970–71	University of California at Berkeley. Guest lecturer.
1972	Bloody Sunday riots in Derry (January). Moves to Glanmore, Co. Wicklow. *Wintering Out.*

1973	Visits Aarhus to see the Bog People.
	Daughter, Catherine Ann, born (April).
	Denis Devlin Award. American-Irish Foundation Award.
1975	*North.*
	Stations.
	Carysfort College, Blackrock, Dublin. Lecturer in English.
	W. H. Smith Prize.
1976	Moves to Sandymount, Dublin.
	Carysfort College. Head, Department of English.
	Duff Cooper Memorial Prize. E. M. Forster Award.
1978	*Robert Lowell: A Memorial Address and Elegy.*
1979	*Field Work.*
1980	*Selected Poems 1965–1975.*
	Preoccupations: Selected Prose 1968–1978.
1981	Resigns Carysfort College position.
	Harvard University. Visiting professor.
1982	*The Rattle Bag.* Anthology for children, edited with Ted Hughes.
	Bennett Award.
1983	*Sweeney Astray.*
	An Open Letter.
	Field Day. Co-founder with Brian Friel, Stephen Rea, Tom Paulin, and others.
1984	Death of mother, Margaret Kathleen Heaney.
	Station Island.
	Harvard University. Boylston Professor of Rhetoric and Oratory.
1986	Death of Father, Patrick Heaney.
1990	Professor of Poetry, Oxford University.
1993	Premio Mondale.
1995	Nobel Prize for Literature.

Major Works

Writings about Seamus Heaney

1965

1 CAREY, JOHN. "Lost and Found," *New Statesman* (December 31): 1033.
   Very brief review of *Eleven Poems,* and of eight other works. Carey finds Heaney to be an assured poet; three poems "are masterly."

2 DEVLIN, POLLY. "Seamus Heaney: poems from the back of beyond," *Vogue* (September 1): 134–35.
   The article contains four poems by Heaney—"The Barn," "Lovers on Aran," "Waterfall," "Ancestral Photograph"—and a brief profile of the poet. Devlin first met Heaney in 1962 and describes his wit as always apt.

3 "Poetry in Pamphlets," *Belfast Telegraph* (September 16): 8.
   "Festival Countdown" notice mentions Heaney's contribution of *Eleven Poems*. It also notes the forthcoming publication of *Death of a Naturalist*.

1966

1 BOLAND, EAVAN. "Three Young Poets," *Irish Times* (January 15): 10.
   Review of three Belfast Festival publications including *Eleven Poems*.

2 BRACE, KEITH. "Time for Poetry?" *Birmingham Post* (June 11): 12.
   Review of *Death of a Naturalist* along with reviews of works by R. S. Thomas, Elizabeth Jennings, and the anthology *Longer Contemporary Poems*. Brace records Heaney's ability to recreate his rural childhood, both pleasant and unpleasant. There is much mature poetry in this collection.

3 COX, C. B. "The Painter's Eye," *Spectator* 216, 7195 (May 20): 638.
   Brief review of *Death of a Naturalist* together with reviews of works by Charles Tomlinson, Randall Jarrell, Louis Simpson, Anne Halley, Herbert Read, Robert Graves, and of *Penguin Modern Poets 8, New Poems 1965,* and

1

Poets on Poetry. This is a new voice, direct and vigorous. His poems give us the color and violence of his childhood on a farm: "the best first book of poems I've read for some time."

4   DALE, PETER. "[Book Review]," *Agenda* 4, 4 (Autumn): 61–63.
      Brief review of *Death of a Naturalist,* and of works by Thomas Kinsella and Jon Silkin. Dale finds that while Heaney uses vivid imagery, the imagery is not always relevant. When Heaney gets to work on this problem, "his next book may be spectacular in the best sense."

5   DELEHANTY, JAMES. "Books," *Kilkenny Magazine* 14 (Spring/Summer): 155.
      Brief notice of *Eleven Poems,* and of Michael Longley's *Ten Poems.*

6   DONOGHUE, DENIS. "Penny Worlds of the Poets," *Encounter* 27, 3 (September): 69–74.
      Review of *Death of a Naturalist* together with reviews of works by Randall Jarrell, Louis Simpson, R. S. Thomas, Conrad Aiken, and Rafael Alberti. Heaney's poems remind us of a forgotten rural world. Images in the poetry are informed by terms associated with war. There is much overwriting but the best poems are true.

7   FITZGERALD, DAVID. "Books," *Dublin Magazine* 5, 2 (Summer 1966): 82–83.
      Review of *Death of a Naturalist.* Fitzgerald assures readers of Heaney's poetry that they will not be disappointed in this volume. None of the poems is a failure and there are many good ones. Heaney is a countryman writing of the realities of rural life in sharp detail. Fitzgerald dismisses the possible complaint that Heaney "is not a distinctively Irish poet."

8   GIBBON, MONK. "The Genuine Article," *Irish Independent* (June 11): 10.
      Short reviews of *Death of a Naturalist* and *Figures Out of the Mist* by Timothy Brownlow and Rivers Carew. This work is full of reminiscences of earthy life on the farm where all is novel and exciting to the young.

9   GIBBS, BARBARA. "Poetry Reviews," *Stand* 8, 3 (1966–67): 71–75.
      Review of *Eleven Poems,* together with reviews of works by George MacBeth, Vernon Scannell, Iain Crichton Smith, Harold Massingham, Christopher Middleton, and Tony Connor. Gibbs sees *Eleven Poems* as a sampling from *Death of a Naturalist.* Some poems indicate the beginnings of a style and strength that may turn out well eventually. Though the poems are good and the writing strong, Gibbs sees them as lacking originality and passion that could, however, develop.

10   HEWITT, JOHN. "[Book Review]," *Belfast Telegraph* (May 19): 10.
     Hewitt praises *Death of a Naturalist* for its language and concrete
     imagery. Heaney is an "authentic countryman" who can broaden his range
     through contact with Ireland's troubled history.

11   HOLLAND, MARY. "Poets in Bulk," *Observer* "Weekend Review"
     (November 21): 12.
     Report on "Festival '65" [Belfast] to which is attached a brief reference
     to Heaney as the "newest star" of the Northern Irish poetry scene. Heaney is
     quoted as saying: "The most important thing that Queen's did for me was to
     make writing seem real."

12   KENNELLY, BRENDAN. "Books," *Dublin Magazine* 5, 1 (Spring): 80.
     Review of *Eleven Poems*, and of *Ten Poems* by Michael Longley. There
     is a distinctive style here, direct poetry recalling little incidents with great clar-
     ity. He recalls incidents from the past to "dramatically illuminate the present."

13   KENNELLY, BRENDAN. "Review of 3 poets, by a fourth," *Irish Press*
     (June 11): 10.
     Review of *Death of a Naturalist* together with two other works: *The
     Northern Fiddler* by Brian Higgins, and *Poems* by Michael Harris. This is a
     well-unified book in tone and content. Heaney realizes that spontaneity has to
     be achieved through dedicated effort. He can write with a dramatic or a light
     touch. This is "a startlingly good collection."

14   "Life in Numbers," *Times Literary Supplement* 65, 3354 (June 9): 512.
     Review of *Death of a Naturalist* together with reviews of works by
     Anne Halley, Ruth Fainlight, Karen Gershon, and Francis Berry. The review-
     er sees the poet's subjects as family, growing up in Northern Ireland, and the
     Irish past. While having problems with the poet's imagery, he commends his
     "convincing observation" and his "fidelity to his rural experience."

15   LONGLEY, MICHAEL. "A Young Ulster Poet," *Irish Times* (May 23): 12.
     Review of *Death of a Naturalist*. The main quality that emerges from
     this collection is Heaney's descriptive power; together with his considerable
     imagination, it changes the focus from the local to a much broader context.
     His vivid obsessions show not only the poetry's strengths but also its weak-
     nesses: he tends toward simile rather than to metaphor, toward expanding of
     precept into concept. His rhythms, however, show him to be "a true poet of
     considerable importance."

1966

16   LUDDY, THOMAS E. "[Book Review]," *Library Journal* 91, 19 (November 1): 5408.
      Review of *Death of a Naturalist*. This is a promising first volume. Its clichés are to be expected. The major themes are the tension between forces in the poet himself and an anti-romantic revulsion from natural things.

17   MacE., P. "Poet gives reading of his work," *Irish Times* (June 4): 8.
      MacE reports on Heaney's reading of his poetry at the Lantern Theatre, Dublin. The poetry has much landscape imagery. The predominant themes are the work of the writer and family relationships. Heaney is good at handling complex meanings. He has a wide range of techniques.

18   MARSH, PETER. "Props for a Proposition," *Observer* (June 19): 12.
      Review of *Death of a Naturalist*, among others. Marsh (i.e., Ian Hamilton) describes the volume as "a strange featureless first collection" which is "deeply mannered."

19   MARTIN, AUGUSTINE. "Twenty for the top shelf," *Manchester Guardian* (December 15): 10.
      In a one-sentence review of *Death of a Naturalist*, Martin notes Heaney's "pungent images."

20   MARTIN, AUGUSTINE. "[Book Review]," *Studies* 55 (Winter): 452–54.
      Review of three works including *Death of a Naturalist*. Heaney seems to have come to maturity in a single stride. Poetry is a piece of work, like framing. A craft must be mastered, so also must experience. His message for poets is "before learning to write you must first learn to live."

21   "Poetry Award," *Belfast Telegraph* (April 4): 8.
      Notice of the Eric Gregory Award to Seamus Heaney, one of the best of today's young poets. His first major anthology, *Death of a Naturalist*, is scheduled for publication by Faber.

22   "Poets American and English," *Times* (August 18): 14.
      Heaney's *Death of a Naturalist* is one of several books reviewed. The reviewer asserts that "descriptions" and "flashing similes" are the most notable aspects of the book.

23   PRESS, JOHN. "Some unacknowledged Legislators," *Punch* 250 (June 22): 928.
      Review of *Death of a Naturalist* notes that Heaney "writes with authority," and also that he is "less violent than Ted Hughes."

24 RICKS, CHRISTOPHER. "Growing Up," *New Statesman* 71 (May 27): 778.
   Review of *Death of a Naturalist*. Ricks sees this collection as about growing up. He examines certain poems and commends them for their simplicity and dignity. Heaney finds beauty "in unexpected places." Ricks terms this an outstanding collection and praises Heaney's "technical fertility."

25 ROSENFIELD, RAE. "Belfast Fortnight of Culture and Gaiety," *Hibernia* 31 (December): 6.
   A report on "Festival '66" [Belfast] that describes a lecture/discussion between Heaney and Professor Daniel Hoffman on the nature of poetry.

26 ROSS, ALAN. "Poetry," *London Magazine* 6, 5 (August): 77–82.
   Review of, among others, Heaney's *Death of a Naturalist*. Heaney, like the best British poets of the past few years, writes about the farming community and the life of nature. The image of the gun, which is present in many of his poems, is not a destructive force. He puts old subjects into new poems with a "pungent whiff." This is a tightly written work of great promise.

27 SADLER, GILES. "Gummidge and others," *The Review* (Oxford) 16 (October): 43–45.
   Death of a Naturalist is one of four books reviewed. For the most part, the review finds Heaney's first book uneven and rough-hewn. Sadler judges much of the volume to be "a fairly flat charting of the moral awakening of his farm childhood." The entire volume suffers from "oppressive sogginess." Sadler finds Heaney's description of the sky over a girl on a date as "a tense diaphragm" slightly humorous.

28 SEALY, DOUGLAS. "Irish Poets of the Sixties—2," *Irish Times* (January 26): 8.
   Review essay on Irish poetry. Heaney is the most promising of the new poets. He writes of the life around him in a simple and direct fashion. Many of his poems are seen through the eyes of a child, but when he writes of the world of his maturity he also inspires our best hopes.

29 SMITH, IAN CRICHTON. "[Book Review]," *Glasgow Herald* (June 11): 6.
   Smith compares Heaney to Hughes in his tendency to name things. The reviewer is, however, skeptical of Heaney's solidity and wonders if he "shouldn't give himself more air." He praises "Churning Day" and "An Advancement of Learning."

1967

1   "[Book Review]," *Choice* 4, 1 (March): 40.
      Review of *Death of a Naturalist.* The lyrics are structured with care and give closely observed details of Irish farm life. The language is clear, the pictures sharp. A promising poet.

2   CHAMBERS, HARRY. "Harry Chambers reviews Festival Poetry Pamphlets," *Phoenix* 1 (March): 50–55.
      Brief reviews of twelve pamphlets including Heaney's *Eleven Poems.* Chambers praises Heaney's successful resonance. The major successes of the book are "Death of a Naturalist," "Follower," "The Diviner," and "Mid-term Break."

3   DELEHANTY, JAMES. "Books," *Kilkenny Magazine* 15 (Spring/Summer): 141–47.
      Review of, among other works, *Death of a Naturalist.* There is little introspection in this collection. Heaney is an acute observer of everyday life on a Derry farm. He is a gifted poet who will in time give us a more searching vision of himself.

4   DOUGLAS, DENNIS. "Self-Consciousness in Contrast," *Age* (October 7): 10.
      Brief review of *Death of a Naturalist,* together with reviews of *African Poetry* compiled by Ulli Beier and *The Northern Fiddler* by Brian Higgins. Douglas sees in Heaney's work the quality of "unselfish directness." He also presents emotion in a pure, unsentimental way.

5   GALLER, DAVID. "Description as Poetry," *Kenyon Review* 29, 1 (January): 140–42.
      Galler finds *Death of a Naturalist* an interesting first book. It is "made up of description which remains exposition." There is, however, some gap between what the poet sees and what he perceives. There is an accumulation of details that does not serve well a poet who is good with sound and rhythm. "An Advancement of Learning," employing dramatic action, is a good poem, as are "For the Commander of the Eliza" and "The Play Way." In the latter "Heaney approaches the method of Philip Larkin, the poet by whose example, more than any other's at this point, he might benefit."

6   JOHNS, B. S. "[Book Review]," *Outposts* 72 (Spring): 29–30.
      In a review of *Death of a Naturalist,* Johns concludes that Heaney is not "an original" nor an "innovator." It is the sense of finality and closure that distinguishes Heaney's poems—"the appearance of being a final version of a particular truth."

7   REED, JAMES. "[Book Review]," *The Use of English* (Summer): 25.
    Reed's brief review of *Death of a Naturalist* judges most successful those poems that consider the "natural world" and "the child's growing awareness of the human condition." However, some poems, such as "Honeymoon Flight" and "Dawn Shoot," barely rise above the level of prose.

8   SERGEANT, H. "Poetry Review," *English* (Summer 1967): 192–95.
    Review of *Death of a Naturalist*, among others. Although Sergeant appreciates Heaney's gritty language, he finds a few of the poems "outright failures" and the book generally uneven. He likes "The Play Way," "Scaffolding," "Churning Day," and "For the Commander of the Eliza."

9   SILKIN, JON. "New Poetry," *Stand* 8, 4: 69–71.
    Review of *Death of a Naturalist* and of *Surroundings* by Norman MacCaig. Silkin sees Heaney's poems as explorations of his Northern Irish roots. He writes much about man's connection with nature. There is also a separation between the child's and the adult's rural experience. Some of the poems are incisive and sharp.
    Reprinted 1985.73.

10 UNTERECKER, JOHN. "Songs of Loss," *New York Times Book Review* (March 26): 4, 27.
    This brief review of *Death of a Naturalist* finds Heaney's poetry "urbane, accomplished, predictable." Heaney's "inoffensive" verse is compared to that of Theodore Roethke.
    Reprinted 1985.73.

1968

1   FIACC, PADRAIC. "Seamus Heaney," *Hibernia* (May): 23.
    Brief interview and sketch of the poet.

1969

1   ABSE, DANNIE. "Myth and Symbol," *Irish Press* (June 21): 10.
    Review of *Door into the Dark*. Abse is very pleased with Heaney's second volume. He finds that Heaney can give a sense of mystery to ordinary things. He gives a feeling of grandeur and myth to the various crafts of the countryside. Some of the symbolism is signalled in advance, but where this is not evident those poems are more subtle. Heaney has a great range of tone and lyricism. This volume is homogenous but not monotonous. It should be read as a whole, the poems complementing one another.

1969

2 BOLAND, EAVAN. "World of Maturity," *Irish Times* (June 21): 10.
Review of *Door into the Dark*. Boland sums up Heaney's success in *Death of a Naturalist* as a discovery of his childhood and his creativity. She wondered would he be able to move on to fresh insights and avoid repetition. He has indeed done so in his new collection. There is a distinct group of poems dealing with women that signals his entrance into the area of sexuality. He has moved into the world of maturity, into the world of love.

3 "[Book Review]," *British Book News*, 1969 (August): 632.
Brief review of *Door into the Dark*. This book confirms the promise shown in *Death of a Naturalist*. Heaney's rural landscape has its own eternal values that are reflected in the lives of the people who live and work there. Readers will find Heaney's poetry easy to understand since it is free from "introspective obscurity."

4 BREDIN, HUGH. "[Book Review]," *Newman Review* 1, 2 (December): 20.
Review of *Door into the Dark*. Bredin praises the earlier collection and sees in the present one a sure development in Heaney's writing. The imagery is now more oblique; there is an unsureness, a sense of alienation. Man and nature now live together in an uneasy relationship. There is a search for "moral vision." Bredin sees this book as a transitional work and looks to Heaney to pursue his "arduous search for meaning."

5 "Fear in a Tinful of Bait," *Times Literary Supplement* (July 17): 770.
Review of *Door into the Dark*. Heaney has been praised in good quarters and poetry as good as his is hard to find. However, "in those poems where we don't feel the brooding vision to be justified by the customary dense beauty of his technique, we are probably in the right to come down hard and send our criticism as close as we can to the man within."
Reprinted 1985.73.

6 JENNINGS, ELIZABETH. "[Book Review]," *Twentieth Century* 177, 1041 (February 24): 44–45.
Review of *Door into the Dark*. Jennings remarks that in his first book of poems Heaney brought back to English poetry a feeling for nature. This he does with added passion and love in his current volume. He resembles R. S. Thomas in his subject matter without Thomas's overt religion. His great strengths are technical skill, compassion, and wonder. This book is a little more hesitant, less open and direct than *Death of a Naturalist*, but it is a fine, strong, new book of poems.

7 JENNINGS, ELIZABETH. "Romantic and Classical," *Daily Telegraph* (September 25): 8.

Brief notice of *Door into the Dark*. There is compassion and imagery in this volume. The poet himself is present in his poetry.

8   JORDAN, JOHN. "Heaney re-visited," *Irish Independent* (July 26): 10.
Review of *Death of a Naturalist*. Jordan prefers this, Heaney's first work, to his second book, *Door into the Dark*. There is much more evidence of Heaney's personality here. Jordan maintains that while his three favorite Heaney poems are in *Door into the Dark*, on the whole he prefers *Death of a Naturalist*.

9   KENNELLY, BRENDAN. "A poet with something to say. . . ," *Sunday Independent* (June 15): 12.
Reviews of *Door into the Dark* and of *On This Athenian Hill* by Jennifer Couroucli. Kennelly finds that this book confirms the achievement of *Death of a Naturalist*. The theme is once again the rural world of his childhood. The keywords to his poetry are "shape" and "music."

10   LEAMING, DELMAR. "Midwestern Book Shelf," *Newton, Iowa, News* (December 13): 10.
Review of *Door into the Dark*. Leaming says that while Heaney's use of words is excellent his subject matter is ordinary—the work of the farm and the people who do it with dignity. An association between nature and craft is always present with Heaney. In fishing "in the hidden stream of the common life [the poet] speaks for us all."

11   NICHOLSON, NORMAN. "Two Modern Poets," *Church Times* (October 10): 9.
This review of *Door into the Dark* compares Heaney's work with that of Robert Frost in its "power of making a plain factual statement sound like a moral judgment."

12   PRESS, JOHN. "Ted Walker, Seamus Heaney and Kenneth White: Three New Poets," *Southern Review* 5 (Summer): 673–88.
Press asserts that these new poets constitute a reaction "against the dominant tradition of English poetry from Eliot to the Movement. They are, in a sense, taking up again a tradition which the Georgians attempted to uphold." They share working-class experiences and public education. Ted Hughes is the forerunner in anti-Movement verse and is a significant influence on the three poets. Heaney is the closest to Hughes in his treatment of Nature and in his un-Wordsworthian attention to the terror of Nature—especially from a child's perspective in *Death of a Naturalist*. Press concludes that Heaney is a "physical poet, dependent upon the earth for his wisdom."
Reprinted 1985.73.

1969

13 RICKS, CHRISTOPHER. "Lasting Things," *Listener* (June 26): 900–901.
    Review of *Door into the Dark*. Ricks asserts that Heaney has proven
himself to be "the poet of muddy-booted blackberry-picking." Shaping the
poet's second volume is his preoccupation with "whatever lasts," that is, with
whatever is "founded." Heaney has dropped his Gravesian love poems and
has picked up a "riddling insidiousness" as in the volume's opening poem
"Night Piece." He ends the review with a consideration of "Undine."

14 SIMMONS, JAMES. "Reviews," *Honest Ulsterman* 15 (July): 26–27.
    Review of *Door into the Dark*. Simmons finds the volume more mature
and marked by a general increase in assurance and variety. Simmons likes
"Requiem for the Croppies," "Elegy for a Still-born Child," and "Mother."
Heaney's use of personification in "Undine" is surprising.

15 SKELTON, ROBIN. "[Book Review]," *Malahat Review* (October): 30.
    Review of *Door into the Dark*. While the descriptive verse here is of a
high standard, it lacks real intellectual power. The imagery, physical details,
and language are as good as that of any poet now writing, yet Heaney makes
few demands on the imagination. Heaney's popularity indicates that British
taste is withdrawing "into safe mediocrity." However, since this is after all
only his second book, and realizing the power of his poetry we must await his
next collection "with anxiety and hope."

16 SYMONS, JULIAN. "New Poetry," *Punch* 257 (July 2): 33–34.
    Review of *Door into the Dark* along with several others. Symons com-
plains that Heaney's language is often "drained of colour" and lacks the "vital
energy" of Robert Conquest. Symons finds Heaney's poems honest ("nothing
deceitful"), but also boring ("nothing very exciting").

17 THWAITE, ANTHONY. "Country Matters," *New Statesman* (June 27): 914.
    Review of *Door into the Dark,* along with several others. Thwaite
admires "the clean language, sensuous delight, concise and modest statements." The appeal of the poetry is greatest for those who know little about
farming. Although Heaney's poems are neater than the other writers
reviewed, he must still be considered a member of the "Tribe of Ted
[Hughes]."

18 "With or without nature?" *Times Educational Supplement* 2822 (June 20):
    2054.
    Review of *Door into the Dark*. Heaney's affinities with Ted Hughes
dominate the commentary. Heaney has changed the formula for nature poetry, partially because he remains modern yet true to his subject.

1970

1   BRESLIN, SEAN. "Ulster's Seamus Heaney," *Reality* (September): 13–16.
    In this affectionate essay Breslin provides a brief overview of Heaney's career including an anecdote concerning a meeting between Heaney and the one-time Prime Minister of Northern Ireland, Major Chichester Clark, whose ancestral home in Castledawson was near that of Heaney's in Bellaghy. Breslin also discusses the politics and poetics of the North and Heaney's unsentimental realism.

2   BROWN, TERENCE. "[Book Reviews]," *Dublin Magazine* 8, 3 (Spring 1970): 107–9.
    Brown reviews *Door into the Dark* and Jon Stallworthy's *Root and Branch*. Brown sees *Door into the Dark* as a development of *Death of a Naturalist* while maintaining its high standard. The book speaks of man's relationship to the earth, to its past knowledge, to women. These are poems in which Heaney begins to give us a way of seeing our earth. Here he is tackling larger themes, and shows himself to be a religious poet.

3   BURNS, GERALD. "Innocent Serpents and a Cunning Dove," *Southwest Review* 55 (Winter): 98–99.
    Burns discusses the Irish weather and *Door into the Dark*. Of the latter he says, "A lot of them are magazine poems in the sense that the thinking doesn't go very deep."

4   CLARKE, AUSTIN. "[Seamus Heaney]," in *Contemporary Poets of the English Language*, edited by Rosalie Murphy (Chicago, London: St. James Press): 487–88.
    Following a listing of biographical details and publications, Clarke deals very briefly with the poetry up to 1973. He commends Heaney's work as being "strong, accurate in observation, and concentrated."

5   FANDEL, JOHN. "[Book Review]," *Commonweal* 92 (September 25): 486.
    Review of *Door into the Dark*. The reviewer senses that the accuracy of the poems tells us about ourselves. "As Seamus Heaney recreates living, we too are recreated through his lovely lithe recreations, our false sentiments displaced by living poetry."

6   FANNING, STEPHEN. "Poetry Bookshelf," *Kilkenny Magazine* 18 (Autumn-Winter): 127.
    Review of, among others, *Door into the Dark*. It continues his exploration of the topics of *Death of a Naturalist*. Darkness, in its various connotations, informs many of these new poems. He celebrates too the world of

1970

people, places, and animals. This work is an exciting successor to his first collection.

7   "Finding Masculine Elements in Yeats," *Irish Times* (August 14): 8.
    Heaney's lecture on Yeats at the Yeats International Summer School is the focus of this unsigned article. The reporter quotes Heaney's comments on Frederico García Lorca's concept of "duende."

8   KIELY, BENEDICT. "A Raid into Dark Corners: The Poems of Seamus Heaney," *Hollins Critic* 7, 4 (October): 1–12.
    Kiely takes a look at the landscape in which Heaney grew up. His poetry comes from this country of farmers and artisans who are made into live images. The old Irish poets in the dark monasteries are of great interest to Heaney. His Catholic childhood was in some ways akin to that of the monks—the self-examination, the penance that "rinsed and renewed."
    Reprinted 1985.73.

9   LONGLEY, EDNA. "[Book Review]," *Phoenix* 6 and 7 (Summer): 145–49.
    In her review of *Door into the Dark*, Longley states that it is a greater achievement than *Death of a Naturalist*. Now we have a universal exploration of the dark places of the human psyche. There is also an advance in technique with more flexible and varied rhythms. His words too are enriched with hybrids and adjective-verbs showing a new energy.

10 MAHON, DEREK. "Poetry in Northern Ireland," *Twentieth Century Studies* 4 (November): 89–92.
    The new poets of Northern Ireland have avoided the provincialism of most current Irish writers. They are not so preoccupied with Ireland that their work loses universal appeal. Mahon comments upon the interrelationship between the "ambiguities attendant upon religio-political alliance" and the cultural situation. He traces the major sources and movements of Northern Irish poetry through the sixties (the fifties were "bleak" times); he develops his argument by comparing Northern poetry to developments in the South. He suggests that the South is wrapped up in "narcissistic provincialism," while poets like Heaney have "something to say beyond the shores of Ireland." Mahon plays with the implications of labeling a poet either "Catholic" or "Protestant." He concludes by claiming that the poets do not have to enter the political arena because the "act of writing is itself political in the fullest sense. A good poem is a paradigm of good politics."

11 SHAW, ROBERT B. "Both Sides of the Water," *Poetry* 117 (November): 108–15.
    Review of *Door into the Dark* with seven other works. His second book is in many ways the best of the eight books being reviewed, its own individ-

ual achievement. At ease with his material, which is rural Ireland, its craftsmen, its animals. There are many things to admire: concise language, clean
vision, technique.

Reprinted 1985.73.

1971

1 LONGLEY, MICHAEL. "Poetry," in *Causeway: The Arts in Ulster*, edited by
Michael Longley (Belfast: Arts Council of Northern Ireland): 95–109.

Heaney's first collection, *Death of a Naturalist*, calls on his rural childhood into which he immerses the reader. *Door into the Dark* is in many
respects a stronger collection. He moves from the local to the national level.
The poems also recall the old territories and promise a return there.

2 MILLER, KARL. "Opinion," *Review* 27, 8 (Autumn-Winter 1971–72):
41–52.

Miller deplores the failure of writers to confront the Irish predicament.
Verbal icons, unless they say something that could be acted on or learned
from, do not amount to the power of a single poem. Miller prints Heaney's
poem, "Craig's Dragoons," which was circulated anonymously at the time
of the Civil Rights marches. Miller refers to a sequence of poems "in a journalistic vein," some of which became the second half of *North*. They are
Heaney's most concerted effort to use a voice that declares the speaker and
his opinions.

3 WALLIS, WILLIAM. "Notes on Five Poets," *Prairie Schooner* 45 (Fall):
278–79.

In this brief review of *Door into the Dark*, along with the work of four
other poets, Wallis notes that Heaney's impressive poems are "turgid with
local colour." The poems reach beyond the local and "speak in echoes of all
ages of childhood."

1972

1 BEER, PATRICIA. "Seamus Heaney's Third Book of Poems," *Listener* 88,
2280 (December 7): 795.

In her review of *Wintering Out*, Beer states that after his first two books
Heaney's landscape is still the Irish countryside. There is little about the present troubles in the book. We get well-made poems here as well as the poet's
brilliant and idiosyncratic technique. His concern is with sound and pronunciation in this impressive collection.

Reprinted 1985.73.

1972

2   BOLAND, EAVAN. "Interim Season," *Irish Times* (November 18): 12.
    Review of *Wintering Out*. Boland sees *Wintering Out* still dealing with
rural matters. There is, however, a turbulence and a loneliness in this work
that make it the most profound of Heaney's books. He is reaching out toward
a certain isolation that gives the work its power. He has avoided the innocence
of his early rural poetry and has instead found conflict in his rural world. This
is an eloquent, moving book.

3   BOLAND, EAVAN. "Poetry of the year: a retrospect," *Irish Times*
    (December 15): 12.
    Boland discusses among other books Heaney's *Wintering Out*. She par-
ticularly appreciates "Summer Home." One of the more important but easily
overlooked themes of the book is "language."

4   BOLAND, EAVAN. "Seamus Heaney in Peacock," *Irish Times* (November
    21): 12.
    Boland reports on Heaney's reading from his new book *Wintering Out*.
In some ways it resembles his earlier collections. Heaney, however, manages
to move away from his previous work and displace his memory in order to
grow. His poetry has real strength, and his reading showed force, meaning,
and humor. He tends to gloss his poems in reading them, but they do not need
this help.

5   BOLAND, JOHN. "Winter of Discontent," *Hibernia* (December 1): 11.
    Review of *Wintering Out*. The expectations we had of a wider range of
poetry and greater depth are not evident here. We find better written poems
but not better poetry. Heaney is accused of being too committed to the short
term, of neglecting the Northern problem. However, Heaney remains one of
the few really good poets writing in Ireland.

6   EWART, GAVIN. "Chicken Soup," *London Magazine* 364 (December
    1972/January 1973): 132–35.
    Brief review of *Wintering Out* along with works by six other poets.
Ewart finds Heaney concerned with the natural world. He speaks of the good
competent poems here. However, the reviewer anticipates seeing the political
poems "we are told he has written, about the troubles of Ulster."

7   GILLESPIE, ELGY. "A Political Stance," *Irish Times* (May 19): 10.
    In this general consideration of Heaney's work, Gillespie incorporates
some comments taken from an interview with the poet. She talks about
Heaney's use of history and his attraction to place-names such as Broagh.

8   JAMES, CLIVE. "A Slough of Despond," *Observer* (November 26): 12.
     Review of *Wintering Out*, and of *Preaching to the Converted* and *After Martial*, both by Peter Porter. James notes Heaney's maturity with the addition of a tragic quality. The comparisons with Yeats will follow. The rhythm, the pace of the argument are just right. In spite of this James finds *Wintering Out* too mannered—the human dimension is missing.
     Reprinted in part 1977.14.

9   KENNELLY, BRENDAN. "Lines on a distant prospect of Long Kesh," *Sunday Independent* (November 26): 14.
     Review of *Wintering Out*, and of *Garden of the Golden Apples* by Peter Kavanagh. Kennelly sees three striking, unforgettable aspects of Heaney's new collection. First, there is the awareness of the horror that is taking place in Northern Ireland. Second, even though he is still writing about childhood memory, it is always accompanied by compassion for those who suffer. Third, there is the "increasing intensity of thought and feeling." The book also has its faults—substituting charm for feeling, and a mixture of literariness and earthiness. Nevertheless, this is an important work that gives us the promise of new directions in his poetry.

10   KILFEATHER, FRANK. "Heaney to quit Q.U.B. post for poetry," *Irish Times* (August 17): 6.
     The article originates in Sligo where Heaney was lecturing at the Yeats Summer School. The article quotes at length from Heaney's lecture on Yeats, "The Choice."

11   MONTAGUE, JOHN. "Order in Donnybrook Fair," *Times Literary Supplement* (March 17): 313.
     Montague, in his review of *The Penguin Book of Irish Verse*, refers to the "epigrammatic neatness" of Heaney's verse as well as that of other Northern writers. He describes Heaney as "naturally sensuous" and argues that Heaney's poems seem to be a "ritualized preparation" for uniting his lost childhood and his adult world.

12   PORTER, PETER. "Poets' places," *Guardian* (November 30): 12.
     In this review of "Christmas Books," Porter treats Heaney's *Wintering Out* in tandem with Stewart Conn. He describes Heaney's poems at their weakest "dossier-poems." He feels that Heaney's poems of country life will be "fatally charming to London's literary tastes." Heaney's use of place-names and dialect obscure "the feelings of the poems they aim to illustrate." Still, he likes "The Last Mummer," "Traditions," and "The Other Side," and he believes that Heaney deserves a "high reputation."

1973

13 SEALY, DOUGLAS. "Appearance and Reality," *Irish Press* (November 25): 14.

In his descriptive review of Montague's *The Rough Field* and of Heaney's *Wintering Out,* Sealy classifies Montague's as a poetry of "statement" and Heaney's as a poetry of "suggestion." The review claims that *Wintering Out* contains a higher percentage of "successful poems" than Heaney's earlier work. Sealy quotes from "Shore Woman" to support his prediction that Heaney's development will draw upon his consideration of "the ways people behave to one another."

14 "Semaphores of Hurt," *Times Literary Supplement* (December 15): 1524.

Review of *Wintering Out.* His earlier books dealt with the sights, smells, and people of a childhood on an Irish farm. In this book the tone is more bleak with a sense of the remote past. *Wintering Out* gives the impression of skirting about topics that the poet is "reluctant to tackle head on."

1973

1 BIDWELL, BRUCE. "A Soft Grip on the Sick Place: The Bogland Poetry of Seamus Heaney," *Dublin Magazine* 10, 3 (Autumn/Winter 1973/74): 86–90.

Heaney has found rich images in P. V. Glob's *Bog People* and sees religious and imaginative parallels with the current violence in Northern Ireland. Heaney asserts that he is not a political poet; however, in the bog poems he is coming to terms with Irish history.

2 "[Book Review]," *Choice* 10 (November): 1384.

Review of *Wintering Out.* The best poetry in the British Isles today is coming from Northern Ireland. This collection shows Heaney closer to Kavanagh than to Yeats. Heaney writes out of his language and culture. Because they are unfamiliar with the background, some readers may miss the strength of the poetry. This collection is recommended for all.

3 BRINTON, GEORGE A. "A Note on Seamus Heaney's *Door into the Dark,*" *Contemporary Poetry* 1, 2 (Winter): 30–34.

The rich simplicity of Heaney's verse derives from a close identification between speaker and subject. This union melds nature and imagination, mystery and myth. Heaney's strength is most easily seen in such poems as "Night Piece," "The Forge," and "Thatcher."

Reprinted 1985.73.

4 BROWNJOHN, ALAN. "Berryman Agonistes," *New Statesman* 85 (February 16): 238.

Review of *Wintering Out*, and of books by John Berryman, Stewart Conn, and John Hollander. Brownjohn sees Heaney dealing with Irish history, landscape, and people with great familiarity and sympathy. This is one of the best volumes of the past year and represents a way for his talent to develop.

5 CHAMBERLIN, J. E. "Poetry Chronicle," *Hudson Review* 26, 2 (Summer): 388–404.

Review of twelve works including Heaney's *Wintering Out*. Comments that Heaney's poems rely on his concrete language and on his melancholic, sensitive mind. Light is a thread throughout these poems. He does not insist on a special logic; he speaks simply and clearly in his own compelling voice.

6 DUNN, DOUGLAS. "Moral Dandies," *Encounter* 40 (March): 70.

Review of *Wintering Out*. This book has disappointed those who expect him to confront the troubles in Northern Ireland. What he says about Ireland is passive. His poems are well-made and he uses Irish-English well.

Reprinted 1985.73.

7 DUNN, DOUGLAS. "The Speckled Hill, the Plover's Shore: Northern Irish Poetry Today," *Encounter* 41, 6 (December): 70–76.

In his preface to *Soundings* (Belfast: Blackstaff, 1972), Heaney defends the non-partisan nature of poetry and offers another purpose for poetry—"the retrieval of ancestry." He holds that poetry can make a new refinement of feelings happen. Dunn remarks that "poetry is the perpetual lost cause."

8 GALASSI, JONATHAN. "Dealing with Tradition," *Poetry* 123, 2 (November): 113–19.

Review of *Wintering Out*. The context is Ulster in the 1970s. Personal life is now drawn in more political terms. Language and the bogland are dealt with in a musical idiom. We find the same originality and precision as in his earlier volumes. His preoccupation with the Ulster tongue "may prove a narrowing influence."

Reprinted 1985.73.

9 GARLAND, PATRICK. "Poets on Poetry," *Listener* 90, 2328 (November 8): 629.

Excerpts from Garland's interviews for the BBC1 Further Education Series, *Poets on Poetry*. Heaney talks of being involved with words. For him the landscape is an image as much as an object of description. He speaks of his fascination with early Irish poetry and with the Anglo-Saxon language. For him a poem is "a completely successful love act between the craft and the gift." He ends up with a discussion of "The Tollund Man" and his avoidance of poetry "as a vehicle for making statements about situations."

1973

10   GRANT, DAMIAN. "Body Poetic: The Function of a Metaphor in Three
     Irish Poets," *Poetry Nation* 1 (November): 112–25.
         Grant maintains that the habit of personification, of treating Ireland as a
     human being, is deeply ingrained in Irish poets. He concentrates on three
     poets—Montague, Heaney, and Muldoon—to prove his assertion. He exam-
     ines their work for "full-dress personification"; for anthropomorphic ele-
     ments; and for a conception "of the Irish landscape as itself somehow
     articulate." He finds that in their interpretation of their world the personifica-
     tion of Ireland occurs as an explicit metaphor which informs a range of relat-
     ed imagery.

11   LONGLEY, EDNA. "Heaney's Hidden Ireland," *Phoenix* 10 (July): 86–89.
         In her review of *Wintering Out*, Longley asserts that Heaney's poetry
     always explores the hidden self, the hidden Ireland, and the hidden artist.
     Door into the Dark showed his fascination with the area where land and water
     meet; this is even more visible in *Wintering Out* where it expresses the per-
     sonal exploration. The imagery of dark yards and outhouses reflects the exis-
     tence of the Hidden Ireland. The circle of lamplight in the yard expresses the
     "the whole poetic process of illumination." "This is not only a very powerful
     but also a very beautiful volume."
         Reprinted 1976.18.

12   LUCY, SEAN. "Three Poets from Ulster," *Irish University Review* 3, 2
     (Autumn): 179–93.
         Lucy reviews Seamus Deane's *Gradual Wars*, Heaney's *Wintering Out*,
     and John Montague's *The Rough Field*. He finds in *Wintering Out* the excel-
     lences of Heaney's earlier work, enhanced with a broader poetic and human
     scope. There are human figures in his landscape, there is also a sequence on
     the Northern conflict. Heaney now faces the choice of continuing to write in
     his established mode, or he can choose "to push further into territory he has
     already partly mapped out."

13   MAXWELL, D. E. S. "Imagining the North: Violence and the Writers," *Eire-
     Ireland* 7, 3 ,2 (Summer): 91–107.
         The essay is primarily about contemporary Northern Irish drama. There
     is one brief reference to Heaney and "The Last Mummer." He quotes from
     Eavan Boland's interview with Heaney: "I didn't mean this to be a poem
     about Northern Ireland, but in some way I think it is."

14   MURPHY, HAYDEN. "[Book Review]," *Dublin Magazine* 10, 1
     (Winter/Spring): 118–20.
         In his review of *Wintering Out*, Murphy notes that Heaney has the abil-
     ity to absorb us in his poetry. In the first and strongest section of the book we

are always aware of violence and loneliness. The most impressive series is the "Northern Hoard," which deals with pain in its many aspects.

15   SILKIN, JOHN. "Bedding the Locale," *New Blackfriars* 54 (March): 130–33.
      In his review of *Wintering Out*, Silken considers the two Irish facets of Heaney's poetry: "self-conscious examination and assumed communal sanity." "Restraint" is the buzzword that runs throughout the review. Silkin cites "Gifts of Rain" as an example of Heaney's traditional concerns. He concludes by arguing that the second half of *Wintering Out* is shaped by Heaney the modernist. In the end, Heaney is almost too accomplished for his own good, since he is unable to "deform his reality" enough to "make it strange."

16   SPENDER, STEPHEN. "Can Poetry Be Reviewed?" *New York Review of Books* 20, 14 (September 20): 8.
      Spender briefly mentions *Wintering Out*. He sees the volume as the product of Heaney's "Dubliners stage." He predicts that Heaney's vision will enlarge since "he comes from Northern Ireland, and the Irish situation must be boiling in him."

17   SWANN, BRIAN. "[Review]," *Library Journal* 98 (April 15): 1290.
      Review of *Wintering Out*. He is a truthful poet not given to trendiness. He does not romanticize Ireland but rather presents the harsh truth.

1974

1   CHAMBERS, HARRY. "The Ulster Poets," *Fortnight* 81 (April 5): 12–13.
      Chambers notes the omission of Ulster poets from *The Oxford Book of Twentieth Century English Verse*, edited by Philip Larkin. He makes the case for the vitality of poetry in the province, and counters the objection that it is the newsworthiness of the Northern conflict which gives the poets their notoriety. He compares Heaney's "Bye-Child" with Adrian Mitchell's "I Saw It in the Papers." He argues that keeping a distance from the conflict which surrounds them might for poets "prove the best safeguard for the preservation of their art."

2   CURTIS, TONY. "Door into the Dark," *Outposts* 100 (Spring): 53–55.
      Curtis reviews Anthony Thwaite's *Inscriptions* and Heaney's *Door into the Dark*. In his brief notice of Heaney, Curtis praises the sharp, economical style and recommends him as a model for writers.

1974

3   FOSTER, JOHN WILSON. "The Poetry of Seamus Heaney," *Critical Quarterly* 16, 1 (Spring): 35–48.

This essay attempts to throw light on Heaney's poetry up to *Wintering Out*. Most of Heaney's poems deal directly or metaphorically with digging. He writes of spading turf, ploughing, divining. He meditates on the past, on confrontations with darkness and fear. In *Wintering Out* we see his first dealing with his emotions in a few love poems. These may be preparations for significant work. Heaney's future will depend on his remaining true to his Irishness in diction, setting, and theme while "taking the emotional risks of. . .Yeats and. . .Thomas Kinsella."

Reprinted 1976.11; 1985.73; 1991.33; 1993.14.

4   GARDNER, RAYMOND. "The Irish Quest," *Guardian* (November 2): 8.

After commenting upon Heaney's career and latest book, *Wintering Out*, and referring to his "hallmark" "abrupt semantics," Gardner includes several remarks by Heaney. Heaney discusses a line from "Gifts of Rain" and talks about "technique." He also describes what being a Roman Catholic from the North means to him and how it inscribes his poetry: "My poetry is not sectarian but it has been deeply affected by the smells of sectarianism." Heaney also discusses the moral responsibilities of the poet.

5   GITZEN, JULIAN. "British Nature Poetry Now," *Midwest Quarterly* 15, 4 (Summer): 323–27.

British nature poetry, which is becoming popular again, departs significantly from its own tradition. The post-World War II poets find that the natural world is not ordained for man's happiness; rather, it threatens him with its immense power. Among the poets treated, Heaney emphasizes the awesomeness of living energy and moves from dread of nature to reconciliation.

Reprinted 1976.13.

6   GRANT, DAMIAN. "Verbal Events," *Critical Quarterly* 16, 1 (Spring): 85–86.

Review of *Wintering Out*. Grant sees in Heaney "the mysterious power of words to recreate in the mind the reality of the physical world." This facility is apparent in his new book. There is a new self-consciousness here both about his language and about Ireland. While Heaney is not a protest poet, he cannot remain indifferent to the violence in his own country.

Reprinted 1976.14.

7   JOHNSTON, DILLON. "The Enabling Ritual: Irish Poetry in the Seventies," *Shenandoah* 25, 4 (Summer): 3–24.

The younger Irish poets after Austin Clarke give evidence that as a group they can make the term "Renaissance" valid. They are concerned with the primacy of experience and have a traditional preoccupation with place and memory.

8   MOLESWORTH, CHARLES. "[Book Review]," *Nation* 218, 11 (March 16): 346–48.
     Review of five books including *Wintering Out*. Molesworth identifies Heaney as a "British poet from Northern Ireland." In *Wintering Out*, the reviewer admires Heaney's powers of observation, which are "so refreshingly accurate as to appear transparent." Heaney differs from the Movement poets because his "tenderness" stands in contrast to the Movement's "ironic brittleness."

9   NUNES, DON. "Who Is Seamus Heaney?" *Virginian Pilot* (January 27): 8.
     In his review of *Wintering Out*, Nunes labels Heaney an "Irish Frost." Nunes considers political poetry to be the poet's weakest area. This poetry often becomes "palsied social commentary," as when Heaney "blunders into the midst of the bloody civil war in Northern Ireland."

10   REDSHAW, THOMAS D. "'Ri' as in Regional: Three Ulster Poets," *Eire-Ireland* 9, 2 (Summer): 41–64.
     This essay explores the relationship between place and the poetry of Heaney, Seamus Deane, and John Montague. An examination of their writing indicates the sense in which they may be called regional poets. Ulster supplies the history, inspiration, culture, and setting which they use in their work. To say regional in this sense is not to charge them with narrow or limited imaginations. Redshaw discusses Heaney's first three volumes. Heaney, he asserts, draws heavily upon images of water. More than mere symbols of the creative urge, in many ways they are connected to Heaney's "sounding" of regional language and his construction of place.

11   TERRY, ARTHUR. "Heaney in Winter," *Prospice* 2: 87–92.
     Terry, in his review, calls *Wintering Out* Heaney's most powerful book so far. At the heart of the book is the poet's "complex and passionate view of history." Terry also notes Heaney's "obsession with the roots of language," and connects this obsession to Heaney's intermingling of "place, history and identity." Language and place, Terry argues, find their metaphoric counterparts in Heaney's attraction to situations where "earth and water converge." Heaney also accurately depicts the "numbness" experienced by Belfast residents.

12   WOOD, MICHAEL. "Now and in England: Larkin's Choice," *Parnassus* 2, 2 (Spring/Summer): 33–55.
     Heaney's *Wintering Out* is one of several books reviewed. Wood judges Heaney's volume to be "far less poised and precise than before, and a good

deal shallower." He finds him to be very talented but his current groping for themes "far less poised and precise than before." There is a concentration on sounds of Irish names which can lead nowhere because the names cannot call up the reality behind them.

1975

1 ALLEN, MICHAEL. "Provincialism and Recent Irish Poetry: The Importance of Patrick Kavanagh," in *Two Decades of Irish Writing: A Critical Survey,* edited by Douglas Dunn (Manchester: Carcanet Press): 23–36.

    Allen's essay discusses Kavanagh's celebration of his own locale and his capacity for an intense engagement with place. He adverts to Seamus Deane's assertion that Kavanagh's influence on recent Irish poetry was greater than that of Yeats. He looks at the work of Montague and Heaney (briefly) as interesting test-cases for this hypothesis.

2 "[Book Review]," *British Book News* (October): 20.

    Review of *North.* Heaney is an important and interesting poet. He can recall the reality of things with original yet familiar phrases. There are good, sombre poems here.

3 BOOTH, MARTIN. "[Book Review]," *Outposts,* 107 (Winter): 33–34.

    In his review of *North,* Booth argues that Heaney is "seeking to establish himself against his past." In his discussion of Heaney's use of nature imagery, Booth finds that in *North* the poet uses this imagery for "impact" rather than subject. He discusses "Belderg" in brief.

4 BOOTH, MARTIN. "Roots of an Irish Poet," *Tribune* (Dublin), (July 18): 6.

    In this review of *North* Booth praises the "patriotic undertones" of the book and describes Heaney's interest in myth as "healthy."

5 BRACE, KEITH. "Poet's view of Ulster," *Birmingham Post* (July 5): 10.

    Review of *North,* and of *The Wearing of the Black* by Padraic Fiacc. Brace feels that Irish poets respond to civil war as if to turn their backs on Catholic sentimentality and Celtic nostalgia. The Northern Ireland conflict is currently inspiring poets to write—some are good some are bad. Seamus Heaney, he says, is one of the serious, gifted poets. In *North* Heaney tries to distance himself from the conflict by proposing a vision derived from prehistory. He looks for some ancient sense and dignity in the daily killings. This is "the most original book of poetry in English, I suspect, since Ted Hughes's *Crow.*"

6 BROWN, GEORGE MACKAY. "Poetry and the Passionate Love of Country," *Education Times* 3 (June 12): 13.

Review of *North*. Brown sees this book as Heaney's reaction to what is happening in Northern Ireland. Heaney is angry at the poet's inability to do anything about it. Heaney's poetry has gained from his study of the agony of Northern Ireland. There is tenderness and love as well as pain in this book. There is no better Irish poet at work today.

7 BROWN, JOHN ALAN. "The Nub," *New Statesman* 90 (July 11): 59–60.

Review of *North*, and of works by Alan Ross, George Macbeth, Donald Hall, and Hugo Williams. Brownjohn sees Heaney in this book linking Irish history with the wider northern European experience. Some of the poems are difficult and distressing for the reader. The approachability of his first two books is not evident here. We hope this new and compromising paring down does not become a habit.

8 BROWN, TERENCE. "Four New Voices: Poets of the Present," in *Northern Voices: Poets from Ulster* (Dublin: Gill and Macmillan; Totowa, N.J.: Rowman and Littlefield): 171–213.

In this essay Brown states that the world of nature as seen by Heaney is a powerful presence, often suggesting feminine sexuality and fertility. Irish history too is seen as a feminine, protecting, preserving landscape. He has explored this latter idea in the series of bog poems, in which the bog is the primary reality, receiving and preserving. More recent poems examine the layers of Irish experience and show that Heaney's sense of the self and of the poetic imagination is similar to his sense of nature and history. The bog poems show the poet consciously beginning to identify with victims and their shame. They indicate that he is coming into his full poetic powers.

Reprinted 1977.4 (in part); 1983.9; 1986.10 (under title "A Northern Voice").

9 BROWNE, JOSEPH. "Violent Prophecies: The Writer and Northern Ireland," *Eire-Ireland* 10, 2 (Summer): 109–19.

A survey of several works of Montague, Brian Moore, Yeats, Macneice, Heaney, Behan, Friel, and others shows that Irish writers vividly predicted the years of violence in Ireland.

10 BUTTEL, ROBERT. *Seamus Heaney* (Lewisburg: Bucknell University Press). 88 pp.

Buttel, after a general introduction to the background against which Heaney wrote, takes us through the first three books. He estimates that by *Wintering Out*, Heaney has arrived at a mature vision which, while being authentically Irish, is not insular. This raises the question of what direction his poetry might now take.

Reprinted (excerpts) 1983.11.

1975

11 CARSON, CIARAN. "Escaped from the Massacre?" *Honest Ulsterman* 50 (Winter): 183–86.
    Carson in his review of *North* accuses Heaney of moving "from being a writer with the gift of precision, to become the laureate of violence." For Carson, *North* is an uneven book. Some of the bog poems do succeed in their honesty of observation. The second half of the book does not quite hang together, yet there is more honesty and humanity here than in the first part. "Everyone was anxious that *North* should be a great book; when it turned out that it wasn't, it was treated as one anyway."

12 DENT, PETER. "Seamus Heaney," *Agenda* 13, 2 (Summer): 59–61.
    Review of *North*. Dent sees here a considerable advancement over the first two volumes, with the promise shown in *Wintering Out* continued. Heaney comes to grips with Ireland as both nurturer and oppressor. The faults of the work lie mainly in the tendency towards inflation and the "search for 'verbal imagery.'" Nevertheless this is a fine book with some great moments.

13 DODSWORTH, MARTIN. "Under Duress," *Guardian* (June 12): 9.
    Dodsworth finds *North* a difficult book to review. The greater part of it deals with man's place in Ireland. The dead represent a history that cannot be shrugged off. The poetry is unhappy, overwhelming but at the same time it is strong and raises questions for the reader. *North* is a testimony to "the power of the imagination under duress."
    Reprinted 1977.7.

14 DUNN, DOUGLAS. "Manana Is Now," *Encounter* 45 (November): 76–81.
    Review of *North*. Heaney's poetry is almost a poetry of a felt philosophy. Some may find Heaney's earlier poetry is his best; they are, however, deluding themselves. He shows that poems can be made from the language of the past. He can conduct a narrative for its best effects.

15 FALCK, COLIN. "Straying to the Savage," *New Review* 2, 17 (August): 61–63.
    Review of *North*. Reviewing his earlier work we find here that his vocabulary and thinking have more effect but the emotion is thinner. There are some hesitant wrestlings with history and archeaeology. Though he is not yet sure of his direction, he can still be convincing in his dealing with the Ulster conflict. Whether his talent can carry him further is an issue to be resolved.

16 FORMAN, JOAN. "A Sense of Life," *Eastern Daily Press*, Norwich, Norfolk (July 25): 10.
    Brief review of *North* together with works by Peter Redgrove, Eavan Boland, George Macbeth, and John Kett. Forman considers these poets, apart

from Redgrove, as apprentices. He admires Heaney's precision as well as his economy. "The anguish of a nation is always an impetus to that nation's poets."

17　GITZEN, JULIAN. "An Irish Imagist," *Studies in the Humanities* 4, 2 (February): 10–13.

Heaney's personal reactions to his subjects are even more self-denying than those of most Imagists. However, his success with the short descriptive poem, the choice of the Imagists, would allow them to accept him warmly.

18　GRIGSON, GEOFFREY. "[Book Review]," *Country Life* 158 (August 7): 355–56.

Review of *North*. For Heaney Irish myth goes far back and embraces both archaeological and modern Ireland. History is always actively present in Ireland. These poems are compact; they are not difficult or obscure. A reader has to master the references.

19　JORDAN, JOHN. "An Inner Emigre," *Irish Independent* (June 7): 8.

In his review of *North*, Jordan judges the poems to be honest responses to the Troubles. "Dazzling" is how he describes "Ocean's Love to Ireland." Heaney's language, Jordan argues, has become more rich and more spare. He concludes that Heaney has "given us a clutch of poems where nobility of language and feeling rises from the compost."

20　KERSNOWSKI, FRANK. "Seamus Heaney," in *The Outsiders: Poets of Contemporary Ireland* (Fort Worth: Texas Christian University Press): 143–48.

Kersnowski speaks of Heaney's locale, which is specific and his alone. Much of Ulster resides in his poetry, and his people are merged with the land and its demands. At this stage his diction is pared down, restrained. His poetry though rooted in the North of Ireland, is more generally Irish than exclusively Northern. Heaney is a poet conscious that he is a political creature even though he may avoid politics as a subject.

21　LELAND, MARY. "Holy Ghosts, Early Voices," *Irish Times* (July 7): 3.

Leland reviews Heaney's RTE radio program on bogs, "The Mossy Banks." She includes several quotations from the program, including Heaney's reflection that he saw the bog as "holding our past embalmed so that time after time a slice with a turf spade opens a door into a different time."

22　LEONARD, TOM. "*North* by Seamus Heaney," *Aquarius* 8: 99–101.

Review of *North*. This work is in two parts, the first dealing with the mythic or historic country, the other with the current conflict in Northern Ireland. The first part is difficult to understand without explanatory notes. The writer's insight does not seem to come naturally; the heavy tone is too strained. However, "The Grauballe Man" makes interesting reading when compared with William Carlos Williams's "A Smiling Dane." The second part of the book is much more accessible. "A Constable Calls" achieves the real menace found in the reconstruction of a personal memory and makes it relevant to the current political situation. Contemporary Irish writing seems conservative, and there is, in addition, an oppressive "literary" climate which poses difficulties for the writer in Ireland. Heaney's talent is probably strong enough to overcome these difficulties.

23 LONGLEY, EDNA. "Fire and Air," *The Honest Ulsterman* 50 (Winter): 179–83.

   In her review of Derek Mahon's *The Snow Party*, Edna Longley in two paragraphs at the end comments on Heaney's *North*. She finds Heaney "a bit longwinded" and guilty of stylistic inflation. She asserts that Heaney, who has already proved his credentials, has no need to include the "topical" material of the second section, in which by far the best poem is "Exposure."

24. McGUINNESS, ARTHUR E. "The Craft of Diction: Revision in Seamus Heaney's Poems," in *Image & Illusion: Anglo-Irish Literature & its Contexts. A Festschrift for Roger McHugh*, edited by Maurice Harmon (Portmarnock: Wolfhound Press): 62–91.

   McGuinness examines the worksheets for four poems which were published in the November 1975 issue of the journal *Quarto*. The poems subsequently published in *North* were "A Constable Calls," "Act of Union," "Punishment," and "Funeral Rights." A study of the worksheets show that the amount of revision varies with each poem. It also reveals that technical accomplishment and tone are the result of Heaney's craftsmanship. The poems as they appear in *North* come from much revision and elaboration.
   Reprinted 1979.25.

25 MAXWELL, D. E. S. "Contemporary Poetry in the North of Ireland," in *Two Decades of Irish Writing: A Critical Survey*, edited by Douglas Dunn (Cheadle: Carcanet Press): 166–85.

   Heaney is one of several poets considered in this overview. Although Maxwell is suspicious of the "development" of poets, he still sees a noticeable increase in the complexity and orchestration of Heaney's poetry in *Wintering Out*. The bulk of the essay is descriptive.
   Reprinted (section on Heaney only, pp. 171–75) 1986.41, under title "Heaney's Poetic Landscape."

26 NÍ CHUILLEANÁIN, EILÉAN. "Book Review," *Cyphers*, 2 (Winter): 49–51.
   Review of *North*. Ni Chuileanain feels that Heaney's "lack of ironic awareness," exemplified in analogies which rely upon sexual metaphors, is a

significant limitation of the volume. She also thinks that Heaney, when working in his "somnambulist" mode, "over-insists" on some topics. Heaney's
sense of his audience has much to do with the limitations of these poems.

27 O'BRIEN, CONOR CRUISE. "A Slow North-East Wind," *The Listener*
(September 25): 404–5.
Review of *North*. Heaney writes about many things: Berkeley, the
English language, Spain, Wicklow, but Derry is always with him. He writes
about the Ulster problem with bleak pessimism. He is being compared with
Yeats. There are resemblances, notably their use of the English language. The
subject matter—the poetry of politics—also points up some similarities, but
Heaney's relationship to the political tragedy is that of one who is "on inti-
mate terms with doom."
Reprinted in part 1977.16.

28 SPENDER, STEPHEN. "Hello, Sailor!" *Sunday Telegraph* (August 24):
10.
Review of *North*. Spender approves both the matter and the manner in
Heaney's book. He is setting out to create an Irish mythology and in doing so
is turning for style to Robert Lowell. His vocabulary is original, "every image
is drawn from an armoury." He is the most striking poet in Ireland since
Patrick Kavanagh.

29 STOREY, MARK. "[Book Review]," *Fortnight* (July 4): 15–16.
Review of *North*. Storey begins his review by emphasizing sound and
the play on words in Heaney's work. In *North* the poet agonizes over his role
in society. Heaney shows his bewilderment thus giving his poetry a moving
quality. There is a bleakness about the poems with their short lines and
rhythms which depend on assonance rather than on direct rhyme. The reviewer sees the strength of *North* as its affirmation of "both the necessity and, yes,
the beauty, of art."

30 THWAITE, ANTHONY. "Neighbourly Murders," *Times Literary Supplement*
3829 (August 1): 866.
Heaney's earlier rural poems were easy to like. With *Wintering Out*
he began to deal with the cruelty of human nature. In *North*, his best book
so far, he contemplates the violence in Northern Ireland in relation to earlier ritual killings and massacres. The poems are sensuous, solid, and beauti-
fully constructed, recognizing tragedy and violence without cheapening
them.

1976

1   "[Book Review]," *Choice* 13 (July): 663.
    Review of *North*. This work continues his explorations of Ireland. In a
rich vocabulary he uses memories of Viking and English invasions to relate to
the current violence in Northern Ireland. His best poetry is in this work.

2   BRESLIN, JOHN B. "A Poet for Ireland," *America* 11, 134 (March 20):
    228–29.
    Breslin talks of Heaney's public readings and of his earlier poetry
before discussing *North*. He notes Heaney's fascination with the earth in his
earlier books. This feeling is more sharp and complex in *Wintering Out* and in
North. In *North* he speaks of the bodies preserved in bogs, each with a story
of punishment or ritual. Authority is brutal no matter where it is wielded. The
message however, about the role of the artist in a world of violence is clear:
"Keep your eye clear / as the bleb of the icicle."

3   BROWN, TERENCE. "Contemporary Irish Poetry," *Ireland Today* 884
    (March 31): 4–6.
    In the course of a survey of contemporary Irish poetry Brown considers
in order the work of Thomas Kinsella, John Montague, Richard Murphy, and
briefly Seamus Heaney's *North*. He deems *North* "a remarkable achievement," as Heaney through a series of poems links the contemporary conflict in
Northern Ireland with the heroic burials of the sagas.

4   CLEARY, A. A. "*North* by Seamus Heaney," *Thames Poetry* 1, 1 (Winter):
    61–69.
    Review of *North*. Cleary recalls the fact that Heaney won his first audi-
ence through the simplicity of his poems. As his work progressed some may
have "mistaken his art for artlessness." As his poetry changed, he resisted
some pressure to write "political poetry." Instead he looked to myth to make
acceptable comment on a sordid and depressing time. He has refused to write
comfortable poetry; instead he writes with strong feelings which will disap-
point those who want only pleasant poems.

5   CONOVER, ROGER. "Book Reviews," *Eire-Ireland* 11 (Summer): 142–46.
    Review of *North*. Conover sees the poems in *North* as the result of an
instructive need, as biologic as artistic. Heaney is defining a landscape he
cannot see. His poems are full of tactile and aural responses to objects
buried underground. This mode has been seen before in his work, but not in
such profusion. There is an alert intelligence that understands the underground world of *North*. One of the recurrent motifs is blindness. The general acuity of other senses in these poems seems to compensate for the loss of
sight.

6   CURTIS, SIMON. "Seamus Heaney's *North,*" *Critical Quarterly* 18, 1 (Spring): 81–83.

Review of *North*. The time-honored imagery of Ireland as female comes off well. Although there are fascinating poems in the first section, the colloquial poems of the remaining sections are preferred. There is much in the book about violence and death, yet the overall message is of endurance and rebirth. Much of this is because of the texture of the language.

7   DEANE, SEAMUS. "The Appetites of Gravity: Contemporary Irish Poetry," *Sewanee Review* 84, 1 (Winter): 199–208.

Reviews of *Wintering Out* and *North* as well as of works by Thomas Kinsella, Derek Mahon, and Richard Murphy. Deane states that Heaney's first two books dealt with the private world of the farm. The two books under consideration are concerned with a larger, more violent, more public landscape. His poems now are about words, bogs, love, and the tensions of his native land. In *Wintering Out*, Heaney associates himself with outcasts and victims; in *North*, he finds a way to hear what they say. Heaney and some other contemporary Irish poets "bring again to mind the Yeatsian possibility of an Ireland which could again become known as 'a country of the imagination.'"

8   EAGLETON, TERRY. "New Poetry," *Stand* 17, 1: 76–80.

Review of *North* together with works by two other poets. Eagleton notes the concern with unearthing history by excavation. The disinterring from Irish bogs is a fertile metaphor for Heaney, drawing landscape and history together, giving an imagery for self-exploration. He uses the sound and sense of words as metaphors for objects, processes, and events. The Irishness of *North* lies in this "conjuncture of material grimness and imaginative grace."

9   "The Editor's Column," *Queen's Quarterly* 83: 159–62.

Review of *North*. *North* confirms the high regard in which Heaney is held. He is taking new directions, going under the earth into his own history as well as into the violence of his native Northern Ireland. The poems in the first part of the book explore the prehistoric world, the nightmare of history. The second part deals with the relationship of the poet with his culture, his society. He is unable to resolve his relationship with his violent culture.

10 FITZGERALD, ROBERT. "Seamus Heaney: An Appreciation," *New Republic* 174, 13 (March 27): 27–29.

Fitzgerald in his survey of ten years of Heaney's poetry finds that in the course of the four books published to date, Heaney's work has broadened. With *North* his gift for writing is fully realized. His poems are grounded in Northern Ireland farm life. He moved out from local matters with a short line and a more selective ear. He deals with the orientation of a poet in Northern Ireland. In the boglands he found a memory bank, a master image and

1976

metaphor for the cycle of violence in Northern Ireland. The following poems by Heaney precede Fitzgerald's text: "Sunlight"; "Bog Oak"; "Mother of the Groom"; "A Drink of Water"; "Thatcher"; "Shoreline"; "Ocean's Love to Ireland"; "The Grauballe Man"; "Kinship"; "Funeral Rites."
Reprinted (without the poems) 1985.73; 1986.21.

11 FOSTER, JOHN WILSON. "The Poetry of Seamus Heaney," *Contemporary Literary Criticism* 5: 170–72.
Reprint of 1974.3; reprinted 1985.73; 1991.33; 1993.14.

12 FOSTER, RICK. "Some Playful, Powerful Poetry," *Daily Californian* (May 14): 9.
Review of *North* and of *Querencia* by Donald Langton. Foster deals essentially with the first part of *North*. Here Heaney speaks about the land itself, as it represents Ireland or as it represents the victims buried and preserved in it. Summing up, Foster says *North* is a strong book which deserves a fuller examination.

13 GITZEN, JULIAN. "British Nature Poetry Now," *Contemporary Literary Criticism* 5: 172–73.
Reprint of 1974.5.

14 GRANT, DAMIAN. "Verbal Events," *Contemporary Literary Criticism* 5: 172.
Reprint of 1974.6.

15 IVERSON, LUCILLE. "Poetry," *Soho Weekly News* (March 18–24): 12.
Review of *North*. Iverson sees Heaney uncovering the history of Ireland in *North*. The remains of men and women preserved in the bog are the remains of those who died for many reasons—some for honor, some ritually killed or murdered. In the same manner Ireland was explored and ravished. Heaney has done well in documenting a centuries-old rage and sorrow.

16 KELLY, CONOR. "Doubled in History: The Poetry of Seamus Heaney and Derek Mahon," *St. Stephen's* 3, 3: 42–56.
This lengthy discussion of Heaney's poetry up to *North* (and Mahon's *Snow Party*), anticipates many of the concerns touched upon by later critics. Using Yeats's concept of "doubling" personal observation with historical and political events, Kelly astutely examines Heaney's search for a "genetic memory" in light of a communal identity. The critic begins with a brief reading of "Digging" followed by a fine analysis of "The Seed Cutters." He talks about Heaney's use of the sonnet and his vocabulary of a "native heritage." The essay contains interesting readings of "The Grauballe Man," "Punishment," and "Exposure"—the final poem Kelly calls a "plangent dejection ode."

17   LONGLEY, EDNA. "Books of the Day: Poetry from the North," *Irish Times*
      (April 21): 8.
           Review of the 50th issue of the *Honest Ulsterman* and other *Ulsterman*
      publications, including Heaney's *Stations*. Longley describes *Stations* as
      prose poems set mostly in Heaney's rural landscape and occasionally dealing
      with the Northern Ireland political scene. The prose poem is an artificial
      form, and further, there is "the exaggerated necessity to point a moral and
      adorn the tale."

18   LONGLEY, EDNA. "Heaney's Hidden Ireland," *Contemporary Literary
      Criticism* 5: 170.
           Reprint of 1973.11.

19   MURPHY, RICHARD. "Poetry and Terror," *New York Review of Books* 23
      (September 30): 38–40.
           Review of *North*. Murphy, in his comments on Heaney's career, men-
      tions that his "words not only mean what they say, they sound like their mean-
      ing." The review dwells upon the first part of *North,* in which the poems are
      composed of elements of beauty and fear. Murphy comments on Heaney's use
      of (archaic) Irish words that "are slipped in, like foreign coins in a meter."
      Murphy claims that the poetry of the first part of *North* "is seriously attempt-
      ing to purge our land of a terrible blood-guilt, and inwardly acknowledging
      our enslavement to a sacrificial myth."
           Reprinted 1985.73.

20   "North Star," *New Society* (November 18): 347.
           Review of *North*. The reviewer claims that Heaney's reputation is
      based on aggressive advertising, The Troubles, and the high quality of his
      poetry. The reviewer hopes that Heaney will leave the bogs behind as well as
      political statements, as exemplified in "What Ever You Say Say Nothing."

21   PRITCHARD, WILLIAM. "More Poetry Matters," *Hudson Review* 29
      (Autumn): 457–58.
           Review of *North*. Pritchard is more interested in Part II, where Heaney
      writes about the Northern Ireland violence with dignity and humor. He sees a
      comparison with Robert Frost. These poems reward with rereading.

22   RIDDELL, ALAN. "Poet of Divided Ireland," *Daily Telegraph* (February
      14): 14.
           Riddle talks to Heaney about the context of the poems in *North.*
      Heaney comments that he felt as if he belonged more "to the mystical Irish
      nation than the mystical British one." There are other statements about
      Heaney's conception of the current violence, cultural "humiliations," and his-
      torical parallels.

1976

23 SHARRATT, BERNARD. "Memories of Dying: The Poetry of Seamus Heaney," *New Blackfriars* 57, 674 (July): 313–21.
    Sharratt adopts a structural reading of Heaney's first two volumes. The author explores the "patterns" which inform the volumes. He describes the organization of *Death of a Naturalist* as "coherently chronological" and shaped by a move towards liberation "from farmer's son to teacher." Sharratt considers *Door into the Dark* an organizational nightmare. The lack of structure is in some ways affected by Heaney's failure in many of the poems to achieve genuine "compassion" with the "other." Instead, the author asserts that Heaney engages in "aimless reflection." Still, Sharratt likes the order and penetration found in "A Lough Neagh Sequence."

24 SHARRATT, BERNARD. "Memories of Dying: The Poetry of Seamus Heaney II," *New Blackfriars* 57, 675 (August): 364–77.
    Sharratt's New Critical reading of Heaney's *Wintering Out* and *North* concludes that "Heaney's work has its impact at a pre- and post-political level."

25 SWANN, B. "Book Reviews," *Library Journal* 101 (May 1): 1124.
    Swann in his brief review of *North* notes the place of myth and history in Ireland in which "the past is a natural presence and present." There is no posturing in Heaney, all is earned.

26 TOULSON, S. "Editorial: A return to the land: the new rural verse," *Stand* 18, 1: 4–6.
    Toulson uses Heaney to illustrate her argument that "rural poetry is vertical poetry in contrast to the horizontal verse of the cities and suburbs." She cites Heaney's "Digging," and mentions the bog poems of *North*.

27 VENDLER, HELEN. "Poet of Silence, Poet of Talk," *New York Times Book Review* (April 18): 6.
    Review of *North*. Heaney's monosyllabic poetry covers the sense and feel of things. The Irish experience is shown through images from different parts of the Northern European experience. His history is not in Celtic legends but in bodies dug up in European and Irish bogs. His meditations on the Ulster violence penetrate past history.
    Reprinted 1985.73.

28 WEBB, W. L. "Irish Poet wins £1,000 Award," *Guardian* (November 16): 5.
    Brief story on the W. H. Smith award which was presented to Heaney for *North*.
    Reprinted 1977.21.

1977

1 BEDFORD, WILLIAM. "To Set the Darkness Echoing," *Delta* 56: 2–7.

From *Death of a Naturalist* onward, the tension between art and reality increased. *Wintering Out* resolved some problems and moved towards what was to be the central theme of *North*—language. The language is moving towards clarity and precision. Art is serious, and the attempt to create order out of chaos has value. *North*'s success depends on the poems and themes explored in the first part of the book. These themes are presented within the framework of the Antaeus legend, an analogy of the struggle for the land which brings historical perspective to the Northern Ireland situation. In Part 2 there is a prosaic flatness in most of the poems. Although *North* is Heaney's finest book—one must ask, is this the direction he should pursue?

Reprinted 1986.3.

2 BEGLEY, MONIE. "The North: Silent Awareness with Seamus Heaney," in *Rambles in Ireland* (Old Greenwich: Devin-Adair): 159–70.

Most of this interview consists of a discourse by Heaney on his background and life in Northern Ireland, Queen's University, the political violence, and the "Bog Poems."

3 BROADBRIDGE, EDWARD. "Radio Interview with Seamus Heaney," in *Seamus Heaney*, edited by Edward Broadbridge (København: Skoleradioen): 5–16.

Heaney talks of growing up in Northern Ireland, local craftsmen, bogs, the sectarian conflict, and the punishments meted out for collaboration, as well as the rituals by which Unionist and nationalist neighbours hide their feelings from one another. The comments serve as an introduction to the printed texts of the following poems: "Digging," with its parody by Hilda Murphy; "The Diviner"; "Bogland"; "Punishment."

4 BROWN, TERENCE. "Summer Home," in *Seamus Heaney*, edited by Edward Broadbridge (København: Skoleradioen): 36.

Reprint in part of 1975.8, which was reprinted in full 1986.6 under title "A Northern Voice."

5 CASEY, DANIEL J. "[Book Review]," *Commonweal* 104 (May 13): 316.

Review of *North*. Casey finds this book to be Heaney's best to date. The vision of the Tollund Man of *Wintering Out* is still present. The poet writes of dark deeds, bodies buried in the bogs, and "neighbourly murders" as he reflects on the Northern Ireland troubles. The poems in the book "are provocative, inspired, and well wrought."

1977

6   DEANE, SEAMUS. "Unhappy and at Home," *Crane Bag* 1, 1 (Spring): 61–67.
   Deane talks with Heaney about Northern poetry and its relationship to the Northern crisis. Major poetry will almost certainly be politically one-sided. Humanism in poetry is dangerous because it tends to detach itself from its origins. They also discuss the idea of an Irish tradition of poetry, Kinsella and this tradition, Yeats and Kavanagh as exponents of the tradition, and finally Heaney's own poetry.
   Reprinted 1982.6.

7   DODSWORTH, MARTIN. "Poetry Reviews: North," in *Seamus Heaney*, edited by Edward Broadbridge (København: Skoleradioen): 49–50.
   Reprint of 1975.13.

8   DONNELLY, BRIAN. "Brian Donnelly talks to Seamus Heaney," in *Seamus Heaney*, edited by Edward Broadbridge (København: Skoleradioen): 59–61.
   Donnelly and Heaney discuss writers in Northern Ireland, comparing them with the Irish Literary Revival; the effect of the political situation on Heaney's writing; the seach for emblems to relate to the Northern Ireland situation, and the notion of Irishness.

9   EAGLETON, TERRY. "New Poetry," *Stand* 17: 76–80.
   Eagleton reviews *North* along with eight other works. He comments on the use of myth, which is a productive metaphor for Heaney. It allows him to bring landscape and history into a complex unity and at the same time gives him imagery for self-exploration. Heaney's poetry has moved away from the sensuous encounters with Nature towards a natural world which "is increasingly mediated by verbal categories." He finds in the evolution of words a way of access to the past and to the dominant alien culture.

10 FOSTER, JOHN WILSON. "Seamus Heaney's 'A Lough Neagh Sequence': Sources and Motifs," *Eire-Ireland* 12, 2 (Summer): 138–42.
   Foster discusses the seven-part poem which occupies the poetic center of *Door into the Dark*. Heaney draws upon scientific knowledge of the eel as well as the superstitions associated with it. The poem is an account of the eel's life and the methods whereby the fishermen catch it. Fact and fiction, science and folklore are all used in Heaney's poem, stressing the circular continuity and the fears which "threaten with ancient, magical, and malign power."
   Reprinted (without footnotes) 1986.22, under title "'A Lough Neagh Sequence': Sources and Motifs."

11 HALL, DONALD. "The Nation of Poets," *Parnassus* 6, 1 (Fall/Winter): 156–60.
    Review of *North* together with *The Book of Irish Verse* and John Montague's *A Slow Dance*. This is Heaney's best book to date. The situation in Northern Ireland and the confrontation with the long dead pervade this volume. It is "a poetry written out of social necessity."
    Reprinted 1985.73.

12 "Introduction to Heaney's Early Poems," in *Seamus Heaney*, edited by Edward Broadbridge (København: Skoleradioen): 44–46.
    Brief survey of Heaney's work, including short quotations from contemporary reviews.

13 "The Irish Quest," in *Seamus Heaney,* edited by Edward Broadbridge (København: Skoleradioen): 46–48.
    Most of this account is devoted to passages by Heaney in which he talks of being Catholic in Northern Ireland. He discusses the absence of sectarianism in his work, and the implications of his move to the Republic.

14 JAMES, CLIVE. "Poetry Reviews: Wintering Out," in *Seamus Heaney,* edited by Edward Broadbridge (København: Skoleradioen): 48.
    Reprint in part of 1972.8.

15 MAHON, DEREK. "The Poetic Renaissance in Northern Ireland," in *Seamus Heaney,* edited by Edward Broadbridge (København: Skoleradioen): 55–57.
    Mahon refers to Northern Ireland in the 1950s with the assertion that no writer of any consequence lived there. Matters changed in the sixties with some Northern men at Trinity College Dublin beginning to write; with Philip Hobsbaum's group seminar in Belfast; with the Belfast Festival; and with the founding of the *Honest Ulsterman*. The religious background of Longley, Heaney, Montague, and Simmons is an indication of political and cultural allegiance.

16 O'BRIEN, CONOR CRUISE. "A Slow North-East Wind," in *Seamus Heaney*, edited by Edward Broadbridge (København: Skoleradioen): 50–51.
    Reprint in part of 1975.27.

17 ROBERTSON, FRANK. "Poem for O-level 'Sick,'" in *Seamus Heaney,* edited by Edward Broadbridge (København: Skoleradioen): 25.
    Excerpts from the *Daily Telegraph* for May 20, 1976, on the reaction to the inclusion of Heaney's poem "Early Purges" in the Cambridge GCE O-level examinations.

1978

18 RUMENS, CAROL. "A Writer for Our Time: Carol Rumens on the Poetry of
Seamus Heaney," *Punch* 272 (January): 36–37.
   Much of Rumen's review of *North* is taken up by a sketch of Heaney's
career and speculations regarding his popularity. She sees the volume as a lit-
eral "kind of culmination" of Heaney's metaphoric genius. Despite the trou-
bling subject matter of the book, which is treated occasionally with ironic
detachment, Rumens claims that *North* "seems at times almost an extended
love poem." She concludes that *North* proves that absorbing "contrary elements" can enrich a culture's (and a poet's) identity.

19 *Seamus Heaney*, edited by Edward Broadbridge (København: Skoleradioen).
64 pp.
   Introduction. - Radio Interview with Seamus Heaney by Edward
Broadbridge. - Growing up in Northern Ireland (prose and verse) by Seamus
Heaney. - Poem for O-level 'Sick,' by Frank Robertson. - Another Side of
Seamus Heaney: The Trade of an Irish Poet. Mother of the Groom. Wedding
Day. Honeymoon Flight. Summer Home, by Terence Brown. "Summer
Home" (poem), - Finding a Subject: The Bog. "The Granballe Man." -
Reviews and Articles about Seamus Heaney and his poems: Introduction to
Heaney's Early Poems. The Irish Quest. Poetry Reviews: *Wintering Out* by
Clive James; *North* by Martin Dodsworth; A Slow North-East Wind by Conor
Cruise O'Brien; Irish Poet wins £1,000 Award by W. L. Webb. Seamus
Heaney. - Seamus Heaney and Northern Ireland: The Poetic Renaissance in
Northern Ireland by Derek Mahon; Brian Donnelly talks to Seamus Heaney, -
Biography - Select Bibliography.

20 WEBB, W. L. "Irish Poet Wins £1,000 Award," in *Seamus Heaney*, edited by
Edward Broadbridge (København: Skoleradioen): 52.
   Reprint of 1976.28.

1978

1 BAILEY, ANTHONY. "A Gift for Being in Touch: Seamus Heaney Builds
Houses of Truth," *Quest* 14 (January/February): 40–49, 110–11.
   The setting for this mostly biographical account of Heaney's career is a
train trip from Dublin to Belfast. The long essay is a composite of published
quotations, reports, and interview material. There is a notable section on
Heaney's "The Act of Union," which first appeared as "A New Life" and
alluded to Roger Casement's diaries.
   Reprinted, in slightly different form, under title "Acts of Union,"
1980.2.

2   BIDWELL, B. "A Sense of Two Nations." Ph.D. dissertation, University College Dublin.

Bidwell refers to Heaney's comment in the *Listener* in 1969 that three Northern Protestant poets—John Hewitt, W. R. Rodgers, and Louis MacNeice—were all "born to a sense of two nations" and that "part of their imaginative effort was a solving of their feelings towards Ireland." Heaney concludes that each found a basis on which he could establish a relationship with the country of his birth and that none of the three surrendered his essential Irishness for an artificial British identity. Bidwell goes on to examine the dilemma faced by the Protestant poet born in Northern Ireland.

3   DONOGHUE, DENIS. "Now & in Ireland: The Literature of Trouble," *Hibernia* (May 11): 16–17.

Heaney looks for his own identity in the past and in pledging himself to the Irish dead. He gives to the reader the present "still in touch with its depth." He emphasizes continuity rather than change. The relation between history and current politics can be separated for a while.

4   LIDDY, JAMES. "Ulster Poets and The Catholic Muse," *Eire-Ireland* 13, 4 (Winter): 126–37.

In the past eight years of violence in Northern Ireland, poets have tried to provide a perspective on the events there. Violence and death have been material for writers such as Montague, Kavanagh, Fiacc, Heaney, and others.

5   McGUINNESS, ARTHUR E. "'Hoarder of the Common Ground': Tradition and Ritual in Seamus Heaney's Poetry," *Eire-Ireland* 13, 2 (Summer): 71–92.

McGuinness discusses *Death of a Naturalist, Door into the Dark, Wintering Out,* and *North* in terms of "the importance of connection in human experience" in relation to the "older more stable reference points" of ritual. One of the themes which unifies Heaney's poetry is the significance of ritual and tradition as a source of meaning and order for one's own experience. This theme is apparent in poems in his first four collections. The first two volumes are less figurative, allusive, and "literary" than *Wintering Out* and *North*. McGuinness notes significant revisions made between the first appearance of poems and their collected forms. The essay includes an examination of the "sacred" in Heaney's work and its relevance to the bog poems. He closes with an examination of the function of "ritual" in Heaney's poetry.

Reprinted 1985.73.

6   "TLS Commentary: The Irish thing," *Times Literary Supplement* (July 14): 796.

The commentator discusses the publicity now attending poets from Northern Ireland. Not all of this publicity is useful. By contrast, the BBC 2 program "A Quiet World," to be shown on July 23, allows some five Northern poets including Heaney to speak about their lives and their art. Heaney admits that now may be a time "of exhaustion and purgation, even of tentative hope."

1979

1   BARCLAY, ANDY. "Abide Wood Quay," *Hibernia* (December) 13: 40.

Barclay describes the Memorial service held for Tom Delaney, during which Heaney recalled his relationship with the archaeologist. Heaney also read his poem in memory of Delaney, "Encounter on Station Island." The service was also reported in *Irish Times*, December 14: 11.

2   BEDIENT, CALVIN. "The Music of What Happens," *Parnassus: Poetry in Review* 8, 1 (Fall/Winter): 108–22.

Review of *Field Work*. Bedient notes that Heaney's strengths lie in his rural childhood, his sense of language, and his steady, reposeful nature. Bedient closely examines a few poems in *Field Work*. "The Skunk" succeeds because Heaney has found mystery in ordinary things and because it is heavily influenced by Robert Lowell. "The Harvest Bow" is a triumph of "unusual scope and power." The "Glanmore Sonnets" constantly demand the ear's attention. He is not a thinking poet, and therefore "he has nothing of particular interest to say about poetry or being a poet."

Reprinted 1983.3; 1985.73.

3   CAREY, JOHN. "Poetry for the world we live in," *Sunday Times* (November 18): 40.

Review of *Field Work* and of Craig Raine's *A Martian Sends a Postcard Home*. Carey comments on the maturing of Heaney's personality in his poetry. He has moved from Northern Ireland. The violence there is commemorated in several elegies for friends murdered in the conflict. These sad poems more than match Yeats's 1916 poems. Heaney's poems about marriage are strong and free of compliments. This book shows Heaney to be a major poet.

4   CROTTY, PATRICK. "An Irishman Looks at Irish Poetry," *Akros* 14, 40: 21–32.

Since Mangan adapted Irish language originals, both the English and Irish languages have contributed much to Irish writing. Kinsella, Montague, Heaney, and Murphy are the first group of poets to be fully at ease with the Anglo-Irish speech.

5   DEANE, SEAMUS. "Talk with Seamus Heaney," *New York Times Book Review* 84, 48 (December 2, sec. VII): 47–48.

Heaney speaks of his rural background and the mixed community of Protestants and Catholics living in harmony. The 1947 Education Act was important especially for members of the Catholic community, making possible secondary and university education. He discusses his reading of poets such as Ted Hughes, R. S. Thomas, John Montague, and Patrick Kavanagh; the tension between talent and the political demands on it; and the critical effect of Northern Ireland violence for the Catholic as opposed to the Protestant writer. His leaving Northern Ireland for the Republic was a way of dealing with political and other pressures.

6   DODSWORTH, MARTIN. "[Book Review]," *Guardian* (October 18): 12.
    Dodsworth says that *North* is in effect a history of the origins of the Irish Troubles, "but history overlaid, history the poet would like to cancel out."

7   DONOGHUE, DENIS. "Poets Who Have Learned Their Trade," *New York Times Book Review* (December 2): 1, 45–46.
    Donoghue in his review of *Field Work* surveys Heaney's earlier work. He sees *Field Work* as continuous with *North* but stronger in craft. He now uses a longer line, bringing a meditative quality to his theme. The strength of the book lies in the personal lyrics. There is in them the feeling that the best part of poetry is not in inspiration, but something you are lucky enough to hear and taste. The poems sound so natural that one could imagine they come without effort. Some readers may want him to write political poems, as in *North*. The poet must, however, come to terms with his own sense of life.
    Reprinted 1985.73.

8   DRUCE, ROBERT. "A Raindrop on a Thorn: An Interview with Seamus Heaney," *Dutch Quarterly Review* 9, 1: 24–37.
    Heaney denies being a nature poet but finds that language comes alive when linked with the natural world. Yeats showed him that personal choice of material maintains private values. Moving to the Republic did not make him more Irish, but it allowed him to relate his public to his private life. He was no longer a Catholic spokesman, and his speech lost political color. Religion and ritual have important values structurally.

9   DURCAN, PAUL. "Heaney in Town," *Cork Examiner* (November 12): 8.
    Review of *Field Work*. Durcan notes that in general most poets do not have a feel for language. In contrast, Heaney's delight in language makes *Field Work* an exciting book. All his senses are at work, but the dominant one is the eye, so richly does he convey the seen world. In this work also the subconscious speaks as Heaney risks more than in his previous books. Durcan applauds the music in Heaney's poetry, particularly in his elegy "The Harvest Bow."

1979

10 DURCAN, PAUL. "Seamus Heaney (2)," *Cork Examiner* (November 19): 8.
    To those who say that Heaney is all description and no thought, Durcan opposes some poems in *Field Work* which are shocking in their clarity. He goes on to show Heaney's skill as a reviser in his attempt to get the arrangement right. The revisions show Heaney's "substituting the actual for the rhetorical."

11 FENTON, JAMES. "A Dangerous Landscape," *Hibernia* (October 25): 14.
    Review of *Field Work*. Most of the review is a revisitation of Heaney's previous work. Fenton begins with a note on the jealousy that Heaney's success has generated among his fellow Irish poets. Fenton approves Heaney's modern pastoral and his use of words. With time Heaney's language has gained in compactness. His success brought pressure in Ireland, as he was expected to comment on the political situation. In *Field Work* we can detect the influence of Robert Lowell, which Fenton sees as quite dangerous. Heaney is working with eloquence in "a dangerous landscape" in a dangerous time.

12 FISHER, E. "New Poetry," *Spectator* 243 (December 1): 28–29.
    Short review of *Field Work* along with reviews of two works by Elizabeth Jennings and of a work by John Fuller. Fisher sees one reason for Heaney's popularity with readers is "the richness, yet rightness, of his vocabulary." He writes well of the violence in Northern Ireland—there is no tokenism here. While disagreeing with two passages in Heaney's translation of the Ugolino passage from the *Inferno*, Fisher nevertheless says "he manages to wear an authority comparable to Dante's tone."

13 FRAZIER, ADRIAN WOODS. "Under Ben Bulben: Irish Poetry after Yeats." Ph.D. dissertation, Washington University—St. Louis.
    Irish poets today are able to appropriate Yeats's poetry in deep and subtle ways. Seamus Heaney gathers together many of the concerns of earlier Irish poets. His sense of the importance of a myth to a poet's work is drawn from Yeats, but his peculiar sort of myth—anthropological and linguistic—is abreast of contemporary thought.

14 HAFFENDEN, JOHN. "Meeting Seamus Heaney: Interview," *London Magazine* 19 (June): 5–28.
    In this wide-ranging interview, Heaney discusses Glob's *Bog People*, his move to Wicklow and Dublin, his teaching, and his religion. He talks about Theodore Roethke writing poetry and the fact that there are no rules for writing poetry; the comforting function of poetry; Frost and Yeats; his forthcoming *Field Work*; his poetry readings and Ted Hughes. He concludes "I look forward to time; all I want is a few hours every day to sit and write, or not write."
    Reprinted 1981.18.

15   HALL, DONALD. "The Music of What Happens," *Nation* 229 (November 10): 472–73.
           Review of *Field Work* and of Thom Gunn's *Selected Poems 1950–1975*. Hall terms *North* a superb work; however, he grants that *Field Work* is a better volume. Heaney's subjects in *Field Work* range from Ireland to California. He speaks of love with tenderness, of violence with intelligence. Of all Heaney's qualities, that of *song* is the most important.

16   HEDERMAN, MARK PATRICK. "Seamus Heaney: The Reluctant Poet," *The Crane Bag* 3, 2: 61–70.
           Wintering Out and *North* are divided into two parts. The first, representing Antaeus, contains his most original and powerful poetry. The second, representing Hercules, contain inferior rationalizations on the Northern crisis. In *Death of a Naturalist* he compares the work of digging with that of writing. He looks for water, the music of the earth. In *Door into the Dark* he will pry into roots; he is the poet of the Dark. In *North* the different metaphors gather together for the interior digging which must be done. Poetry speaks from a place of language, and Hercules and Antaeus represent two different kinds of poet. The new image of the poet makes us look forward to his next collection.
           Reprinted 1982.12.

17   JOHNSTONE, ROBERT. "We Still Believe What We Hear," *Fortnight* 174 (December-January): 20–21.
           Johnstone's review of *Field Work* finds Heaney tackling the Northern Ireland conflict, the poet's response to it, and the relationship of the artist with his public. Johnstone admits to certain resistance to Heaney's work because he feels that Heaney's poetry asserts "one 'tribes' point of view." Nevertheless, he considers that Heaney may indeed be one of the few "to use poetry to salve our wounds." Immediately following Johnstone's review is a note purportedly from a school principal in the form of a report on the Hedge School, Glanmore. Heaney is assigned first place but is advised to revise, and leave the dictionary aside; nationalism does not need another voice.

18   KING, P. R. "I Step Through Origins," in *Nine Contemporary Poets: A Critical Introduction* (London: Methuen): 190–219.
           King looks at the first four books of poetry, giving more attention to *Death of a Naturalist* and *Door into the Dark* than to *Wintering Out* and *North*. The clarity of his early poetry has created a difference of opinion among critics and is often underestimated by reviewers. He describes his rural background in many of his poems, yet it would be a mistake to view him as a nature poet. The first two books show his skill in handling image, rhythm, and language, while adding a tautness of line and a spareness of diction. *Wintering Out* has poems about the isolation of the poet. There are also poems about the names of places, poems which capture the land's identity and speak for the

past in Ireland. *North* shows the poet digging down into a past, which is sometimes violent. He discusses the bog's peculiar power to preserve Ireland's troubles, past and present.

Reprinted 1986.34.

19 LASK, THOMAS. "The Hold of Ireland on One of Its Poets," *New York Times* (April 22): 63.

Lask talked with the poet in Harvard and discovered that he is not contemplating a move to the United States. He insists that Ireland is the source of his poetry, "the ground of my imagery." He speaks of the Irish bogs as "a landscape that remembered everything that had happened to it." His first influence was Gerard Manley Hopkins, as well as the litany of the Virgin Mary and Anglo-Saxon verse. They were all absorbed into his poetry, which is his own voice.

20 LELAND, MARY. "Heaney on Heaney," *Irish Times* (December) 18: 8.

Leland reports on a reading given by Heaney in Cork. Heaney was introduced by John Montague, whom the reporter quotes as saying that *North* had sold more than *Lallah Rookh*. Heaney's introductory comments for several of his poems make up the bulk of the essay, including "Casualty," "Triptych," "The Badgers," and "The Skunk."

21 LLOYD, DAVID T. "The Two Voices of Seamus Heaney's *North,*" *Ariel* 10 (October): 5–13.

The two parts of *North* reveal differences in technique, tone, approach, and subject matter. Heaney's own attitude, however, to the central issues and his preoccupations with the role of the poet in strife-torn Northern Ireland show *North* as a completely unified work.

22 LOGAN, WILLIAM. "Dramas of observation," *Library Journal* 104 (November 1): 2353.

Logan in his brief review of *Field Work* comments on Heaney's sharp expression, his complex intelligence, and his luminous imagery. His precision allows him "to make meaning from the idiosyncrasy of his vision."

23 LONGLEY, EDNA. "Stars and Horses, Pigs and Trees," *Crane Bag* 3, 2: 54–60.

Longley in the course of reading Frank Ormsby's *Poets from the North of Ireland*, Heaney's *Field Work*, and Derek Mahon's *Poems 1962–1978* reflects on the questions: Is there a Northern poetry? Have different achievements been linked together by violence? Is there a tradition to which the poet can relate? Longley pleads for a recognition of Northern poetry as a source of strength in twentieth-century poetry. Heaney, Mahon, and Muldoon show the diverse personalities and the new shapes they have brought to the English

lyric. Ormsby, Paulin, and Carson show signs of the problems of belonging to a new generation. Northern poets are very much aware of one another, and the Troubles provide a shared experience. For Heaney, *Field Work* is a return to pastoral and personal concerns after *North*. Longley wonders if too much is asked of him.
  Reprinted 1982.18.

24 LUCY, SEAN. "Irish Poetry in English 1978," *Irish University Review* 9, 1 (Spring): 142–62.
  At the end of this essay Lucy devotes a paragraph to Heaney. He commends Heaney's individual sensibility and talent. He comments favorably on the poet's "linked series of poems" in *North*, where Heaney explores Irish-Ulster history and landscape.

25 McGUINNESS, ARTHUR E. "The Craft of Diction: Revision in Seamus Heaney's Poems," *Irish University Review* 9, 1 (Spring): 62–91.
  Reprint of 1975.24.

26 MAY, DERWENT. "Peace in Ireland?" *Listener* (November 22): 720–21.
  May contends in his review of *Field Work* that the many elegies are more than personal tributes but "mythical representatives of Ireland at peace." Peace, then, becomes the dominant theme of the poems, which are about "the creation of an Irish Harmony." Challenging this peace are the inner turmoils of "conscience" and the outer disruptions of politics. Heaney's view is fatalistic in the end. Lowell's influence helps some poems, such as "Leavings," but hurts others because Lowell's "grittiness" does not mix well with Heaney's "suppler movement." May particularly likes "The Guttural Muse."

27 MERRILL, THOMAS. "Seamus Heaney," in *Dictionary of Irish Literature*, edited by Robert Hogan (Westport: Greenwood Press): 288–90.
  Merrill's essay comprises a short biography, an evaluation of the works through *North*, followed by a bibliography.
  Reprinted 1980.24.

28 MORRISON, BLAKE. "Out from the Shoal," *New Statesman* 98 (November 9): 722–23.
  In his review of *Field Work*, Morrison praises the quality of the volume but regrets Heaney's decision to write poems that are more private. In contrast to *North*, Morrison finds *Field Work* less ambitious, more geographically restricted, reduced in its time-scale, and less urgent in tone. The circle, according to the reviewer, is the central image in the volume and signifies "artistic perfection," "confinement and artistic self-enclosure," and the "infernal circles" of Dante.

1979

29 O'DRISCOLL, DENNIS. "In the Mid-Course of his Life," *Hibernia* (October 11): 8.

Part review of *Field Work,* part conversation, O'Driscoll looks at Heaney at forty. The article mentions that some of the poems of *Field Work* were written while putting together *North.* However, since Heaney once intended *Field Work* to be made up only of sonnets, he did not include them in the earlier volume. Of Robert Lowell, Heaney comments: "I felt that he was telling me things sometimes, silently." He also mentions his relationship with a few contemporary Irish painters, such as T. P. Flanagan, Colin Middleton, and Barrie Cooke. O'Driscoll alludes to a verse-play written by Heaney for the BBC, entitled *Munro,* and asks if Heaney has considered writing a play. Heaney says that he was worried about the personal "I" in *Field Work* since he was "bored to tears by a lot of English verse with domestic settings."

30 PINSKY, ROBERT. "[Book Review]," *New Republic* 181 (December 22): 31–33.

In his review of *Field Work,* Pinsky describes the book as "a less original, less heroically stretched work than *North.*" Nonetheless, *Field Work* is marked by its more prosaic and explicit approach. Pinsky admires Heaney's treatment of human nature in "Casualty," a nature not heroic but "glorious in its individual persistence." Heaney's volume is "literary" in both the positive and negative senses of the word, according to Pinsky. He enjoys the "comic sense" that also informs some of the poems, as in "The Guttural Muse."

31 RANDALL, JAMES. "An Interview with Seamus Heaney," *Ploughshares* 5, 3: 7–22.

Randall talks to Heaney about living in Belfast as a poet and about Heaney's move to the South. Heaney says that he was uncomfortable with being perceived as a spokesperson for the Catholic minority. Heaney comments upon "The Group." He calls Derek Mahon the "Stephen Dedalus of Belfast." Heaney says that he had begun to write before he met Hobsbaum. Randall asks numerous questions about Heaney's opinion of various aspects of Yeats and his public life. Heaney comments upon the differences between *Field Work* and his earlier volumes. He talks at length about the significance of the "bog" to his work and angrily states: "I'm very angry with a couple of snotty remarks by people who don't know what they are talking about and speak as if the bog images were picked up for convenience instead of being . . . a deeply felt part of my own life, a revelation to me." Heaney concludes by describing his 1970–71 stay in Berkeley and by identifying the people and circumstances behind the elegies in *Field Work.*

Reprinted 1985.73.

32 RICKS, CHRISTOPHER. "The Mouth, the Meal and the Book," *London Review of Books* (November 8): 4–5.
      Review of *Field Work*. This is an even better book than *North*. In *North* the poems were enlightened; here he shows that there is something more primary than enlightenment. Heaney is a poet of trust. It shows in this work in the love poems and in the poems of an Ireland torn by mistrust, such as "After a Killing." Heaney's trust in his influences (other poets) is a central element of his work.

33 SHAW, ROBERT B. "High Notes and Low," *Poetry* 129 (January): 233–39.
      Review of four works including *North*. Better than his previous three, it shows a new departure in its concern with public events. Heaney, however, is not a "political zealot" or "journalistic commentator." He places events in their historical context and makes them understandable. His "explanations" of the bog are forays back into the long and bloody history of Ireland. He acts out the civil war in his own mind. Diction, vivid phrases, and conciseness are much evident in this book. This is a work of balance: he deals with public concerns but will not "degenerate into fanaticism."

34 SILVERLIGHT, JOHN. "Brooding Images," *Observer* (November 11): 37.
      In his profile of Heaney, Silverlight discusses *North, Stations*, and *Field Work*. He describes the poet as "a hefty man (very conscious of his waistline)." Silverlight quotes Heaney as saying the decision to leave Belfast "was taken almost somnabulistically." He also cites the poet's comment that "I am very conscious of being set up as the fall guy," when talking about the comparison with Yeats and his success.

35 SMYTH, GERARD. "Change of Idiom," *Irish Times: Weekend Supplement* (October 20): 6.
      Smyth opens his review of *Field Work* by declaring that in Heaney's previous two books the poet has "over-harvested the buried past." Despite this severe limitation, Smyth likes what he sees in *Field Work*, especially the influence of Dante. He appreciates Heaney's intermingling and mirroring of love and nature—the human and non-human realms. The least successful poem in the volume, he argues, is "The Toome Road," but he likes the elegies to Lowell and O Riada.

36 STEIR, VIVIAN. "An Interview with Seamus Heaney," *The Advocate*: 4–9.
      Heaney responds to questions about the influence of the Irish and English traditions upon his work. He finds that the distinction can be an "artificial one." He talks about the place-name poems of *Wintering Out* as a way of dealing with "cultural and political differences through language." John Montague's essay "The Primal Gaeltacht" is referred to, as well as works by Ted Hughes. Heaney says that he did not join "The Peace Movement, the

1979

Troops Out Movement or the SLDP" because he wants to respond to the situation "in my own way." The process of revision, his move to the Republic, and his writing practices are also touched upon.

37   STEVENSON, ANNE. "The Recognition of the Savage God: Poetry in Britain Today," *New England Review* 2 (Winter): 315–26.
         A. Alvarez's concept of the savage god (A. Alvarez, *The Savage God: A Study of Suicide.* London: Weidenfeld, 1971), informs Stevenson's discussion of the poetry of post-Movement, post-Group poets Ted Hughes, Peter Redgrove, and Seamus Heaney. Although Stevenson agrees with Alvarez's argument that contemporary "British" poetry is rooted in the primitive and the violent, she concludes that Hughes, Redgrove, and Heaney have managed to avoid the self-sacrificing, self-destructive energies and conventions which have harmed other poets. One reason these three poets have survived, according to Stevenson, is because of a general shift from Freudian to Jungian paradigms. She refers specifically to *North* and *Field Work*.
         Reprinted (brief excerpt) 1983.41.

38   TAYLOR, ROBERT. "Book-making," *Boston Globe*, Book Page (June 17): 1.
         Taylor quotes Heaney and Mahon in this brief article. Heaney talks about leaving the North and about reading "wallops of American Indian poetry" in preparation for his anthology with Ted Hughes.

39   TAYLOR, ROBERT. "The Reflections of Poet Seamus Heaney," *Boston Globe* (December 12): 72.
         Taylor remarks in his review of *Field Work* that by moving to Glanmore, Heaney "chose the harder path of allegiance to poetry" instead of political alliance in the North. Taylor divides the volume into three parts: semipublic, the Glanmore Sonnets, and private poems.

40   WATERMAN, ANDREW. "Ulsterectomy," in *Best of the Poetry Year 6*, edited by Dannie Abse (London: Robson): 42–57.
         Waterman asserts that poets in Northern Ireland have benefited from Heaney's star quality and from the interest generated by the "troubles." What has come into being is "a banana republic of letters." He notes Heaney's distinctive "talent for verbal realization" of his subject-matter. The so-called Ulster "literary renaissance" does not search into itself; it is "poetic wallpaper."

41   ZOUTENBIER, RITA. "The Matter of Ireland and the Poetry of Seamus Heaney," *Dutch Quarterly Review* 9, 1: 4–23.
         Heaney's poetry starts from a sense of displacement, which leads to a search for identity through language. There is a continuous development in the four volumes so far published, in which he increasingly submits himself to Ireland's history. Heaney's poetry is based upon a sense of personal and cul-

tural displacement; consequently he searches for his roots and his identity. Heaney has constructed an identity out of language itself. An analysis of each volume follows. In various poems one can see the influence of Hopkins, Frost, Yeats, and Joyce.

Reprinted 1986.59.

1980

1   ALVAREZ, A. "A Fine Way with Language," *New York Review of Books* 27 (March 6): 16–17.

Review of *Field Work*. Alvarez ponders on Heaney's unprecedented acceptance by readers and critics and attributes it to the lack of "contemporary English taste." They are besotted with Heaney for his way with words, for his being a rural poet, and because he writes in a recognizable tradition. He is also a very literary writer and this sometimes leads him into pedantry—his verbal affectations intrude. In *North* he seemed to have found an absorbing theme which he treated in simple poems. That is absent from *Field Work* where he plays the verbal showman. His strength is in modest little poems, such as "The Skunk." He is appreciated in England because he does not upset or scare; he writes beautiful minor poetry.

Reprinted 1983.1; 1985.73.

2   BAILEY, ANTHONY. "Acts of Union," in *Acts of Union: Reports on Ireland, 1973–79* (New York: Random House): 123–38.

Reprint, in slightly different form, of 1978.1, where it appeared under title "A Gift for Being in Touch: Seamus Heaney Builds Houses of Truth."

3   BAILEY, ANTHONY. "Irish Miles," in *Acts of Union: Reports on Ireland 1973–79* (New York: Random House): 170–209.

Reprint, in a slightly different version, of 1980.4.

4   BAILEY, ANTHONY. "A Reporter at Large: Walk along the Boyne," *New Yorker* 56 (June 2): 92, 95–122.

Bailey describes a walk with Heaney along the Boyne river from Trim to Bective, to Tara, to Slane, at which point Heaney returns to Dublin. Along the way there is much talk of history, archaeology, landscape, the Irish character, and inevitably the weather.

Reprinted, in a slightly different version, 1980.3.

5   BAYLEY, JOHN. "Seamus Heaney's prose: What started him as a poet was 'the slap of soggy peat,'" *Listener* 104, 2688 (November 20): 691–92.

Bayley, in his review of *Preoccupations*, says Heaney is the exception to those poets who comment on their own work—he is interesting and he has a feel for good manners. The mythology of the bog gave him the images and subject matter for some of his important poetry. He contemplates the need to escape the pull of nation, religion, and culture. He has a confidence and reassurance in his use of ordinary language which "is something to be grateful for and to admire."

6   BEDIENT, CALVIN. "New Confessions," *Sewanee Review* 88: 482–83.
    Brief note on Heaney's poetry pointing out its strengths as well as its lack of being "strugglingly innovative like Hughes and Kinsella."

7   BLOOM, HAROLD. "The Voice of Kinship," *Times Literary Supplement* (February 8): 137–38.
    Review of *Field Work*. Bloom looks back at Heaney's five books of poetry. *Death of a Naturalist* speaks of the earth and the redemption of poetic work. *Door into the Dark* was mostly a repetition in a finer tone. In *Wintering Out* the poet questions his own language. In *North* and *Field Work* he compares Heaney to Yeats. Heaney's problem now is how to avoid becoming entangled in politics.
    Reprinted (excerpts) 1983.4; reprinted 1985.73; 1986.5 (under title "Introduction").

8   "[Book Review]," *Choice* 17 (May): 388.
    Very brief review of *Field Work*.

9   BRESLIN, JOHN B. "Poetry of the Five Senses," *Washington Post Book World* (January 6): 5.
    Review of *Field Work*. Breslin finds that Heaney's poetry celebrates the sensuous part of life, friendship, and civil war. The elegies for relatives and friends killed through political violence point out the randomness of the deaths as well as the personal loss. In *North* the Nordic sagas had prominence; here Dante is the informing personality. Heaney's great gift for music is shown in the "Glanmore Sonnets" sequence. Heaney belongs at the front of contemporary poets.

10 BROWNJOHN, ALAN. "An Unprovincial Province: New Poetry," *Encounter* 54, 1 (January): 64–70.
    Review of ten books of poetry including *Field Work*. Death is present in this appealing book. However, in every poem of sorrow there is also life and hope. The personal poems are now more complex; the range and control are impressive.

11 CASEY, DANIEL J. "Ireland, Poetry and Prose," *America* 142 (February 2): 86.

Review of *Field Work*. Casey sees in Heaney a fascination with things of the earth as there is with the subsoil of language—words. Violence is present and has to be acknowledged. The centerpiece, the "Glanmore Sonnets," is a set of well crafted meditations. This book "shores up our flagging faith in language and the land," and secures Heaney's reputation as a major poet.
Reprinted 1985.73.

12 CONOVER, ROGER. "Book Reviews," *Eire-Ireland* 15, 1 (Spring): 149–52.
In his review of *Field Work*, Conover asserts that the poet has given readers a "door into the light." The reviewer also feels that the "spell of the bog is broken." Heaney has also left behind the mythological foundations of earlier work and now writes about real people. Animals are a central concern of the book, as in "The Badgers," "The Otter," and "The Skunk." Heaney still does not write pressurized love poems. Conover believes that the Dante translation at the end of the book reflects Heaney's concern with the concept of "Catholic Poet."

13 COTT, JAMES L. "Ireland's Second Coming," *Harvard Crimson* 171, 7 (February 6): 2.
Review of *Field Work*. Cott describes the work as imbued with Heaney's leaving Belfast and with political images. The poet tries to reconcile the life of the family with that of the artist, a dilemma which he never resolves. Many of the poems are elegies, but Cott sees the "Glanmore Sonnets" as the high point of the collection. Heaney puts words together as a musician does with notes. There are problems with line breaks and with the coupling of abstractions. Nevertheless, this is a strong achievement.

14 CURTIS, SIMON. "[Book Review]," *Critical Quarterly* 22, 4 (Winter): 81–82.
Brief review of *Field Work* and of Roger Frith's *Immortality Farm*. Curtis sees the work as a chastening and an inspiring one: chastening in the descriptions of the violence in Northern Ireland; inspiring in the descriptions of the solace of love, friendship, and the continuities of rural life. Heaney's use of language is rich and confident, and he is prepared to take risks.

15 DONNELLY, BRIAN. "The Artful Voyeurs—Aspects of Northern Irish Poetry," *Meddelelser fra Gymnaieskolernes Engelskalererforening* 88 (May) 25–40.
Donnelly selects the poetry of Heaney and Derek Mahon to illustrate "the diversity of response to events in the North [of Ireland] over the last decade." He sees Heaney's first two books as hinting at the directions of the later poetry in pointing to his awareness of the antiquity of Irish history and the potential of the bog as metaphor in his attempt to define his own feelings about the Northern conflict. This approach raises the problem of distancing the

poet and his audience from the reality of the events he describes. This tension between isolation from the events and their actuality produces some of his best poetry.

16   EWART, GAVIN. "[Book Review]," *British Book News* (February): 116–17.
      Ewart in his review of *Field Work* finds the work elegaic in tone while not ignoring the current tragic situation. The rhyme and assonance of the "Glanmore Sonnets" give them a certain freshness which is marred somewhat when the rhymes vanish completely.

17   GROSHOLZ, EMILY. "Poetry Chronicle," *Hudson Review* 33, 2 (Summer): 292–308.
      Review of fourteen works including *Field Work*. In her brief review, Grosholz is not surprised that political violence and senseless death are the subject of some of the poems. The book, however, is not overshadowed by death; life is dealt with "particularly in a series of lovely, unsentimental and very moving poems to the poet's wife."

18   LONGLEY, EDNA. "Heaney—Poet as Critic," *Fortnight* (December): 15–16.
      Review of *Preoccupations* and of *Selected Poems* 1965–1975. These books "complement one another perfectly, almost too perfectly." Heaney's criticism is that of a poet, and he is not tempted by theory. His poetry is ultimately also about poetry. The development of the prose underlines that of the poetry, in showing Heaney as "increasingly perplexed between feminine and masculine, instinctive and conscious. . .vowel and consonant. . . ."

19   LYNCH, BRIAN. "Poet on the brink," *Sunday Press* (January 20): 22.
      Review of *Field Work*. Lynch comments on Heaney's gift for the sounds and meanings of words. For Lynch, the best book by Heaney up to this time has been *Door into the Dark*. The forces of nature, particularly the bog, calmed and also weighed on the poet's mind in the following books. In *Field Work* there is a new maturity as the poet seeks to justify poetry's place in the world. Lynch admires the shape of the work in spite of some weaknesses. There are public poems, elegies, and poems of marriage and love, all written with "the old understanding for words and the new maturity of consciousness." This book will be looked on as a landmark in Heaney's career.

20   McAULEY, LIAM. "Premier in a crop of premieres," *Sunday Times* (London, October 5): 39.
      In this brief notice, McAuley reviews *Selected Poems 1965–1975* and *Preoccupations*. He quotes Heaney as saying he was tempted to change a line in "Digging." Heaney does not say which line.

21 MARTEN, HARRY. "'Singing the Darkness into the Light': Reflections on Recent Irish Poetry," *New England Review* 3: 141–49.

Marten looks at the recent work of five contemporary Irish poets, including Heaney's *Field Work*. Marten places Heaney's volume somewhere between Kinsella's inner journeys and Longley's and Mahon's "prismatic surfaces." The author points out that the "Glanmore Sonnets" celebrate "creative renewal" in a language he describes as "verbal love-knots."

22 MEGERLE, BRENDA POWELL. "Contemporary Poets: The Quest for Value Beyond Nihilism." Ph.D. dissertation, University of California-Berkeley.

Reading the works of Ted Hughes, Gary Snyder, James Dickey, Thom Gunn, and Seamus Heaney in conjunction becomes a process of focusing on a general trend within the contemporary poetry of the English-speaking world. These poets find a common cause in their attempt to reestablish meaning and value beyond the nihilistic atmosphere which followed in the wake of God's funeral.

23 MERRILL, THOMAS. "Seamus Heaney," in *The Macmillan Dictionary of Irish Literature*, edited by Robert Hogan (London: Macmillan Press): 288–90.
        Reprint of 1979.27.

24 MILLS, GEORGINA. "Interview with Seamus Heaney," *Strawberry Fare* (Autumn): 14–18.

In this interview Heaney identifies several quotations from other writers which appear in the poems found in "North." He discusses Wordsworth and "The Ministry of Fear," Tacitus in "North," Yeats in "Hercules and Antaeus," and Katherine Mansfield in "Fosterage."

25 MONTAGUE, JOHN. "Poet's Workshop," *Guardian* (November 27): 10.

Review of *Selected Poems 1965–1975* and *Preoccupations*. Montague writes mostly in generalizations about the two books, which he sees as consciously interactive and cross-referencing. In the spirit of Yeats and Eliot, Heaney's *Preoccupations* serves as a "running commentary" on his *Selected Poems*. Midway in his review, Montague deduces: "Finally, of course, Heaney sees us all trying to salvage something through a common language, with different accents." He finds the essays as a whole "both thoughtful and sensuous, an occasional episcopal seriousness. . .leavened with near laughter. . . ." Montague ends by revealing his uneasiness over Heaney's mythic use of "bog burials" and "ritual sacrifice" since they "have played little part in Irish history."

1980

26 MORRISON, BLAKE. "Speech and Reticence: Seamus Heaney's *North*," in *British Poetry since 1970: A Critical Survey*, edited by P. Jones and M. Schmidt (Manchester: Carcanet Press): 103–11.

Although Morrison's essay is a survey of Heaney's work up to 1980, he focuses upon *North*. Heaney's career has been shaped by an increasing public awareness, which can be seen in *North*. However, the division of *North* produces a "false gap between the past and present, private and public." Heaney's response to violence (existential and political) is one of "sympathy and resignation." Morrison argues that the "rustic" material of the first two volumes encourages caricaturing by British critics. In his overview of *North*, Morrison argues that Heaney strives to produce images in the bog poems which are "simultaneously linguistic, historical, geographical and sexual." The bog poems present a defense of Republicanism; they "give sectarian killing in Ulster a historical respectability." In many of these poems Heaney's "prejudices or loyalties as an Irish Catholic" are revealed as well as his "resentment of Protestant colonization."

27 MOTION, ANDREW. "Glow and Haze," *New Statesman* 100, 2591 (November 14): 22–23.

Review of *Preoccupations* and of *Selected Poems 1965–1975*. Motion finds that in both his prose and his poetry Heaney repeatedly looks back to his childhood in such a way as to register both affection and distance at the same time. In almost every essay Heaney discusses this debate between intellect and instinct. Since the outbreak of violence in Northern Ireland he has searched for "images and symbols adequate to [his] predicament." This has resulted in his "Bog Poems." One of his special strengths is that he always keeps reason and instinct before him.

Reprinted 1985.73.

28 O'CONNELL, SHAUN. "Seamus Heaney: Poetry and Power," *New Boston Review* 5, 5–6 (August-September): 3–5.

From the beginning Heaney has kept away from writing poetry with a political purpose. He is also ill at ease with those who would use his poetry for political purposes. Some of his poetry has an oblique relation to the Northern Ireland crisis where he speaks of the conflict but without partisanship. His work is well balanced between personal poems and those poems that cast a wider net— tensions through which his poetry gains its force. There are those who see him as a symbol of hope, and there are those who see him as the darling of the critical establishment, who moves across the boundaries between poetry and politics. Heaney "remains interesting from the risks he chooses to run."

Reprinted 1983.27.

29 PARINI, JAY. "Seamus Heaney: The Ground Possessed," *Southern Review* 16, 1 (Winter): 100–123.

Parini examines the basic images, themes, and formal aspects of Heaney's first four volumes. In them Heaney moves meditatively between the "private arena" of autobiography and Ireland's history. Thus he repossesses a heritage—personal, national, linguistic—that redeemed by time "will [make] living possible in today's violent world." The poet, beginning in a folk-pastoral mode but moving through his first four collections into "a stinging new version of reality," voices increasingly political yet private protests in poetry.

Reprinted (excerpts) 1983.30; reprinted 1985.73; 1986.48 (under title "The Ground Possessed").

30 PETTINGELL, PHOEBE. "Spirits of Place," *New Leader* (January 14): 16–17.

In her review of *Field Work,* Pettingell argues that the book is concerned with the "transplanting" of the poet in the South and the anxiety over leaving the turbulence behind. She admires many of the poems, such as "Casualty," "The Badgers," and "In Memory of Francis Ledwidge." However, Pettingell is critical of those poems which she feels have been most misguided by the influence of Robert Lowell. In addition, she finds the elegy for Lowell "sentimental and weak."

31 PINSKY, ROBERT. "The Prose of an Irish Poet," *New York Times Book Review* (December 21): 4.

In his review of *Preoccupations*, Pinsky asserts that poet-critics have an intense focus, their insights come from concern with composition. Heaney deals with this in exciting ways. His best moments are when he meditates on his own and his country's past. He writes with authority and persuasiveness on the poets who are close to him. If there is anything to mar the book it is the occasional tone of the literary journalist.

Reprinted 1983.35; reprinted 1985.73.

32 RATINER, STEVEN. "Seamus Heaney: Poet of the Irish land and mind," *Christian Science Monitor* (February 6): 17.

Ratiner's review of *Field Work* concentrates on the structure of Heaney's verse and not the content, partially because "Heaney is not really a political poet." Even though the reviewer admires and approves of Heaney's "masterly craftsmanship," he finds that the poet's technical skill "occasionally contradicts the rough beauty of the poem's subject and brings a falseness to the final creation."

1980

33 SCHIRMER, GREGORY A. "Seamus Heaney: Salvation in Surrender," *Eire-Ireland* 15, 4 (Winter): 139–46.

Seamus Heaney has worked out a way to write poetry that is based in his local area as well as written to an audience far beyond the island of Ireland. "The principle of excavation" is responsible for this expansiveness since it allows the poet to dig into both his personal and cultural past. The author disagrees with A. Alvarez's critique of Heaney and especially with Alvarez's conception of Heaney's audience as aesthetically complaisant (1980:1). His latest work, *Field Work* (1979), also relies on the archetypal power of poetry to lift it out of the local.

Reprinted (excerpts) 1983.40.

34 SCHMIDT, MICHAEL. "Seamus Heaney," in *Eleven British Poets: An Anthology* (London: Methuen): 206–7.

Schmidt comments upon Heaney's "primitive trust in the force of ono-matopoeia" in the early poems and upon the general feeling of "evocation" one senses in the majority of his work. These elements of Heaney's verse are rooted in the "chants of his childhood."

35 "Seamus Heaney, 1939–," in *Contemporary Authors: A Bio-Bibliographical Guide to Current Writers* 85–88 (Detroit: Gale): 247–48.

A brief biographical guide is followed by a listing of the poet's principal publications. This is followed by "Sidelights," a short evaluation of his work up to *North*. Finally there is a very brief listing of "Biographical/Critical Sources."

36 SMITH, DAVE. "Trimmers, Rounders and Myths: Some Recent Poetry from English Speaking Cousins," *American Poetry Review* 9 (September-October): 30–33.

Review of *Field Work* together with the work of seven other poets. Smith comments on the expectations of some readers that Heaney's work should be political and partisan. That would silence his talent. He has to free "himself from Yeats, from the English, and from the public roles expected of him." *Field Work* is the result of his leaving Northern Ireland to live in the Republic. The poems in this book are about freedom and the responsibility of carrying on in the face of death. There is the backward look at loyalties, the sources of self-knowledge. Though this work may be for Heaney "an interlude," he "speaks for all poets who must draw from the darkness of the universe, an authoritative, personally verifiable myth of knowledge. . . ."

37 SMITH, STAN. "Seamus Justin Heaney," in *Contemporary Poets*, 3d ed. (New York: St. Martin's Press): 670–72.

Revised 1985.77; 1991.66.

38 STEVENSON, ANNE. "To the editor: Seamus Heaney," *Times Literary Supplement* 4013 (February 22): 208.

  Stevenson in her letter takes issue with Harold Bloom's review of *Field Work*, and in particular his interpretation of the poem "The Harvest Bow."

39 SWEENEY, MATTHEW. "[Book Review]," *Aquarius* 12: 122–23.

  Sweeney in this review of *Field Work* comments on the references to the violence in Northern Ireland, and on the elegies for victims of the violence as well as for friends of the poet. In spite of this the tone is one of affirmation. Heaney's language has continued to develop in his finest collection to date.

40 THWAITE, ANTHONY. "The Hiding Places of Power," *Times Literary Supplement* (October 31), 1222.

  Review of *Preoccupations: Selected Prose 1968–1978* and *Selected Poems 1965–1975*. Thwaite finds Heaney "all of a piece" in his poetry and prose, which in part is the result of his ability to join technique and craft in a happy marriage. The reviewer notes that Heaney's prose pieces—like those of T. S. Eliot—are often the product of his "enthusiasms" for his "shaping spirits and personal exemplars." He states that *Preoccupations* is informed by Heaney's "generousity of spirit [and] acuteness of mind." Thwaite argues that the best piece in the book is "Englands of the Mind." He says very little about *Selected Poems, 1965–1975.*

  Reprinted 1983.42; 1986.55.

41 WRIGHT, DAVID. "A Poet's Prose: David Wright on Seamus Heaney," *Times Educational Supplement* (November 14): 20.

  Short review of *Selected Poems* and of *Preoccupations*. Wright comments on the quality of Heaney's prose and ranks him "a serious critic in the class of Yeats."

  Reprinted 1983.43.

1981

1 ANDREWS, BRIAN. "Hearing Voices," *Honest Ulsterman* 68: 57–61.

  Review of *Preoccupations* and of *Selected Poems, 1965–1975*. Andrews, applying Faulkner's dictum to Heaney, asserts that when poets write criticism, in "revealing others they often reveal themselves." Most of the review is concerned with *Preoccupations*. The pieces in Section I are fragments of autobiography, while Section II is composed of literary essays and lectures. Heaney's main preoccupation is with the poetic voice. His choices for the *Selected Poems* are what could be expected, though the omission of the entire text of longer poems is bothersome. However, "minor carping should not be allowed to detract from the fineness of this selection."

1981

2   BERKE, ROBERTA. "'The Voyage of Recovery': Recent British Poetry," in *Bounds Out of Bounds: A Compass for Recent American and British Poetry* (New York: Oxford University Press): 144–45.
    Heaney often writes about rural life. He also writes about remains of prehistoric peoples, showing that old customs persist in our own times. His descriptions in his earlier work were not always sufficiently sustained; he has counteracted this by writing longer sequences of short poems.

3   "[Book Review]," *Choice* 18, 8 (April): 1098.
    Review of *Poems, 1965–1975*. This collection allows the reader to trace Heaney's development and style and to observe his increasing political involvement. The best work here is *North*, in which Heaney lays bare the layers of meaning and shows that violence is always present.

4   "[Book Review]," *Choice* 18, 8 (April): 1100.
    Review of *Preoccupations: Selected Prose 1968–1978*. The reviewer stresses the importance of this collection of prose for the light it casts on Heaney's growth and the landscape which inspired him, as well as for the discussions of other poets. Heaney's arguments are clear, and his insights are interesting. However, his literary judgments tend to be less critical than they might be, and this is a real shortcoming.

5   BRADBROOK, MURIEL. "Doing Literature on Dover Beach," in *The Humanist as Citizen*, edited by John Agresto and Peter Riesenberg (Chapel Hill: National Humanities Center): 117–32.
    Bradbrook, in a general essay on poetry, looks at Heaney at the end of her presentation. She calls Heaney "perhaps the most articulate voice in English poetry today." Hopkins and Wordsworth were the first voices to teach him to "raid the inarticulate." For Heaney this has been the discovery of dread. His poems on the bog victims in Denmark present a horror appropriate for Northern Ireland. The richness of his poetry found a new voice, a new image, linking the immediate present dread with factual history. It also "carries the power to change those who read it."

6   BRADLEY, ANTHONY G. "Pastoral in Modern Irish Poetry," *Concerning Poetry* 14, 2 (Fall): 79–96.
    Bradley discusses certain elements of the pastoral tradition in selected poems by Yeats, Kavanagh, Montague, and Heaney. He reads "The Seed Cutters" and "Sunlight" in relation to what he calls the "realistic" pastoral movement of post-Yeatsian Irish poetry. This realism is the result of keen observation and produces a painterly quality in the poems that is unsentimental in subject and treatment.

7 BRAVERMAN, KATE. "Poetry from an Irish shaman," *Los Angeles Herald Examiner* (June 7): F6.

Review of *Field Work.* Braverman comments on the power of the poetry and on the sense of Ireland in this book. She senses that the political stance of the poetry comes from the violence which is part of Ireland. She commends Heaney's gift with language, making music from words.

8 BROWN, MARY. "Seamus Heaney and North," *Studies* 70, 280 (Winter): 289–98.

In *Death of a Naturalist,* Heaney explores his own growing up in rural Ireland. His sensibility makes him a poor farmer but enables him to be a poet. In *Death of a Naturalist* he expands his interest in the processes of nature and examines man's place in nature's cycles. In *Wintering Out* he is concerned with the divided culture, particularly as it is shown in language, and develops a poetry which will now carry ideas. Going back in time, he also sees a connection between the human sacrifices of the past and those of the present. He pursues this further in *North* and explores Ireland's preoccupation with martyrdom and sacrificial death. In *North* he also raises the problem of the responsibilities of the poet in a world of violence and death. In these poems he places art and moral judgment on opposite sides of the scale, and art loses out. The hope is that he will resolve the doubts about his art and use his fine gifts in another direction.

9 COTTER, J. F. "Outer and Inner Poetry," *Hudson Review* 34, 2 (Summer): 277–89.

Review of *Poems 1965–1975* and of *Preoccupations* together with reviews of the work of some sixteen other poets. Cotter sees in Heaney's writings about poetry a healthy self-knowledge and a catholic taste in reading. The essays have a unity that makes for pleasurable reading. In his poetry, speech, both country and city, is important. His maturity shows in his sketches of farm life. Cotter notes that Heaney writes of the Northern conflict as "a reflective, non-participant."

10 CURTIS, TONY. "A More Social Voice: Seamus Heaney's *Field Work,*" *Poetry Wales* 16, 3: 79–101.

Curtis sets out "to analyse Seamus Heaney's skill in responding to the challenge of events in Ireland, to consider the extent that his latest book exhibits a growth in his stature as a poet, and to judge the extent to which, over the last five collections, Heaney's craft has developed to match his vision."

Reprinted 1982.1; 1982.4; 1985.3; 1985.17.

1981

11 DEANE, SEAMUS. "Seamus Heaney," *Ireland Today* 977 (June): 2–5.
    Heaney's poetry shows the effects of study of the work of a variety of poets, such as Hopkins, Frost, Hughes, Wordsworth, and Robert Lowell. It is not, however, imitative. From his first book he has become an individual voice. In Northern Ireland the pressures of past history are ever present, just as the landscape itself preserves layers of previous civilizations. This is his preoccupation in *Wintering Out*. It is continued in *North*, which has in addition a more direct contemplation of the political situation in Northern Ireland. The recreation of atrocity as poetry dominates the first half of of *Field Work*. Another kind of poetry "of deep and silent patience" also appears here in the "Glanmore Sonnets" sequence. Heaney has shown us a landscape and a vocabulary and discovers for us their dark energy.

12 DES PRES, TERRENCE. "Emblems of Adversity: Seamus Heaney: Politics and Poetics," *Harper's Magazine* 262 (March): 73–77.
    In the violent society of Northern Ireland, the dilemma facing the poet is: "How with this rage shall beauty hold a plea?" Des Pres argues for a reading of Heaney's work which engages the politics of his time. Heaney's poetry is "a fusion of history and the land, politics colliding with life's daily round." The landscape holds the memory of "spilled blood" and this in Heaney's hands takes on dignity and sweetness and helps us to endure and bear adversity.

13 DI PIERO, W. S. "Digs," *American Scholar* 50, 4 (Autumn): 558–62.
    Review of *Poems 1965–1975* and of *Preoccupations*. Heaney takes his work as a poet seriously. In his poetry and prose he goes deep into the layers of Irish history, into the Irish landscape and into the lives of the people who live there. However, in his later work he pays too much attention to the "noise of language" over that of theme. He needs to take care not to substitute "fine craft for true feeling."
    Reprinted 1983.14; 1989.12 (under title, "Digs: On Seamus Heaney").

14 EHRENPREIS, IRVIN. "Digging In," *New York Review of Books* 28, 15 (October 8): 45–46.
    In his review of *Poems 1965–1975* (in addition to two other volumes by different poets), Ehrenpreis argues that the theme of "self-definition" dominates Heaney's work. The reviewer also sees the politicizing of the Irish landscape in Heaney's work as a positive equation: "Nationality becomes landscape; landscape becomes language; language becomes genius." "Freedman," "A New Song," "The Skunk," "Punishment," and "Traditions" are cited in support of Ehrenpreis's argument.
    Reprinted 1986.18.

15 GRIMES, CLAIRE. "Seamus Heaney's Irish Idyls," *Irish Echo* (March 14): 25.

    This article includes several comments taken from Grimes's interview with Heaney. The poet comments upon politics and poetry and mentions Joyce and Bertolt Brecht. Heaney says "I think most writers don't have that purely political intelligence [that Brecht has]."

16 GROSHOLZ, EMILY. "Writing Landscape: Five Poets," *New England Review* 3, 4 (Summer 1981): 604–16.

    Grosholz recommends Heaney's collection of prose writings, *Preoccupations*, to those who have already acquired his *Poems 1965–1975*. She does this not only for the light *Preoccupations* sheds on his own work, but also for its valuable commentary on British and Irish poetry. She selects the essay "Feelings into Words" for its discussion of the "bog poems," the emblems of political struggle, and the distinction the poet makes between craft and technique in writing.

17 HADLEY, ERIC. "[Seamus Heaney and Translation]: Seamus Heaney and Dante," *Present Tense* 2 (Winter): 28–39.

    Hadley compares Heaney's "Ugolino" (*Field Work*) with the original from Dante's *Inferno* (cantos xxxii 124–39—xxxiii 1–90). The translation teaches us more about Heaney than it does about Dante. Heaney tends to mark each moment as important when one wishes he would be ordinary. He charges and loads everything while Dante is calm and unfrenzied. There is also a coarseness in the translation which is not there in the original. With Dante we feel that for his dead souls this is their sole chance to speak with a living person, yet at this moment Heaney's feeling for human speech is absent. What we have is "a failure of his [Heaney's] critical sense. . .there are no short cuts to profundity in the Dante." Heaney fails most where it is clear how much Ugolino the man matters to Dante.

18 HAFFENDEN, JOHN. "Meeting Seamus Heaney: An Interview," in *Viewpoints: Poets in Conversation with John Haffenden* (London: Faber & Faber): 57–75.

    Reprint of 1979.14.

19 HILL, MARK. "Seamus Heaney and Translation: Seamus Heaney and Charles Baudelaire," *Present Tense* 2 (Winter): 22–27.

    Hill finds reading Heaney's work unsatisfactory, though not entirely without rewards. In this essay he compares "The Digging Skeleton" (*North*) with the original Baudelaire poem, "La squelette laboureur." The best part of "The Digging Skeleton," the absorbed questioning, comes from Baudelaire. The language is typical of Heaney and much less powerful than that of

Baudelaire. For Baudelaire's fear, Heaney gives us "a kind of detached pity." Baudelaire is wholly possessed by the picture while Heaney sidles up to it. Hill is impressed by the quality of "The Digging Skeleton" compared with the rest of the poetry in *North*. He attributes its preeminence to Baudelaire, who "seems so much more a contemporary."

20 JOHNSON, MANLY. "Collected Works," *World Literature Today* 55, 4 (Autumn): 677.

Review of *Preoccupations* and of *Selected Poems 1965–1975*. Johnson sees the conflict in Heaney's poetry as reflecting the Irish conflict, that is, how to reconcile the fruit of art, "peace," with war. Johnson asserts that the Northern conflict pushes Heaney into partisan poetry. The essays in *Preoccupations* he sees as Heaney's struggle to establish poetry as the center of his life. The two volumes under review give us a feeling of promise that art "is part of the creative push of civilization itself."

21 JONES, D. J. "Myth and History in the Poetry of Geoffrey Hill, Seamus Heaney and George MacKay Brown." Ph.D. dissertation, University of Wales.

22 KEARNEY, TIMOTHY. "[Book Review]," *Furrow* 13 (February): 127, 129.

In his review of *Preoccupations*, Kearney compares Heaney to Pope Paul II, because the Irish poet embodies the marriage of "the masculine and the feminine." The reviewer praises Heaney's emphasis on "craft" and his delightful prose style.

23 KROLL, JACK with ROSEMARY BRADY. "Bard of the Irish Soul," *Newsweek* (Feb. 2): 53–54.

The review of *Poems 1965–75, Field Work*, and *Preoccupations* relies heavily on Irish stereotypes and cliches. The reviewers identify the source of Heaney's power and success in the "classic Irish gift of revelatory gab." He is the poet of the "unfake."

24 LLOYD, DAVID T. "Seamus Heaney's *Field Work*," *Ariel* 12, 2 (April): 87–92.

Lloyd sees this work as both a consolidation of and an advance on Heaney's earlier collections. New ground is broken in his response to the political violence in Northern Ireland. This he does through greater use of assonance and longer verse lines. The *Field Work* poems are arranged by thematic concerns. In the overall context, however, Lloyd sees poems from each section as having a political dimension. In the rural-based poems we see again the complexity of that world, full of both frail and dangerous elements. This collection does not offer solutions for Northern Ireland's political problems. Rather, in this, his best work to date, Heaney seeks to have us share the human emotions which bring us together.

25 McCULLOUGH, DAVID W. "Seamus Heaney," in his *People, Books & Book People* (New York: Harmony Books), pp. 78–80.

A conversation with Heaney in which the poet discusses his admiration for Yeats as a strategist handling the tension between the writer and the public figure. Heaney solves the problem of the political role by abandoning it. He talks of his familiarity with the bog and with Glob's *Bog People* as well as the symbolic possibilities of the bog. Ireland's roots in Northern Europe and the bodies found in Jutland became an obsessive image—people with a religion going out to kill. The conversation was first recorded in the *Book of the Month Club News* (1976).

26 McKEEN, CATHERINE. "Seamus Heaney: The Eloquent Earth," *America* 144 (June 20): 503–4.

McKeen's brief sketch of Heaney's poetry and career is related to a series of readings the poet gave in the United States during the year.

27 MENAGH, DIANE. "[Book Review]," *America* 144 (March 21): 234.

Menagh's brief review of *Preoccupations* is pure praise for the volume. She primarily summarizes the contents of the book and comments that Heaney is concerned with the poetic process and its consequences.

28 O'BRIEN, DARCY. "Seamus Heaney and Wordsworth: A Correspondent Breeze," in *The Nature of Identity: Essays Presented to Donald D. Haydon by the Graduate Faculty of Modern Letters, the University of Tulsa*, edited by William Weathers (Tulsa: University of Tulsa): 37–46.

O'Brien mentions that Heaney told him in December 1973 that he had "'been getting a lot out of Wordsworth lately.'" The specific poem was *The Prelude*. O'Brien looks closely at the Wordsworthian elements of "Exposure" and the "Glanmore Sonnets." In the former it is "self-revelation and confession" which correspond to Wordsworth, while in the latter it is the landscape, the relationship between man and nature, and the celebration of the rejuvenated relationship between husband and wife. O'Brien concludes by referring to *North* and *Stations*.

29 O'CONNELL, SHAUN. "Tracing the growth of a poet's mind," *Boston Sunday Globe* (January 25): 23.

Review of *Preoccupations* and *Poems: 1965–1975*. The review focuses upon the similarities and differences between Heaney and Yeats. "These books define Heaney in the midst of a great career. . . ."

30 O'SHEA, HELEN. "Interview with Seamus Heaney," *Quadrant* (Sydney) 25 (September): 12–17.

Heaney and O'Shea discuss the so-called "Northern School" of poetry, the influence of Kavanagh, Hughes, and Lowell ("the first major voice"); the

1981

role of the poet in addressing realities other than the purely aesthetic. Cultural continuity and loyalties and political viewpoints are treated in some detail, as is the bog mythos. Heaney talks of a new phase beginning with *Field Work* and the effects of "home life" on poetry. He concludes: "The activity of writing poetry—finally, it is the thing that you pursue."

31 PERLOFF, MARJORIE. "Seamus Heaney: Peat, Politics and Poetry," *Washington Post Book World* (January 25): 5, 11.

Perloff challenges those critics who praise Heaney's poetry and prose in her review of *Poems 1965–1975* and *Preoccupations*. She considers Heaney's prose "bland" and filled with Romantic clichés and domestic commonplaces. For example, Heaney's autobiographical accounts lack the "tough reasonableness" of Donald Davie's "A West Riding Childhood." She particularly disapproves of Heaney's "textbook" treatment of Yeats. When discussing the poetry, Perloff finds Heaney's verse contrived. She makes an interesting comparison between "Follower" and Theodore Roethke's "The Premonition." Reprinted 1983.32; 1985.73.

32 PYBUS, RODNEY. "Matters of Ireland: Recent Irish Poetry," *Stand* 3: 72–78.

The essays in *Preoccupations* seem to be occasional pieces by a freelance journalist, but they are none the worse for that. Heaney is widely read and respected in England because of his vivid recall of rural Ireland, which appeals to urban readers. He avoids English-Irish problems and is more inclined to deal directly with the pain of contemporary Ulster. He has been a consistent new voice for Irish poetry, which is also fortunate in also having writers such as Montague, Murphy, Mahon, and Longley. Reprinted 1983.36.

33 RICHARDS, MAX. "Fit for Digging: Seamus Heaney," *Helix* 9/10: 20–22.

In his review of *Preoccupations*, Richards notes Heaney's initial genuflection before the classic canon of English poetry until, while reading Hopkins, he came to recognize his own potential voice. He writes of his poetic elders and peers, both local and international, as well as of the playwright Brian Friel. His deepest preoccupation is the sacral or sacramental. He shows his intimacy with the power of language, in its glamour as well as in its menace. The readings that matter to Heaney go back to Wordsworth and to the Táin, but also to the face of Ireland. Poetry does well to recover and cultivate the sacramental aspect of the landscape.

34 STUART, RORY. "Heaney in Prose," *English* 30, 137 (Summer): 204–7.

In his review of *Preoccupations*, Stuart states that "the division of himself" is one of the poet's preoccupations. He tells us about himself and expresses himself with precision, yet his criticism lacks sharpness. He sees himself in relation to Yeats, and his essays on Yeats are interesting from that standpoint. We like the essays because Heaney writes attractive prose rather than for the intrinsic value of the essays themselves.

35 VENDLER, HELEN. "The Music of What Happens," *New Yorker* (September 28): 146–57.

In this long review, Vendler looks at *Poems 1965–1975*, *Preoccupations*, and *Field Work*. She focuses on the development of Heaney's "coming of age" and not on specific poems or volumes. Vendler sees Heaney's writing life as an ever-expanding circle which becomes more social as it loses its childhood innocence. She finds Heaney's "experiments with native sounds"—the "Gaelic solution"—"too programmatic." After discussing Heaney's poetry of "verbs," she concludes that "Heaney wants his social voice to make its way into his poetry, joining that voice of secret brooding in which he first found a poetic self."

Reprinted 1988.76, where it is combined with her essay "Echo Soundings, Searches, Probes" (1985.80) to form the essay "Seamus Heaney."

36 WARNER, ALAN. "Seamus Heaney," in his *Guide to Anglo-Irish Literature* (Dublin: Gill and Macmillan): 260–68.

Warner examines Heaney's work up to *Field Work*. He appreciates the poet's "vivid sensuous apprehension" and the "variety of mood and mode," especially in the early volumes. Warner quotes from a BBC interview with Heaney in which he discusses the "dark centre. . .the hidden core" in relation to "Personal Helicon." The author considers "Punishment" the finest poem in *North*.

37 WATERMAN, ANDREW. "Somewhere, Out There, Beyond: The Poetry of Seamus Heaney and Derek Mahon," *PN Review* 8, 1: 39–47.

As the author reiterates throughout, this article is an "insider's" reading of Heaney's tribal solidarities—solidarities which typically compromise the poet's vision and verse: "[Heaney] has tended too much to crave his 'tribe's endorsement." The article examines Heaney's work up to and including *Field Work*. The author concentrates on the lapses, limitations, and excesses of Heaney's verse: "'Act of Union'. . .is geographically inept. . .and becomes grotesque." In addition to spotlighting the poet's misconceptions, the article argues that although Heaney often becomes boring and monotonous in *North*, he displays a new vitality in *Field Work* as a result of looking into his heart.

1982

1 *The Art of Seamus Heaney*, edited and introduced by Tony Curtis (Bridgend: Poetry Wales Press). 150 pp.

Contents: "Introduction" by Tony Curtis. "*Death of a Naturalist*" by Roland Mathias. "*Door into the Dark*" by Dick Davis. "Craft and Technique in *Wintering Out*" by Philip Hobsbaum. "*Stations*: Seamus Heaney and the Sacred Sense of the Sensitive Self" by Anne Stevenson. "The Manuscript Drafts of the Poem 'North.'" "*North*: 'Inner Emigre' or 'Artful Voyeur'?" by Edna Longley. "A More Social Voice: *Field Work*" by Tony Curtis. "The Peace Within Understanding: Looking at *Preoccupations*" by Anne Stevenson.

Revised edition 1985.3.

2   CLUYSENAAR, ANNE. "Formal Meanings in Three Modern Poems," *Dutch Quarterly Review of Anglo-American Letters* 12, 4: 302–20.

Cluysenaar discusses three poems: Heaney's "Personal Helicon," "Hawk Roosting" by Ted Hughes, and Philip Larkin's "Mr. Bleaney." Heaney's poem has lexical items growing around wells such as fungus, moss, roots, ferns, etc. The stress falls on effects like fertilizing and reflecting. "Hawk Roosting" is unrhymed; "Mr. Bleaney" is fully rhymed; Heaney's poem is off-rhymed.

3   CURTIS, TONY. "Introduction," in *The Art of Seamus Heaney*, edited and introduced by Tony Curtis (Bridgend: Poetry Wales Press): 7–9.

Curtis rehearses Heaney's publishing career, commenting briefly on *Death of a Naturalist, North,* and *Field Work.* The book seeks to illuminate the qualities of Heaney's work by tracing thematically and chronologically his development since his first work. The collection of essays includes distinct, diverse, and sometimes opposed views of Heaney's poetry.

Reprinted (revised version) 1985.16.

4   CURTIS, TONY. "A More Social Voice: *Field Work*," in *The Art of Seamus Heaney*, edited and introduced by Tony Curtis (Bridgend: Poetry Wales Press): 97–127.

Reprint of 1981.10; reprinted 1982.1; 1985.3; 1985.17.

5   DAVIS, DICK. "Door into the Dark," in *The Art of Seamus Heaney,* edited and introduced by Tony Curtis (Bridgend: Poetry Wales Press): 27–34.

The natural world is seen as feminine—a fruitful, threatening lover. The exploration, digging, going inward and downward is typical of the poems in Heaney's first three books. The way into the dark is the way into the obscurity of the past, which the poet can explore without that fear of the darkness of the natural world. Heaney's explorations into darkness suggest that he sees the poet as a finder and also as a craftsman. He presents his subjects in almost wholly physical language. His is a poetry at ease with his temperament.

Reprinted 1985.20.

6   DEANE, SEAMUS. "Unhappy and at Home: Interview with Seamus Heaney," in *The Crane Bag Book of Irish Studies, 1977–1981* (Dublin: Blackwater Press): 66–72.
Reprint of 1977.5.

7   "First Degree coming of Age for Seamus," *Irish News and Belfast News* (July 8): 10.
This unsigned article covers the awarding of an honorary degree to Heaney at Queen's University, Belfast. The article quotes from statements made at the ceremony regarding Heaney's relationship with the university.

8   FITZGERALD, MARY. "A Seamus Heaney Harvest," *Irish Literary Supplement* 1, 1 (Spring): 18.
Fitzgerald comments on the omissions in *Selected Poems* and establishes its difference from *Poems*. *Preoccupations* is a search for answers: how and what to write, what is the poet's relationship to the world and his own heritage. *Field Work* is a turning point; Heaney moves South to the Republic and to the warmth of Italy. It has his best poem, "The Harvest Bow." The comparison with Yeats is not useful—Heaney is his own voice.

9   FLANAGAN, THOMAS. "The Poetry of Seamus Heaney," in *Poems and a Memoir* by Seamus Heaney (New York: Limited Editions): ix–xvi.
Flanagan sees Heaney as a poet of territory. His territory is the farmland of south Derry in Northern Ireland. Heaney's work shows his fascination with the natural world and with language. For a time, bogs were potent images for him and provided "symbols adequate to our predicament," the violent life of Northern Ireland. This culminated in his collection *North*, in which he declares himself free from political and other encroachments on his work as a poet. In *Field Work* the poet conducts a dialogue with himself—"an Antaeus strong within his territory, but as artful as much-travelled Hercules."

10   GAFFNEY, ELIZABETH. "Poems on Poetry: Heaney and Plath." Ph.D. dissertation, SUNY-Stony Brook.
Gaffney gives a reading and analysis of specific poems on poetry by Heaney and Plath. The poems represent chronologically each poet's full career. Unlike most contemporary poets, Heaney and Plath are well known to the general public, but the attention focused on their lives often distracts from their work. This study emphasizes that both are poets, first and foremost. Some of Heaney's poems on poetry are exhortations to the poet to be faithful to his ideals for his work. For Heaney, writing poetry is an ordinary activity, such as digging, farming, etc. While his early poems celebrate the delights of writing, his later poems talk of the "betrayals" and the pain involved.

1982

11   GREVER, GLENN A. "Seamus Heaney," in *Critical Survey of Poetry: English Language Series* (Englewood Cliffs: Salem Press): 1264–73.

Grever surveys Heaney's life and work under various headings: Achievements, Biography, Analysis. The thrust of the essay is in the "Analysis," where Grever discusses each volume of poetry up to and including *Field Work*. Grever sees excavation as dominant in Heaney's poetry— "digging below the surface of the natural world, of Ireland, and of the self."

Revised edition by James Livingston: 1992:31.

12   HEDERMAN, MARK PATRICK. "Seamus Heaney, The Reluctant Poet," in *The Crane Bag Book of Irish Studies, 1977–1981* (Dublin: Blackwater Press): 481–90.

Reprint of 1979.16.

13   HOBSBAUM, PHILIP. "Craft and Technique in *Wintering Out*," in *The Art of Seamus Heaney*, edited and introduced by Tony Curtis (Bridgend: Poetry Wales Press): 35–43.

Heaney's craft is very certain. It reminds us of Hopkins, Hardy, and Frost, which is what the reviewers like. In poems such as "The Other Side," where his instructor is Patrick Kavanagh, language is medium and meaning. Heaney is more inclined to give us elsewhere craft and not technique. He is always good and has moments which transcend the merely good. Hobsbaum concludes, "What present day critics hail as achievement, the future may look upon as promise."

Reprinted 1985.37.

14   KELLY, MARY PAT. "The Sovereign Woman: Her Image in Irish Literature from Medb to Anna Livia Plurabelle." Ph.D. dissertation, City University of New York.

The study focuses on major works from various periods in Irish literature. The qualities of the ancient heroines appear in the works of the writers of the 20th century Irish Literary Revival. They appear again in Joyce's women. Joyce's work in turn influences the present generation of Irish writers— Thomas Kinsella, John Montague, and Seamus Heaney—in whose poetry and translations from the ancient literature, the sovereign woman lives again.

15   KINAHAN, FRANK. "Artists on Art: An Interview with Seamus Heaney," *Critical Inquiry* 8, 3 (Spring): 405–14.

This interview was conducted at the University of Chicago on March 8, 1981. Heaney talks about being an Irish poet and what it entails, as well as about Joyce's contribution to Irish writing as distinct from that of Yeats. He discusses his early attempts at poetry and the meetings with other poets in Belfast when Philip Hobsbaum came to teach at Queen's University. He describes his first three books as "the trace element of a hopeful learning experience." *North* was to some extent designed, while *Field Work* was an attempt to do something deliberately, to change the note and lengthen the line. There is a shift from *North* to *Field Work*, a learning to trust melody and art.

16   LAFFERTY, JAMES J. "Gifts From The Goddess: Heaney's 'Bog People,'" *Eire-Ireland* 17, 3 (Fall): 127–36.
     Heaney's poems about the ancient bog people suggest that the atrocities, sacrifices, and punishments of this race prefigure the anguish of the Irish and of modern man in general.

17   LONGLEY, EDNA. *"North*: 'Inner Emigré' or 'Artful Voyeur'?" in *The Art of Seamus Heaney*, edited and introduced by Tony Curtis (Bridgend: Poetry Wales Press): 63–95.
     Longley agrees with Heaney's view of *North* as a culmination, especially in terms of merit as well as development. She observes, however, that "the slightly aggravated young Catholic male" has surfaced before *North* and *Wintering Out* in such poems as "At a Potato Digging" and "Requiem for the Croppies." He became aware of poetry as "a mode of resistance." Longley sees this kind of poetry pervasive throughout *North*, defining the battlefield in Catholic and Nationalist terms. Longley surmises that Heaney's move to the Republic distanced some thoughts but brought others closer—*Wintering Out* was written from a Northern perspective; *North* was written from a Dublin/Wicklow and Nationalist perspective.
     Reprinted 1985.47; 1986.35 (with additional material).

18   LONGLEY, EDNA. "Stars and Horses, Pigs and Trees," in *The Crane Bag Book of Irish Studies, 1977–1981* (Dublin: Blackwater Press): 474–80.
     Reprint of 1979.23.

19   McCRUM, SEAN. "Directly from the Elements to the Pigments," *Sunday Tribune* (August 22): 21.
     McCrum reviews the Ulster Museum exhibit which produced Heaney's pamphlet *A Personal Selection.* The review comments upon Heaney's attitude towards the visual arts.

20   MAHONEY, PHILLIP. "Seamus Heaney and the Violence in Northern Ireland," *The Journal of Irish Literature* 11, 3 (September): 20–30.
     After a brief survey of Heaney's treatment of violence in the earlier works, especially in *North*, Mahoney considers *Field Work* at length. He argues that while "Croppies" from *Door into the Dark* is essentially "legend," "Punishment" from *North* "deals with the reality of the situation as he knows it actually exists." Heaney's attitude is "remarkably pessimistic" in *North*. In *Field Work* he presents himself as "an anti-British nationalist"—most clearly in "Triptych" and "Toome Road." Mahoney concludes that although Heaney

1982

adopts a "nationalistic statement, his final and most important statements" are "condemnations of terrorism and murder."

21   "The Manuscript Drafts of the Poem 'North,'" in *The Art of Seamus Heaney*, edited and introduced by Tony Curtis (Bridgend: Poetry Wales Press): 53–62.
      The various drafts of the poem are reproduced. There are two manuscript versions, five corrected typescripts, and the final printed version.
      Reprinted 1985.56.

22   MATHIAS, ROLAND. "Death of a Naturalist," in *The Art of Seamus Heaney*, edited and introduced by Tony Curtis (Bridgend: Poetry Wales Press): 11–26.
      Mathias examines the influence of Ted Hughes upon Heaney's first volume. Hughes's animal poems were enabling for Heaney because of their unsentimental depiction of the natural world. Heaney differs from Hughes, however, because Heaney's poetic center is always human; Hughes only provided the subject matter of Heaney's early poems. Mathias also comments upon the formal qualities of the volume's poems—that is, the texture of the language and structure of the poems. The author concludes that the dominant theme and impulse of *Death of a Naturalist* is "self-discovery," and not simply a loss of innocence.
      Reprinted 1985.57.

23   MAXWELL, D. E. S. "Semantic Scruples: A Rhetoric for Politics in the North," in *Literature and the Changing Ireland*, edited by Peter Connolly (Gerrards Cross: Colin Smythe; Totowa, N.J.: Barnes & Noble): 157–74.
      Maxwell examines the work of several modern and contemporary Irish poets, including Heaney, Mahon, and Longley whom he quotes as being referred to as "the tight-assed trio." Maxwell examines the various rhetorical options open to Irish poets writing under complex political pressures. In his brief discussion of Heaney, Maxwell focuses on "Roots," a poem which appears in the sequence "A Northern Hoard" from *Wintering Out*. The article concludes that one rhetorical stance is to expose the various paradoxes behind the Irish situation, as Heaney does in this poem.

24   MORRISON, BLAKE. *Seamus Heaney* (London: Methuen): 96.
      Morrison's book explores the sources, contexts, and receptions of Heaney's poetry up to *Field Work*, including a section on *Stations*. Morrison uses first appearances of poems in his arguments as a way of decoding some of Heaney's more politically ambiguous poems. He places Heaney in relation to Movement poets and his American contemporaries. After noting that Heaney has a "safe reputation but also a reputation for safety," Morrison asserts that Heaney is more complex and postmodern than many critics think. Refering to Heaney's politics, the author states that there are "important ques-

tions to be asked about Heaney's role as historical witness." This issue appears in many of Morrison's readings of Heaney's poems. For instance, the author concludes of "Kinship" and "Punishment" from *North*: "like it or not, his poetry grants sectarian killing in Northern Ireland a historical respectability which it is not usually granted in day-to-day journalism." Also of *North*, Morrison claims that the "structure of the book is its meaning." Morrison sees the early Heaney concerned with silence versus articulation, while the later, mid-Heaney becomes more vocal and public. *Field Work* represents a conscious withdrawal from the world of *North*.

Chapter 5, reprinted 1985.73; 1986.44.

25 MOYNAHAN, JULIAN. "Tongues of the Land," *New Republic* 186 (May 19): 38–39.

In his review of *Irish Poetry after Yeats*, edited by Maurice Harmon, Moynahan discusses each of seven poets Harmon selects for his anthology. Moynahan refers to Heaney's poetry as "pat" and "predictable." He also argues that Heaney has unfortunately mastered that "punchy mid-Atlantic style." Singling out Heaney's "At a Potato Digging," the reviewer suggests that the poem is over-cooked and pure contrivance.

26 O'KANE, DANIEL FINBAR. "The Myth of Irish Identity." Ph.D. dissertation, Drew University.

Irish history is the raw material of individual and racial biography, and the process of its transformation and appropriation is both autobiographic and mythic. This manner of living the myth is exemplified in the literature in Ireland that is individually and collectively biographic. The prose of James Joyce and the poetry of Seamus Heaney are considered relevant examples, which are paradigmatic of the socially creative act that is work-in-progress ongoing.

27 PARKINSON, THOMAS. "Poetry Is Alive and Well in Ireland," *Georgia Review* 36, 3 (Fall): 662–68.

This review essay on contemporary Irish poets mentions Heaney's *Field Work* and *Poems 1965–1975* only in passing because, as the author explains, he treats Heaney at length in his "Serious Work."

28 PARKINSON, THOMAS. "Serious Work: The Poetry and Prose of Seamus Heaney," *Southern Review* 18 (Spring): 442–47.

Parkinson reviews Heaney's *Poems 1965–1975*, *Preoccupations: Selected Prose 1968–1978*, and *Field Work*. Noting that Heaney's poetry becomes more oriented towards public issues with each new book, *North* then is the culmination of this outward motion: "it all coheres in a fierce quiet splendor." Parkinson is intrigued by the lack of intensity and the "interim tone" of *Field Work*. The author concludes: "Heaney has developed a power-

1982

ful instrument that is perhaps too powerful to become the servant of occasions, even [as in]. . .his 'Elegy' for Robert Lowell."
Reprinted 1987.54.

29   PEARSON, HENRY. "Seamus Heaney: A Bibliographical Checklist," *American Book Collector* 3, 2 (March/April): 31–42.
A comprehensive listing of the books and pamphlets by Heaney up to 1981, as well as of books with contributions by him.
Reprinted (New York: Moretus, 1982, 12 pp.) in the American Book Collector Bibliographic Checklist Series.

30   REGAN, STEPHEN. "The Poetry and Prose of Seamus Heaney," *University of Toronto Quarterly* 51, 3 (Spring): 306–13.
Review of *Selected Poems 1965–1975* and of *Preoccupations: Selected Prose 1968–1978*. The poems show us the poet's sense of his responsibilities, his private fears of exposure to public issues, and his commitment to his personal vision in a time of social and political unrest. The craftsman must remain true to his work. *Preoccupations* shows a concern with place, language, and customs and with the poet's relationship to them. The question of land is particularly vital in Northern Ireland. His critical sense and insights are shown in the section of literary reviews.

31   "Seamus Heaney," *Current Biography* 43, 1 (January): 9–12. Collected in *Current Biography Yearbook 1982* (New York: H. W. Wilson Company): 148–51.
Biographical details with analysis of his work up to *Field Work* and *Preoccupations*.

32   "Seamus of the Bogs," *Monthly Letter of the Limited Editions Club* 530 (November): 1–4.
This edition of the *Newsletter* deals with the edition of Heaney's *Poems and a Memoir* published by the Limited Editions Club in 1982. There is a section providing details on his life and poetry. Thomas Flanagan, who contributed a preface to the edition, is featured in a short biographical account. Henry Pearson, who made the selections for the book and who also contributed eight illustrations, is also commemorated . Finally, those people who were involved in the production of the work are listed: John Anderson of the Pickering Press, who planned the format; Robert A. Burlen, the binder; and Daniel Keleher at the Wild Carrot Press, who printed the illustrations. The paper for the edition was made at the Mohawk Mills, Cohoes, New York.

33 STALLWORTHY, JON. "The Poet as Archaeologist: W. B. Yeats and Seamus Heaney," *Review of English Studies* 33, 130 (May): 158–74.

Stallworthy examines the "digging" tropes in Heaney's work up to and including *Field Work,* occasionally in explicit comparison with Yeats. The essay begins by analyzing Yeats's and Heaney's complicated appreciation of Edmund Spenser. Stallworthy also looks at how Heaney subverts Yeats. Finally, the author draws a few specific comparisons between poems by Yeats and Heaney, such as their elegies.

34 STEVENSON, ANNE. "The Peace within Understanding: Looking at *Preoccupations,*" in *The Art of Seamus Heaney*, edited and introduced by Tony Curtis (Bridgend: Poetry Wales Press): 129–37.

Reading Heaney's critical essays in light of T. S. Eliot's arguments in "The Perfect Critic," Stevenson concludes that Heaney would not fit into Eliot's two main categories: impressionistic critics and analytical critics. According to Stevenson, Heaney writes out of an "androgynous understand-ing" which is the result of "marrying and balancing intelligence and feeling." She also uses Dante to illustrate her points regarding Eliot and Heaney and Heaney's concern for the spiritual state of Ireland and the world. There is no attempt made to discuss all of the essays in *Preoccupations*.

Reprinted 1985.78.

35 STEVENSON, ANNE. "*Stations*: Seamus Heaney and the Sacred Sense of the Sensitive Self," in *The Art of Seamus Heaney*, edited and introduced by Tony Curtis (Bridgend: Poetry Wales Press): 45–51.

Stevenson explores the dilemma facing Heaney, whose source of suc-cess and possible failure is the strength of his self-awareness. She suggests one way Heaney has responded to this dilemma is "to speak publicly of his failure. . .'failure' which in our time has become a hall-mark of honesty," as in *North*. *Stations*, according to Stevenson, is important then in terms of "fail-ure" because the prose poems challenge the myth that "the 'self' can be sal-vaged by art, from failure." She also comments that the artificial language and hyper-self-consciousness of *Stations* is a serious limitation of the volume.

Reprinted 1985.79.

1983

1 ALVAREZ, ANTONIO. "A Fine Way with Language," *Contemporary Literary Criticism* 250: 247–48.

Reprint of 1980.1; 1985.73.

1983

2   BAYLEY, JOHN. "Social Arrangements," *London Review of Books* (December 30): 3, 5, 6.
    The Rattle Bag is mentioned briefly at the end of this long review, which focuses on *The Penguin Book of Contemporary British Poetry*. Heaney is also discussed in the review of *The Penguin Book of Contemporary Poetry*.

3   BEDIENT, CALVIN. "The Music of What Happens," *Contemporary Literary Criticism* 25: 242–43.
    Reprint (excerpts) of 1979.2; reprinted 1985.73.

4   BLOOM, HAROLD. "The Voice of Kinship," *Contemporary Literary Criticism* 25: 246–47.
    Reprint (excerpts) of 1980.7; reprinted 1985.73; 1986.5, under title "Introduction."

5   BOLAND, EAVAN. "Heaney's Sweeney," *Irish Times* (December 10): Weekend 4.
    Review of *Sweeney Astray*. The poem deals with one of the oldest types in European literature—the estranged creative individual. The best parts are the lyric passages. Perhaps Sweeney is shown too much in a literary way; nevertheless, this is "a moving and satisfying piece of work."

6   BOOTH, MARTIN. 'Anthology Time,' *Tribune* (London), (January 7): 10.
    Hughes and Heaney's *The Rattle Bag* is one of several books reviewed. Booth argues that the editors have avoided the traps of limited ranges or semi-academic work which often affect other anthologies. Consequently, *The Rattle Bag* "shows the true internationalism of poetry."

7   "Bowman awarded prize for book," *Irish Times* (December 15): 12.
    Seamus Heaney presented the 1983 Ewart-Biggs Memorial Prize to John Bowman for his book *DeValera and the Ulster Question 1917–1973* and praised Bowman for his sensitivity to DeValera's ambivalent position. On the one hand, DeValera was capable of conciliatory gestures to the Ulster Unionists while on the other hand; he pursued policies which were the result of his dream of an Irish-speaking, separatist republic.

8   BRADLEY, ANTHONY. "Landscape as Culture: the Poetry of Seamus Heaney," in *Contemporary Irish Writing*, edited by J. D. Brophy and R. J. Porter (New Rochelle: Iona College Press; Boston: Twayne): 1–14.
    Bradley concentrates on the way in which Heaney's poetry goes from the natural to the cultivated. At the same time, he asserts that there is an opposite pull in the poetry, which is especially valuable for people living in a technological age who have lost touch with nature and the rural scene. Heaney

gives a strong sense of the Irish cultural landscape and unifies the earth and the intellect.

9   BROWN, TERENCE. "Four New Voices: Poets from Ulster," *Contemporary Literary Criticism* 25: 240–41.
    Reprint (excerpts) of 1975.8; reprinted 1977.4; 1986.6, under title "A Northern Voice."

10 BUCKLEY, VINCENT. "Poetry and the Avoidance of Nationalism," in *Irish Culture and Nationalism 1970–1950*, edited by Oliver MacDonagh, et al. (New York: St. Martins): 258–79.
    The myths of nationality and conflict still live in Ireland, and it is to be assumed that they will also exist in poetry. Buckley examines Conor Cruise O'Brien's charge that Heaney is too nationalist, a charge which is supported by other commentators. Buckley maintains that Heaney is not really a political or a republican poet—such opinions are propagandist and serve no creative purpose.

11 BUTTEL, ROBERT. "Seamus Heaney," *Contemporary Literary Criticism* 25: 241–42.
    Reprint (excerpts) of 1975.10.

12 CLINES, FRANCIS X. "Poet of the Bogs: Seamus Heaney, Ireland's Foremost Living Poet Commands a Growing Audience," *New York Times Magazine* (March 13): 42–43, 98–99, 104.
    Clines in this general essay talks about Heaney's popularity, his life in Ireland, his teaching at Harvard, and his familiarity with and his reverence for writers such as Wordsworth, Yeats, Hopkins, Graves, Lowell, and Whitman. Of the Irish political scene, he notes Heaney's current project, *Station Island*, where he hopes to face the Northern situation and put it behind him.
    Reprinted 1985.73.

13 CROZIER, ANDREW. "Thrills and Frills: Poetry as Figures of Empirical Lyricism," in *Society and Literature 1945–1970*, edited by Adam Sinfield (New York: Holmes & Meier): 199–233.
    Crozier in his essay discusses the canon of contemporary literature, 1945–1970. He examines Blake Morrison's placing of Heaney, Hughes, and Larkin in that canon.

14 DI PIERO, W. S. "Digs," *Contemporary Literary Criticism*, 25: 250–51.
    Reprint of 1981.13; reprinted 1989.12, under title "Digs: On Seamus Heaney."

15 DONOGHUE, DENIS. "A Playwright, Three Poets, an Actor, and a Walking Saint," *Inside Tribune* (Dublin), (October 2): 4.

Donoghue reviews Field Day Company's new pamphlets, including Heaney's *An Open Letter*. The reviewer comments that "Heaney's protest came slowly" and that "Heaney is too nice to be a satirist."

16 ENGLE, JOHN. "That Always Raised Voice: Séan O Riada and Irish Poetry," in *Contemporary Irish Writing*, edited by James D. Brophy and Raymond J. Porter (New Rochelle: Iona College Press; Boston: Twayne): 33–47.

During his lifetime the Irish musician and composer Séan O'Riada touched the best Irish poets of his generation. In the years following his death in 1971, Kinsella, Montague, and Heaney wrote elegies reviewing their relationship with him. Heaney's elegy is an ambivalent response to an ambiguous personality. Heaney acknowledges his comradeship with O'Riada, whose preoccupation with the Irish musical tradition is akin to Heaney's own interest in the native word. Heaney's poetry of restraint and quiet observation is contrasted with O'Riada's "instinctive side." The elegy "reads like the work of someone drawn to O'Riada 'thematically' but not personally." His poetic relationship can be styled as keeping one's distance; Montague's is warmer, while Kinsella shows a sense "of an almost total personal and artistic kinship."

17 FITZGERALD, MARY M. "Modern Poetry," in *Recent Research on Anglo-Irish Writers: A Supplement to Anglo-Irish Literature: A Review of Research* (New York: Modern Language Association of America): 299–334.

In her essay Fitzgerald considers "poets who were contemporaries or successors of Yeats." The section "Studies of Individual Poets" includes works about Heaney from 1968 to 1982.

18 GIFFORD, TERRY, and NEIL ROBERTS. "Hughes and Two Contemporaries: Peter Redgrove and Seamus Heaney," in *The Achievement of Ted Hughes,* edited by Keith Sagar (Athens: University of Georgia Press): 90–106.

This essay examines the relationships between Ted Hughes and two important contemporaries. The three put their faith in an inward source; they are highly conscious of language. They associate the female with some form of rebirth. For Heaney the meanings of Celtic mythology are immanent in contemporary history, while for Hughes they have to be met through an imaginative journey. Hughes and Heaney have developed an autobiographical poetry. Heaney's "Skunk" recalls Hughes's "The Thought Fox." "Neither poem would be the same if the poets had not explored archetypes and myths as seriously as they have," in a quest to keep faith "with the world of things and the world of spirits equally."

19 GRAVIL, RICHARD. "Wordsworth's Second Selves?," *Wordsworth Circle* 14, 4 (Autumn): 191–201.

Gravil's theme is the presence of Wordsworth in contemporary British poetry, particularly as seen in the work of Geoffrey Hill, W. S. Graham, R. S. Thomas, Seamus Heaney, and Ted Hughes. Granvil points out that from *Death of a Naturalist* through *Field Work* and in his prose writings, Heaney, in his attitude to nature, in his sense of the poet as diviner, in his belief in poetry as a revelation of the self to the self, and in his moral intelligence, shows the influence of Wordsworth. In the "Glanmore Sonnets" Wordsworth is seen as model and warning. Indeed, throughout *Field Work* the poet is faced with a choice between isolation or becoming embroiled in tribal divisions. This preoccupation for the poet is Wordsworthian. What direction Heaney's art will take we must wait and see.

20 GREEN, CARLANDA. "The Feminine Principle in Seamus Heaney's Poetry," *Ariel: A Review of International English Literature* 14, 3 (July): 3–13.

Heaney's best poetry is achieved by a wedding of the feminine (Irish, Celtic, emotional, inspirational) with the masculine (English, rational, intellectual) element. Green sees this feminine principle of Heaney as that which pulls man toward the nurturing earth and toward woman. The feminine principle was established in Heaney's early poetry; later, in *Wintering Out*, she becomes the bog goddess. She is again recalled in *North* and gives the poet a context to view the current violence in Northern Ireland. In *Field Work* the cultural past is "the lens through which Heaney looks at the present," as he goes to the Earth Mother as the source of understanding and renewal. The male must ally himself with this female principle because it is "the regenerative, spiritual principle of life."

Reprinted 1986.25.

21 HARMON, MAURICE. "Seamus Justin Heaney," in *20th-Century Poetry* (London: St. James/Macmillan): 219–20.

Brief assessment of Heaney's poetry, prefaced by biographical data and a list of publications. Harmon speaks of Heaney's poetry as rooted in his rural background. The dark centres of the past found an eloquent metaphor in the bogs, a process which broadened the scope of his poetry.

Reprinted 1985.35.

22 "Heaney to publish epic poem," *Derry Journal* (September 6): 5.

This unsigned article describes Heaney's plans to publish *Sweeney Astray*. The article also reports information on the poem provided by the poet. There is some mention of *Field Day*.

1983

23 KELLY, CONOR. "Seamus Heaney Naming His Nation," *Magill* 7, 5 (Christmas): 40–45.

Kelly says that much of Heaney's work is concerned with the different traditions facing the people born in Northern Ireland. In his preoccupation with language, the poet looks to find a form to contain it. He laces his poetry with place-names which "declare shored, often divided allegiances." The hidden Ireland is discovered in place-names in his collection *Wintering Out*. Yet he needed a coherent mythology, which he found in *North* in his great series of poems based on Stone Age corpses uncovered in a Danish bog. *North* was followed by *Field Work,* which Kelly asserts is his most accomplished and humane work to date. The process of naming his country is also to be seen in *Sweeney Astray*, in which the poet translates the placenames of the the medieval poem into their modern equivalents. There is also his naming of Irish trees, stags, birds, animals, and food. Kelly notes Heaney's assertion of Sweeney as a figure of the displaced, guilty artist and quotes Heaney as saying: "It is possible to read the work as an aspect of the quarrel between free, creative imagination and the constraints of religious, political, and domestic obligation."

24 MARTIN, GRAHAM. "John Montague, Seamus Heaney and the Irish Past," in *The Present*, vol. 8 of *The New Pelican Guide to English Literature*, edited by Boris Ford (Harmonsworth: Penguin Books): 380–95.

Martin relates the emergence of Northern Irish poetry and Heaney in particular to a shift in cultural power from London to the "provinces." English poetry, the author asserts, gave Heaney a means to escape the oppression of the "Ulster Protestant state" and the Roman Catholic Church. Heaney's sense of the Catholic tradition, Martin concludes, "derives more from family living than from theology or ethics." Martin mentions the influences of Hughes and Lawrence on Heaney's poetry. "Evocative description" and "metaphorical vitality" are striking features of Heaney's poetry. Concluding with a discussion of *North* and *Field Work,* Martin suggests that the latter is written from "a condition of pastoral withdrawal." The land in *Field Work* is "simplified" and does not reverberate with the political struggles of *North*.

25 MILLIGAN, BRYCE. "An Interview with Seamus Heaney," *Pax* 1, 1: 41–47.

Heaney discusses the responsibility of the poet with authority and his role as an "ambassador." He also talks about the Irish-Catholic fear of the "bad word." "Bogland," according to Heaney, links up ideas of sacrifice with "the mythos of Irish republicanism." Heaney comments upon his understanding of what is meant by the "muse" and its connection with inner freedom. In addition, Heaney refers to the work of Kinsella, Milosz, Sefaris, and Austin Clarke.

26 MONTAGUE, JOHN. "Tarzan among the Nightingales," *Fortnight* 200 (December): 27.
    Review of *Sweeney Astray*. Montague feels that Heaney's sharpening up and cleaning up the text of the Sweeney story is done because it is written for "an audience that can no longer relish the peculiarities of Irish literature." While Heaney has written well *about* early Irish nature poetry, he does not think in Irish when it comes to translating it. Austin Clarke and Flann O'Brien were obsessed with Sweeney, and in both there is a wildness which is not matched by Heaney.

27 O'CONNELL, SHAUN. "Seamus Heaney: Poetry and Power," *Contemporary Literary Criticism*, 25: 248–49.
    Reprint of 1980.28.

28 O'HAIRE, HUGH. "A Touch of the Irish Poet on L.I.," *New York Times* (May 22, sect. 21): 19.
    The occasion of this article is the Stony Brook Foundation's honoring of Heaney for his distinguished contributions to higher education. The article also describes Heaney's familiarity with Long Island and includes comments on Heaney by Long Island residents Louis Simpson and Thomas Flanagan (in whose home Heaney stayed while translating *Sweeney Astray* in 1981). There is also a brief remark by Heaney in which he describes his favorite places on the Island.

29 O'TOOLE, FINTAN. "Heaney's Sweeney," *Inside Tribune* (Dublin), (November 20): 12.
    O'Toole talks to Heaney about his recently published *Sweeney Astray*. Heaney's first impulse was to select the lyrical high points for translation. Having decided to do the entire work, he was unhappy with his first attempts and left the poem aside for seven years. Now that he has completed the work he has used Sweeney as a mask for his own voice: "I would hope that to inhabit Sweeney or be inhabited by him would be a bonus in the writing."

30 PARINI, JAY. "Seamus Heaney: The Ground Possessed," *Contemporary Literary Criticism* 25: 244–46.
    Reprint (excerpts) of 1980.29; reprinted 1986.48, under title "The Ground Possessed."

31 PAULIN, TOM. "Shorter Reviews," *New Statesman* (January 14): 27.
    Paulin, in his review of *The Crane Bag Book of Irish Studies*, quotes from Heaney's introduction to the volume and refers to Heaney in passing.

32　PERLOFF, MARJORIE. "Seamus Heaney: Peat Politics and Poetry," *Contemporary Literary Criticism* 25: 250.
　　　Reprint of 1981.31; reprinted 1985.73.

33　PETTINGELL, PHOEBE. "Poetry's Performance," *New Leader* 66, 20 (October 31): 14–15.
　　　Pettingell comments on Faber's new series of poetry tapes by Heaney, Tom Paulin, Ted Hughes, and Paul Muldoon. Heaney reads fewer poems than the others but talks more about them. The pronunciation and inflection that the voice supplies brings a new energy to the written word, which sometimes makes "a poem different and better than the one that was actually written."

34　PINE, RICHARD. "Finding the right words," *Sunday Press* (September 25): 12.
　　　Pine outlines the publications that launched the Field Day project. Among them, Pine refers to Heaney's *An Open Letter*. Pine concludes that finding himself in the *Penguin Book of Contemporary British Poetry* ("a colonial annexation"), Heaney saw the situation as one "which puzzles, perplexes, amuses him, rather than offending."

35　PINSKY, ROBERT. "The Prose of an Irish Poet," *Contemporary Literary Criticism* 25: 249–50.
　　　Reprint of 1980.31; reprinted 1985.73.

36　PYBUS, RODNEY. "Matters of Ireland: Recent Irish Poetry," *Contemporary Literary Criticism* 25: 250.
　　　Reprint of 1981.32.

37　QUINLAN, KIERAN. "Forsaking the Norse Mythologies: Seamus Heaney's Conversion to Dante," *Studies in Medievalism* 2, 3 (Summer): 19–28.
　　　Tracing Dante's presence through Heaney's *Field Work*, Quinlan first asserts that Heaney's appropriation of Dante grows out of the Irish-Italian (visionary) tradition, which includes Yeats and Joyce. Quinlan then examines Heaney's attraction to and appropriation of Dante in terms of Heaney's preoccupation with the underground/underworlds; the poet's concentration on the "victims" of the "Northern Irish Hell"; Dante's and Heaney's interest in dialect, language as an historical/political map; and both poet's political awareness and sense of exile. The essay concludes with a brief discussion of the first appearances of poems from the forthcoming "Station Island" sequence.

38　QUINLAN, KIERAN. "Unearthing a Terrible Beauty: Seamus Heaney's Victims of Violence," *World Literature Today* 57, 3 (Summer): 365–69.

This essay examines a few key poems from *North* and *Field Work*. Quinlan places Heaney in the "Ulster Literary Revival," which he contrasts with the "Irish Literary Revival." He argues that the "Ulster" revival is informed by a resigned sadness in the face of Ireland's violence. He also argues that Heaney's poetry suggests that peace will only come from "exhaustion" and "weariness"—key moods in Northern Ireland. He sees *Field Work* as a move from the mythic to the real and domestic. He concludes by identifying Heaney's poetry as that of "an apolitical pagan religious vision."

39   ROULSTON, STEWART. "Past Tense, Present Tension: Protest and Poetry and Ulster History," *Eire-Ireland* 18, 3 (Fall): 100–123.
      Heaney appears as an intermittent cultural (read "Catholic") reference point in this essay on contemporary Protestant poetry from Ulster: "the land of Ireland can be a resting-place [for Heaney] in a way seemingly impossible for the Ulster Protestant."

40   SCHIRMER, GREGORY A. "Seamus Heaney: Salvation in Surrender," *Contemporary Literary Criticism* 25: 243–44.
      Reprint (excerpts) of 1980.33.

41   STEVENSON, ANNE. "The Recognition of the Savage God: Poetry in Britain Today," *Contemporary Literary Criticism* 25: 242.
      Reprint (brief excerpt) of 1979.37.

42   THWAITE, ANTHONY. "The Hiding Places of Power," *Contemporary Literary Criticism* 25: 249.
      Reprint of 1980.40; reprinted 1986.55.

43   WRIGHT, DAVID. "A Poet's Prose," *Contemporary Literary Criticism* 25: 249.
      Reprint of 1980.41.

1984

1   ALCORN, ALFRED. "Seamus Heaney Named to Boylston Professorship," *Harvard University Gazette* 80, 14 (December 7): 1, 4.
     The essay begins with tributes to Heaney from William Alfred and Helen Vendler. Alcorn then goes on to give some biographical details of the poet and a general introduction to his poetry. He ends with some comment on the Boylston Chair and lists its former incumbents.

1984

2 ANNWN, DAVID. *Inhabited Voices: Myth and History in the Poetry of Geoffrey Hill, Seamus Heaney and George Mackay Brown* (Frome, Somerset: Bran's Head Books). 243 pp.

A critical study of the part played by myth and history in the work of three contemporary poets whose poetry is deeply rooted in their national past. For Heaney it is Irish history which he uses to show his love of the country. Much of the work is devoted to a summing up of others' criticism.

3 BREDIN, HUGH. "A Language of Courage and Love of Objects," *Fortnight* 209 (November): 18, 20.

Review of *Station Island*. Bredin asserts that Heaney in this book is as good as ever and possibly better. The lyrical poetry of the first section deals with a wide range of themes—sex, childhood, age, and above all, the meaning of objects. For Heaney, objects and their relation to people define the world. The "Station Island" sequence involves meetings with people—some literary, some exemplary. Shadows of more distant voices are there too—Dante, Horace, St. John of the Cross. These are rich and complex poems and the Lough Derg setting is particularly felicitous. In the "Sweeney Redivivus" poems Heaney moves from the lyric to the dramatic and shows Sweeney as strong and tempered by adversity. Heaney is one of the few poets who can, in the words of Matthew Vendome, "stimulate the understanding, refresh the attention, awaken goodwill, resonate in his listeners, and nourish the appetite for knowledge."

4 BYRNE, J. M. "The Significance of Landscape and History in the Poetry of Seamus Heaney, Derek Mahon, and John Montague." Ph.D. dissertation, University of Newcastle-upon-Tyne.

5 CAREY, JOHN. "The Joy of Heaney," *Sunday Times* 8358 (October 14): 42.

Review of *Station Island* and of *Sweeney Astray*. Carey sees Heaney's encounters with life as random, yet he weighs each meeting to discover what it has done to himself. Each object in his life comes adorned with its past. This insight, when applied to people, prevents him from giving the quick, simple answer which seems appropriate from a political point of view. The "Station Island" sequence is an act of self-accusation because of the poet's silence as a Northern Ireland Catholic. In *Sweeney Astray* the main character stands for the displaced, guilty artist. Heaney's poetry is not polemic, but it makes itself felt without deceiving with false hope.

6 CARSON, CIARAN. "Sweeneys Ancient and Modern," *Honest Ulsterman* 76 (Autumn): 73–79.

Review of *Sweeney Astray*. Irish writers writing in English inherit a linguistic dilemma—that of the Irish language. That language underlies this entire work. Carson examines Heaney's version of the medieval tale with reference to O'Keeffe's translation and Flann O'Brien's verson in *At Swim-Two-Birds*. Heaney's version sometimes gives us Heaney's voice rather than that of Sweeney. When, however, we consider the neglect of the tale until Heaney made his version, we can only commend Heaney's work.

Reprinted 1985.12, in a revised and expanded version under title "*Sweeney Astray*: Escaping from Limbo."

7   CLYDE, TOM. "Station to Station," *North* 3 (October): 15–16.
Review of *Station Island*. In the first part of the book we are in familiar territory; the best poems are those inspired by inanimate objects. Dante's spirit is very much present in the second part of this important work. In the third part the poet questions his ambitions and values. This is Heaney's most interesting work to date.

8   COTTER, JAMES FINN. "Poetry Marathon," *Hudson Review* 37, 3 (Autumn): 496.
Brief review of *Sweeney Astray*. In his version of the tale "Heaney delivers all the drama of the hero 'on the run,' an unforgettable figure."

9   DAVIES, RUSSEL. "The Grand Poetry Tour," *Observer Review* (October 21): 21.
The article describes day-by-day the reading tour made by Heaney and Craig Raine. Heaney was launching *Station Island* and *Sweeney Astray*.

10   DE BREADUN, DEAGLAN. "Comfortable image belies the serious poet," *Irish Times* (September 13): 13.
De Breadun talks with Heaney in the poet's Dublin home. They discuss his writing pattern, his forthcoming book *Station Island*, and the appearance in it of William Carleton and Heaney's cousin Colum McCartney. The poet talks of his life as a student in Derry and Belfast, his father, the neighborly Protestants and their disquieting paramilitaries, his move to the Republic, and his teaching at Harvard. He speaks of his admiration for Czeslaw Milosz and his friendship with Robert Lowell and Brian Friel. The Field Day enterprise is also touched on, as well as "the contemporaneity of all history in Ireland."

11   DONOGHUE, DENIS. "A Mad Muse," *New Republic* 190, 3615 (April 30): 27–29.
Review of *Sweeney Astray*. O'Keeffe chose the most important of the three manuscripts for his edition of the poem. This is the version with which Heaney worked. He omits some of the material and turns some of the prose passages into verse. His concern is with the spirit of the original.
Reprinted 1985.73; 1986.14, under title "Heaney's Sweeney"; 1986.15 (in part, untitled).

1984

12 DUNN, DOUGLAS. "Heaney Agonistes," *London Magazine* 24, 8 (November): 92–95.

Review of *Station Island* and of *Sweeney Astray*. Dunn asserts that Heaney's poetry is distracted by the urgency of Irish nationality. Both *Station Island* and *Sweeney Astray*, the latter indirectly, deal with the relationship between poetry and politics. The "Station Island" sequence has twelve substantial poems in which the poet meets people from his own and his country's past, some of whom offer him advice. *Sweeney Astray* tells of "a harrowing fall from repute and acclaim." It should be read "as a measure of the inroads made on Heaney's mind by the times in which he lives."

Reprinted 1986.16.

13 GAFFNEY, ELIZABETH. "[Book Review]," *America* 150 (June 30): 495–98.

Review of *Sweeney Astray* and of two other works. Gaffney considers it a striking poem. Sweeney is confused. He blames God for his misfortune while at the same time he celebrates the natural world. He is a figure for the outsider, the artist. He has two voices, the narrator and the poet. The poem is full of love of the landscape. In his poetry Heaney "has always found words to praise the ordinary."

Reprinted 1985.73.

14 HILDEBIDLE, JOHN. "The Provocative Ghosts of Seamus Heaney," *Boston Globe* (December 16): B49, B51.

Review of *Station Island*. Hildebidle sees this book as bringing together Heaney's "ghosts": the voices of Sweeney, of Chekhov, Joyce, and other "familiars." For these voices poetry and politics are facts. Heaney's problem is how to write fairly and justly of his birthplace which has destroyed many of the voices who visit him. Dante, whose life was full of similar family conflicts, is a strong presence in these poems. They speak of a world of treachery from which Heaney has removed himself far enough to see it clearly.

15 JENNINGS, ELIZABETH. "The Spell-Binder," *Spectator* 253, 8159 (November 24): 30–31.

In her review of *Station Island* Jennings comments briefly on Heaney's first five books of poetry. *Field Work* was a true advance in themes and forms. There is much that is new in *Station Island,* where we find the poet in complete command of language, image, and form. He shows great virtuosity; he never reaches pat solutions; he belongs to that great masculine tradition of Yeats and MacNeice.

Reprinted 1986.29.

16 JOHNSTON, CONOR. "Poetry and Politics: Responses to the Northern Ireland Crisis in the Poetry of John Montague, Derek Mahon, and Seamus Heaney," *Poesis* 5, 4 (September): 12–35.

Johnston examines how three Northern Ireland poets—John Montague, Derek Mahon, Seamus Heaney—respond to the agony and strife in the province. He looks at the relationship of the poets' work with the ongoing civil strife, and what that relationship should be. Montague confronts the crisis in a bitter, sad, despairing, passionate voice; Mahon recognizes the legitimate demands of community; Heaney's responsibility to community remains unresolved.

17 KEANE, MICHAEL JAMES. "Private and Public Voices in Irish Poetry: W. B. Yeats, Patrick Kavanagh and Seamus Heaney." Ph. D. dissertation, University of Michigan, 271 pp.

Although Yeats, Kavanagh, and Heaney represent different generations and traditions of twentieth-century Irish poets, their poetry shares the impulse to project both public (essentially political) as well as private (essentially spiritual) voices. Individual chapters of the dissertation examine how images of "place" in the poets' works transform private feelings into public statement.

18 KEARNEY, J. A. "Heaney: Poetry and the Irish Cause," *Theoria* 63 (October): 37–53.

Kearney sets out to trace the changing relationship between Heaney's sense of himself and his sense of the Irish situation as seen in *Selected Poems 1965–1975*. The attempt to recapture childhood fears shown in *Death of a Naturalist* is further expanded in *Door into the Dark* with the additional sense of the Northern violence. In the same way, "Bogland" in *Door into the Dark* is preparing us for the poems inspired by the Danish bog burials. *Wintering Out* shows Heaney grappling with the increasing bloodshed and bitterness in Northern Ireland. The attempt to bring together contemporary and archaic death by violence involves "an underlying hope." In *North* he has arrived at a stage where he deals directly with the Northern troubles and posits a sense "of what it means for him to be a poet in such a context."

19 KEARNEY, RICHARD. "Annual Review '84: Literature: The Year of 'The Gigli Concert,'" *Irish Times* (December 31): 6.

Includes discussion of Tom Murphy's *The Gigli Concert* and Heaney's *Station Island*. Kearney views Heaney as exploring the relationship between poetry and politics. In the "Station Island" sequence Heaney feels guilty at his lack of political involvement until Joyce's ghost assures him that such guilt and involvement is a waste of time. In the final section Sweeney is seen as the liberated poet. Heaney refuses to choose between guilt and the carefree imagination. Kearney endorses Heaney's stance of viewing the political reality

1984

from several angles—"words not only mirror reality. . .but actively shape and reshape it."

20 KENNELLY, BRENDAN. "Soaring from the Treetops," *New York Times Book Review* 89 (May 27): 14.
    Review of *Sweeney Astray*. As in the original, Heaney in his version of the poem mixes poetry and prose. Kennelly sees the work as "a compelling poem of human pain." While some of it is flat, the poetry of pain is balanced by the poetry of praise. His best praise is for the Irish landscape.
    Reprinted 1986.33 (untitled).

21 KENNY, ADRIAN. "Heaney's Quest," *Sunday Press* (October 21): 18.
    Review of *Station Island*. Kenny sees the poems in this work reliving past experience. The Lough Derg pilgrimage is Heaney's return to his past in which he meets mentors and accusers. In the Sweeney poems the poet is never at peace; he must follow his craft whatever the struggle.

22 KIBERD, DECLAN. "Breech birth of a naturalist," *Sunday Tribune* (October 28): 20.
    Review of *Station Island*. Kiberd poses the question for Heaney: Does the beauty of poetry have a place in a painful world? Nature, which did so well in Heaney's early poetry, does not suffice; neither does religion. There is an empty space where the poet walks and from which he can be tempted by making a political commitment. He adopts the position of impartiality instead, by listening to the voices of the dead of Northern Ireland. Some accuse him, but he is absolved by the ghost of Joyce. He must forget the past and strike his own note. He must also smile a smile that may well be the smile of modesty and self-effacement. However, when he should create his own passage of beauty, he gives us an extract from Dante.

23 KIELY, NIALL. "Warm Praise for a Gentle Poet," *Irish Times* (December 21): 8.
    Kiely quotes extensively from Heaney's comments on the appointment of Ted Hughes as British Poet Laureate. Heaney commends the choice as a move away from "the usual middle-class establishment." Hughes is interested in the role of the poet in society. According to Heaney, poets represent "an alternative source of authority." Heaney sees no problem in the choice of Hughes, whose images from nature are in stark contrast with the poetry of Philip Larkin, who had been widely predicted as the choice for the position.

24 LONGLEY, EDNA. "Old Pewter," *Honest Ulsterman* 77 (Winter): 54–58.
    Review of *Station Island*. Longley maintains that Heaney's approaches in *Station Island* share similar virtues and faults. The first section contains some beautiful poems, while in other poems Heaney attempts unsuccessfully to assuage his guilt. More than Kavanagh, Devlin, and other poets Heaney

concentrates on the confessional potential of Lough Derg while his guilt is "a useless *poetic* emotion." In the third section the Sweeney persona allows Heaney to explore a wide range of feeling. The book proves that when a poet is responsible to language, "other responsibilities look after themselves." The book is too long by a third.

25 McAULEY, LIAM. "Poets go on the superstar circuit," *Sunday Independent* (August 12): 15.

The brief article describes Faber and Faber's plan to use a helicopter during the "Heaney/Raine British Tour, 1984." McAuley also includes some interesting comments made by Faber's marketing specialists.

26 McELROY, JAMES. "Poems that Explode in Silence: A Meditation on the Work of Seamus Heaney," *Studia Mystica* 7, 2 (Summer): 40–44.

The essay meditates upon Heaney's religiosity in relation to images of light and dark, as in "In Gallarus Oratory." Heaney, according to McElroy, is simultaneously "the enemy and captive of a Christian monastic tradition" as exemplified in Mad Sweeney. Heaney's poetry is infused with a "mystical urge," a "radical, spiritual element" that cannot be quelled.

27 McELROY, JAMES. "Seamus Heaney: Skull Handler and Parablist," *Greenfield Review* 12 (Summer/Fall): 200–213.

McElroy chides Heaney for not being true to his Celtic roots. The author approves of the "mystical union" between the poet and the world in his poetry. The essay concludes "Heaney has finally come to his senses" and has "reclaimed and reaffirmed" the "submerged tradition" in the "Glanmore Sonnets."

28 McGRAIL BROWN, M. "Art Can Outface History: A Study of the Development of the Poetry of Seamus Heaney." Ph.D. dissertation, New University of Ulster.

29 McKNIGHT, JAMES. "A Foolish Hack," *Fortnight* (November): 15.

The article describes an exchange between a journalist and Heaney, who was giving a reading in Belfast with Craig Raine. The journalist accused the poets of manufacturing their "megastar" positions and not living the life of the starving poet. Heaney responded that poets have to fight against the language of "megastar journalists." McKnight quotes another journalist as pointing out that Heaney's comment stressed that "the fight against cheap language and cheap thoughts" was precisely the mission upon which poets were engaged.

1984

30 MASON, DAVID. "Seamus Heaney's Guttural Muse," *Mid-American Review* 4, 2 (Fall): 101–5.

    Mason discusses the importance of voice in *Field Work* and uses "Casualty" as a main example. He also examines Heaney's vocabulary and relates it to the poet's "etymology of being."

31 MATHEWS, AIDAN CARL. "All he touches turns to guilt," *Sunday Independent* (November 18): 20.

    In his review of *Station Island*, Mathews argues that what matters most in *Station Island* (and in all of Heaney's work) is "the shadow side of the Midas touch. . .that what he touches also turns to guilt." Mathews concludes that Heaney is our "guiltiest poet" and that *Station Island* is a conversation with our whole cultural nature.

32 MAY, DERWENT. "One feels the iron swerving out of control," *Listener* 112, 2889 (December 20–27): 53–54.

    In her review, May catalogues the many weaknesses she finds in Heaney's *Station Island*. Arguing that Heaney overworks the theme of "guilt," May feels that Heaney's poems thrust private problems on the readers with a sense of self-importance. Heaney is too "coy" when writing about sex and too "over-intense and sentimental" when writing about his childhood. May also thinks that many of the poems' situations are inflated, particularly in terms of the analogies Heaney produces. Finally, she believes that the language is often over-charged, especially when Heaney attempts in a "Lowell-like" fashion to recreate the "immediacy of a feeling." May also mentions *Sweeney Astray* in passing.

    Reprinted 1986.42.

33 MEARES, PETER. "'Ah Poet, Lucky Poet': Seamus Heaney's *Station Island*," *Agenda* 22, 3/4 (Autumn-Winter): 90–96.

    Review of *Station Island*. Meares outlines the three-part arrangement of the work. He lists his favorite poems in Part One and discounts others for various reasons. He sees Heaney exploring his bad conscience and the pain of Ireland in the "Station Island" sequence, in which he feels that the writing sometimes lacks conviction. In Part Three the presence, voice, and consciousness of Sweeney speak severally and sometimes merged. The concluding poem, "On the Road," attempts to sum up and integrate all that has gone before. Usually the language in the book is plain and idiomatic, and the text is vibrant. Some readers may not like the author showing his inner turmoil. Others will be grateful for this book and will have expectations for Heaney's work in the future.

34 MEDWICK, CATHLEEN. "[Book Review]," *Vogue* 174 (May): 236.
    Review of *Sweeney Astray*. In this brief review Medwick calls Sweeney "one of literature's great holy fools." Heaney is particularly adept at capturing Sweeney's "anguish."

35 MOONEY, BEL. "Poet, pilgrim, fugitive. . .The Times Profile: Seamus Heaney," *Times* (London, October 11): 8.
    Mooney's profile includes several quotations from Heaney, which include reflections on his childhood, *Station Island*, and *Sweeney Astray*. Heaney talks primarily about inner and outer divisions and the struggle for artistic freedom.

36 MORRISON, BLAKE. "Encounters with Familiar Ghosts," *Times Literary Supplement* (October 19): 1191–92.
    Review of *Station Island* and of *Sweeney Astray*. Morrison chooses "Making Strange" as a synecdoche for the entire *Station Island* volume since it is what we have come to recognize as "typically Heaney-ish" as a result of "weighing loyalties" and "puzzling through some moral dilemma." Morrison observes that we often associate the concepts of "dependable" and "reliable" with Heaney and that we "depend on him to charm us with stony truths." The reviewer finds the book "religious" in its concentration on "atonement" and extremely "Hardyesque." According to Morrison, although Sweeney in the book's third section is the "'new man' Heaney becomes," the poetry doesn't "let off enough steam." Morrison feels that *Sweeney Astray* is important because it allows Heaney to "practice his own inventive glosses."

37 MULDOON, PAUL. "Sweaney Peregraine," *London Review of Books* 6, 20 (November 1–14): 20–21.
    Reviews of *Station Island*, *Sweeney Astray*, and Craig Raine's *Rich*.
    Muldoon has a few words of wisdom for Heaney as well as making a few critical judgments. Muldoon argues that the real success of *Station Island* can be found not in the title sequence, but in the opening short lyrics (particularly in "Widgeon"). He finds the title sequence weakened by "arbitrary/obligatory sex scenes." More neutrally, Muldoon asserts that the "fatalism" of both Irish Catholicism and Irish nationalism have deeply influenced Heaney. Muldoon finds the "Sweeney Redivivus" poems either "unintelligible" or too "intelligible." His words of advice to Heaney are to keep a clear eye; forget about "general absolution"; and "resist more firmly the idea that he must be the best Irish poet since Yeats, which arose from rather casual remarks by the power-crazed Robert Lowell and the craze-powered Clive James. . . ."
    Reprinted 1986.45.

1984

38   MULLEN, FIONA. "Seamus Heaney: The Poetry of Opinion," *Verse* 1, 1: 15–21.
    Mullen provides a brief overview of the contemporary responses to *North*. She disagrees with Conor Cruise O'Brien's and Ciaran Carson's critiques of the volume. She argues that the political nature of Heaney's poetry is in his selection of materials which embody nationalist cultural values. After arguing that Heaney *is* a political poet, Mullan concludes with a short analysis of *Stations*.

39   O'DONOGHUE, BERNARD. "Singing Responsibly," *Poetry Review* (April): 57–59.
    This review of *Station Island* explores the volume's dominant themes of artistic freedom and religious affiliation and anxiety. In relation to the first theme, O'Donoghue comments: "The desire for abstract, artistic liberation is a recurrent and sympathetic yen; but by implication it is always rejected in the end because it is a lower thing than artistic conscientiousness." The reviewer is troubled by the inaccessibility of a few of the poems, especially in the book's first and third sections. O'Donoghue is impressed by Heaney's "daring, serious punning" in the "afterlife" poems. The review concludes by noting that Heaney's poems have none of "Dante's grimness."

40   O'TOOLE, FINTAN. "A Pilgrim's Progress," *Inside Tribune* (September 30): 1–3, 6.
    O'Toole talks with Heaney shortly before the publication of *Station Island*. O'Toole declares that the work is the pattern of the poet's life, in which he sees himself as a pilgrim "in search of atonement and renewal." As a Northern Catholic, Heaney was seen by many as a cultural spokesman. The self-accusations in *Station Island* underline the problems of the artist in the face of history and politics and express his desire to free himself of these entanglements. The poet sums up: "It's impossible to get back to the first innocence again, but it might be possible to get a second innocence."

41   PARINI, JAY. "Poet of Ireland," *Horizon* 27, 5 (June): 26–27.
    Parini refers to well-known facts about Heaney's career and the sources of the Irish poet's vast reputation. Parini includes a few unidentified quotations, including one from a Harvard undergraduate.

42   PONSOT, MARIE. "[Book Review]," *Commonweal* 111 (November 30): 666.
    Sweeney Astray is one of several books mentioned in this brief essay. Ponsot appreciates the "kinetic power" of Heaney's writing.

43   ROBINSON, PETER. "A Local Habitation: The Sense of Place in Contemporary British Poetry." Ph.D. dissertation, University of York (Canada).

Wordsworth emphasized specific locality and the use of observed detail and developed the meditative lyric, with its characteristic tension between observer and landscape. With Hardy an imagined place, grounded in reality, brought historical depth and continuity to the sense of place. Pound's development of Modernist techniques introduced the idea of a landscape constructed from fragments of history, literature, geography, and archaeology. The six poets discussed in this dissertation —Tomlinson, Larkin, Bunting, Hughes, Heaney, and Hill—illustrate how these themes and techniques have become an essential part of the contemporary sense of place.

44   RUSSELL, NOEL. "The Best of Heaney," *Irish News* (October 29): 4.
      After claiming that *Station Island* is Heaney's "best collection to date," Russell in his review of the book discusses its "wit" and the "joy and reveling in craftsmanship. . .celebrated throughout. . . ." Russell concentrates on the book's central sequence and argues that the encounters with the ghosts "are restorative, revivifying the poet's confidence and his powers." Initially uneasy with the seemingly self-conscious force of the volume, Russell accepts this force as ultimately necessary.

45   SHAPIRO, ALAN. "Crossed Pieties," *Parnassus* 11, 2 (Spring/Summer): 336–48.
      Review of *Poems, 1965–1975* and of *Preoccupations: Selected Prose 1968–1978*. Shapiro comments upon the tension between Irish culture and the English language which informs Heaney's early poetry. Although he finds many of the early poems marred by a "formal awkwardness" which results from the poem's subject fighting with the form, he sees Heaney's use of descriptive language as "a way of preserving his own identity" while asserting his religious allegiance. Shapiro argues that the use of free verse in *Door into the Dark* liberates Heaney. He also asserts that the "ambivalence" between "reverence" and "disgust" informs the best of the bog poems. However, Shapiro feels that many of the poems in *North* suffer from the "stale predictability of mannerism."

46   SLOTKIN, E. M. "[Book Review]," *Choice* 22 (September): 96.
      Brief review of *Sweeney Astray*. This is not a word-for-word rendering of the original Irish text. Heaney does, however, give us the storytelling and the poetry of the original. He recreates for us the oral narration and gives us a rich experience.

47   STOLER, PETER. "Singing of Skunks and Saints," *Time* 123 (March 19): 82, 84.
      This is a pre-publication announcement of Heaney's *Sweeney Astray*. Although there is only one cursory reference to the work, Stoler does record some interesting comments made by Heaney, whom he says looks as if he

1985

"might pass as an immigrant long-shoreman or an off-duty officer." For example, he quotes Heaney: "I have long insisted that the artist who works within the university system pays his way in society."

48 "Sweeney Astray," *Publishers Weekly* (March 23): 60.
    Brief review of *Sweeney Astray*. Sweeney resembles Lear in his stub-born defiance and in his love of nature. Heaney produces moments of great emotion in this sweeping translation, which "recaptures Sweeney for the modern imagination."

49 TROTTER, DAVID. "Declarative Voices: The development of Philip Larkin's 'voice.' Seamus Heaney and the Troubles," in his *The Making of the Reader: Language and Subjectivity in Modern American, English and Irish Poetry* (New York: St. Martin's Press): 177–95.
    Trotter notes that Heaney uses the phrase "declarative voice" to describe his own attempts to write a more public poetry. That voice was notable in its description of the Bog People in *North*. It was also used to explain cultural conflicts in terms of gender, which, Trotter argues, prevents any political understanding of national or sexual differences. The poems in the second half of *North* do speak out, but "they lack the buoyancy and finality of declarative utterance." Trotter sees "Casualty" as Heaney's finest attempt at a public poem.

50 WILLIAMSON, ALAN. "The Values of Contemporary European Poetry," *American Poetry Review* 13, 1 (January/February): 28–36.
    As the article's title suggests, Williamson includes Heaney in his discussion of several European poets and argues that Heaney has been "thoroughly Balkanized." These poets, according to Williamson, unlike their American counterparts, do not artificially divide life into simplistic and mutually exclusive binary categories. Poets like Heaney effectively intermingle (or often do not distinguish between) the personal, emotional, and linguistic with the historical, rational, and abstract. The article looks at two poems from *North*—"Punishment" and "Funeral Rites." The author appreciates Heaney's skeptical myth-making; and he concludes that Heaney, like other European poets, uses the primitive to get beyond destructive energies of chauvinistic primitivism.

1985

1 ANDERSON, NATHALIE F. "Survivor Beast, Politicized Terrain: Mythic Approaches in the Poetry of Ted Hughes and Seamus Heaney." Ph.D. dissertation, Emory University.

Ted Hughes and Seamus Heaney offer revealing examples of the application of myth to private and social ends. Each elaborates a single dynamic symbol: Hughes, the insatiable substratum uniting man and beast; Heaney, the landscape which exacts blood sacrifice from its inhabitants.

2   ANDREWS, ELMER. "The Gift and the Craft: An Approach to the Poetry of Seamus Heaney," *Twentieth Century Literature* 31, 4 (Winter): 368–79.

For Heaney, according to Andrews, poetry is secret and natural even though it must exist in a brutal world. The sense of self, too, depends on a sense of place and history. Another love is words. All these go towards finding a poetic voice. This voice is sensitive to the opposition between intelligence (male) and instinct (female) which Heaney uses to describe the tension between English influence and Irish experience. Then there is the problem of politics. The great model is Dante, who could, in Heaney's words, "place himself in a historical world yet submit that world to scrutiny from a perspective beyond history."

3   *The Art of Seamus Heaney,* 2d ed., edited and introduced by Tony Curtis (Bridgend: Poetry Wales Press; Chester Springs: Dufour Editions). 180 pp.

Reprint of 1982.1, with the addition of the following new essays: "*Sweeney Astray*: Escaping from Limbo" by Ciaran Carson, pp. 139–48; and "Meeting the Myth: *Station Island*" by Barbara Hardy, pp. 149–63.

4   BATTERSBY, EILEEN. "Stirring the cultural pot with a wooden spoon," *Irish Times* (June 5): 5.

Battersby's account of Heaney's election as Professor of Poetry at Oxford University includes comments by the poet himself, as well as by Benjamin Zephaniah, one of the challengers for the position.

5   BAX, MARTIN. "[Book Review]," *British Book News* (January): 52.

Review of *Sweeney Astray* and *Station Island*. Bax maintains that the two works have a close affinity—Sweeney appears again in *Station Island*. *Station Island* describes the pilgrimage of the poet. We are introduced to life in Northern Ireland and to love itself. Bax finds *Sweeney Astray* to be "rather laborious material," while *Station Island* is "a major achievement" that "strengthens Heaney's reputation as a poet of international stature."

6   BLAKE, JAMES J. "Leirmheas," *An Gael* (1984–85): 24–25.

Blake reviews *Sweeney Astray* along with *Suile Shuibhne* by Cathal O'Searcaigh. The review is in Irish with an English translation. Blake summarizes the poem and discourses on anti-clericalism in Irish literature and folklore. He also discusses the revival of the Irish language from the end of the 19th century.

1985

7   BOLAND, EAVAN. "Have Poets Forgotten Lessons of the Past?" *Irish Times* (July 24): 10.

As part of a series on the state of literature in Ireland today, Boland looks at several contemporary poets, including Heaney. Boland considers the fact that no Irish poet over sixty is a negative force on younger poets, who have perhaps forgotten the lessons of the past. She says that Heaney typically turns the "original physical territory" into a "metaphysics." She considers "Station Island" and his pamphlet "Hailstones" to be among his best work so far.

8   BOOTH, MARTIN. "[Seamus Heaney]," in his *British Poetry 1964 to 1984: Driving Through the Barricades* (London: Routledge & Kegan Paul): 222–26.

Booth argues that Heaney's ability to write in a vital way about his personal landscape has been the backbone of his writing. With *Wintering Out* he showed a strong sense of history together with a brutal comprehension of the realities of life. In *North* and *Field Work*, poems based on the Northern violence, his poetry reached new audiences. His success lies in his Irishness and in his facility with words. He writes of the present, and "he is not a self-indulgent poet."

9   BRESLIN, JOHN B. "[Book Review]," *America* 152 (March 9): 202–03.

Review of *Station Island*. Breslin comments on the division of the book into three parts. The first part consists of matters familiar to readers of Heaney's poetry. The poems in the second section are preoccupied with self-discovery, as different spirits of the dead remind Heaney of the problems of a land at war with itself. In the final section, Heaney assumes the voice of Sweeney in order to state the beauty of total commitment to one's art.

10 BUTTEL, ROBERT. "Hopkins and Heaney: Debt and Difference," in *Hopkins Among the Poets: Studies in Modern Responses to Gerard Manley Hopkins*, edited by Richard F. Giles (Hamilton, Ontario: International Hopkins Association): 110–13.

Buttel takes an early poem by Heaney, "October Thought," to illustrate the influence of Hopkins on the young poet. Heaney became increasingly subtle in the use of highly accentuated alliteration and assonance as he came to be more certain of his own strength. Heaney himself points out the affinity between his own dialect and the heavily accentuated, consonantal poetic voice of Hopkins. In his essay on Hopkins, *The Fire i' the Flint*, Heaney distinguishes between Hopkins's masculine forging and his own feminine emphasis. Buttel concludes that Heaney now moves in another direction but does not disown Hopkins's effect on his early development.

Reprinted (updated) 1992.11.

11 BUTTEL, ROBERT. "Seamus Heaney," in *Poets of Great Britain and Ireland since 1960*, part 2, *Dictionary of Literary Biography* 40, edited by Vincent Sherry (Detroit: Gale): 179–201.

    Buttell reviews Heaney's life and work, concluding with *Station Island* (1984). He also includes comments on Heaney's work by other critics. While praising the work so far achieved, Buttell poses the question of where Heaney goes now. Will we see new directions in subject matter and technique?

12 CARSON, CIARAN. "*Sweeney Astray*: Escaping from Limbo," in *The Art of Seamus Heaney*, edited and introduced by Tony Curtis (Bridgend: Poetry Wales Press; Chester Springs: Dufour Editions): 139–48.

    Revised and expanded version of 1984.6, where it appeared under title, "Sweeneys Ancient and Modern."

13 CHRISTOPHER, NICHOLAS. "A Pilgrim in County Donegal," *New York Times Book Review* 90 (March 10): 9.

    Review of *Station Island*. Christopher asserts that these poems are for the ear rather than for the eye. There is confidence here and an assured energy; the lines are rarely overloaded; his triplets and quatrains make the poems move. Some of Heaney's finest work is in this book.

    Reprinted 1986.8.

14 COLE, WILLIAM. "Four Fine Poets," *Saturday Review* 11 (July/August): 67.

    Brief review of *Station Island* together with works by X. J. Kennedy, Molly Peacock, and Ted Kooser. Heaney explores the Irish soul in poems that are lyrical and which show his "love for the odd word. . .that jolts."

15 CONDINI, NEREO. "Vision as Resistance," *CrossCurrents* 35 (Summer/ Fall): 339–41.

    Review of *Station Island*. Condini sees Heaney's work as the seeking for loyalty to one's calling. There are meditations on Ireland and nature, on people doing penance on Station Island, and on the poet's obligation to write unhampered by political or other peripheral considerations.

16 CURTIS, TONY. "Introduction," in *The Art of Seamus Heaney*, edited and introduced by Tony Curtis (Bridgend: Poetry Wales Press; Chester Springs: Dufour Editions): 7–10.

    Reprint (revised version) of 1982.3.

17 CURTIS, TONY. "A More Social Voice: *Field Work*," in *The Art of Seamus Heaney*, edited and introduced by Tony Curtis (Bridgend: Poetry Wales Press; Chester Springs: Dufour Editions): 53–62.

    Reprint of 1981.10; reprinted 1982.1; 1982.4; 1985.3.

1985

18 CURTIS, TONY. "Station Island," *Poetry Wales* 20, 3: 91–95.

  Curtis in his review of *Station Island* refers to *Sweeney Astray,* in which the poet sees a model for his own predicament, while here he reviews his life and art. The central sequence shows the poet revisiting the painful ground of his personal history as the pilgrims in their turn tread the stony, hurting paths. The eighth poem in the sequence is the most unsettling, in which the poet is confronted by his own second cousin, a victim of a random assassination. With each new collection, Heaney shows that he "contributes not only to our awareness of Ireland, but also to the nature of poetic discourse itself."

19 DAVIES, DIANE. "Knowing Their Place: A Reflection on the State of Contemporary Anglo-Irish Poetry," *Poetry Wales* 21, 2: 43–50.

  Contemporary, troubled Ireland has produced many good poets. Writers such as Montague, Heaney, Mahon, and Muldoon are all concerned with Ireland as a place with a past. They each, however, approach it in various ways, often transforming elements of their homeland into their own private mythology.

20 DAVIS, DICK. "Door into the Dark," in *The Art of Seamus Heaney*, edited and introduced by Tony Curtis (Bridgend: Poetry Wales Press; Chester Springs: Dufour Editions): 29–34.

  Reprint of 1982.5.

21 DEANE, SEAMUS. "A Noble Startling Achievement," *Irish Literary Supplement* 4, 1 (Spring): 1, 34.

  Review of *Station Island*. Deane finds that Heaney's internal debate is always fruitful. Here it is on betrayal in some of its many forms—experience, privacy, political commitment, what it is to be an Irish poet. The freedom of the poet in this case demands a high price. Great poetry carries a great risk, which Heaney performs "to the point where it begins to convert itself into freedom."

22 DEANE, SEAMUS. "Seamus Heaney: The Timorous and the Bold," in *Celtic Revivals: Essays in Modern Irish Literature 1880–1980* (London: Faber): 174–86.

  Deane reflects on Heaney's tentativeness in beginning to write poetry and on his boldness as he gained confidence in his writing. These aspects are seen in his first books, where he records rural activities and crafts which were in the process of dying, an old wisdom that was fading. Politics enter in with *Wintering Out*, where the poet's sympathy is with those who were executed because of their beauty or sinfulness. Heaney brings the ritual deaths to light so that he himself can face death and violence. From *Field Work* on, he has looked at his literary heritage in the light of his Northern Irish experience and has sought to deal with it as a poet.

  Reprinted 1993.11.

23 DE LA VARS, GORDON JOHN. "A Nation Found: The Work and Vision of John Hewitt," Ph.D. dissertation, Ohio State University.

   John Hewitt has confronted in his work those issues basic to understanding Ulster's turbulent past as well as its violent, tenuous present. His vision of a saner, stronger, freer Ireland has inspired other writers, most notably John Montague and Seamus Heaney who, although they approach these issues from different perspectives and backgrounds, share with Hewitt his recognition of the need for mercy and trust as a prerequisite for any political solution.

24 ELLMANN, RICHARD. "Heaney Agonistes," *New York Review of Books* 32, 4 (March 14): 19–21.

   Unlike Yeats, Heaney does not overwhelm his subjects; instead he allows them a certain freedom. His sounds are contained, definite; his rhythms are subdued; his images are apt and unexpected. The situation in Northern Ireland plays a large part in these poems, where the poet shows compassion, not partisanship. The central "Station Island" sequence represents his most ambitious work. His model is not Yeats but Joyce. His great talent is flowering in this work.

   Reprinted 1985.73; 1986.20.

25 FRAZIER, ADRIAN. "Pilgrim Haunts: Montague's *The Dead Kingdom* and Heaney's *Station Island,*" *Eire-Ireland* 20, 4 (Winter): 134–43.

   It is almost expected that a Northern Ireland poet should write about the Troubles. Heaney is very much aware of the conflicting demands of literature and politics. Of the three sections of *Station Island*, Frazier maintains that the best are the first and the last. In the last he adopts the mask of Sweeney which frees him to express his thoughts.

26 FUNSTEN, KENNETH. "In Verse," *Los Angeles Times* (February 10): 5.

   In this brief review of *Station Island*, Funsten comments on Heaney's use of metrical verse, as well as internal rhyme and off-rhyme, to give his sound a fuller suppleness.

27 GARRISON, DAVID. "Transient Fixities," *Commonweal* 112 (July 12): 410–11.

   Garrison in his review of *Station Island* says that Heaney continues to surprise us with poetry about the external and internal world. He outlines the three sections of the work. In the first section the concern is always the connection between the world, perception, and language. The "Sweeney Redivivus" poems are concerned with the poet's work—making poetry. The finest poems in this fine book are in the "Station Island" sequence, in which Heaney confronts his ghosts. At length we have the sense of a poet preparing himself to find his own songs and visions.

1985

28 GLEN, HEATHER. "Geoffrey Hill's 'England of the Mind,'" *Critical Review* 27: 98–109.
    Heaney, in his essay "Englands of the Mind," takes the work of three contemporary English poets—Larkin, Hughes, and Hill—and discusses their work as presenting a vision of England as a distinctive, historical, geographical, and social landscape with its own character and distinctive language. Glen uses Heaney's essay as a starting point to discuss Geoffrey Hill's vision of the England he inhabits.

29 GRANT, DAMIAN. "The Voice of History in British Poetry, 1970–84," *Etudes Anglaises: Grande-Bretagne, Etats-Unis* 38, 2 (April-June): 158–79.
    Despite assertions to the contrary, history remains a potent force in the work of several contemporary poets. Seamus Heaney and Derek Mahon make use of Irish and European history, respectively. Other poets do likewise.

30 GREVER, GLENN A. "Seamus Heaney, 1939," in *Research Guide to Biography and Criticism,* vol. 2 by Walter Beacham (Washington: Research Publishing): 565–68.
    Author's study guide under headings: chronology, bibliography, biography, criticism, and other sources.

31 GRIFFIN, CHRISTOPHER. "[Book Review]," *An Gael* 3, 1 (Summer): 49–50.
    Review of *Station Island*. Griffin states that following Heaney's career we see the steady growth of a poet. Images in earlier poetry are the seed of future growth. *Station Island* has many fine poems, but it does not seem to Griffin to be a development or a breakthrough. There is, however, the relish of textures, the hoard of words which make his poetry rich and sometimes difficult.

32 GROSS, JOHN. "Be it English or Irish, the poem's the thing," *New York Times* (January 31): C21.
    This is Gross's response to correspondents who objected to his describing Seamus Heaney as a British poet.

33 GROSS, JOHN. "Books of the Times," *New York Times* 134 (January 11): C26.
    Gross in his review of *Station Island* sees powerful images and compelling rhythms. He notes the pressures on Heaney from his native Ulster and from Irish history. The central sequence of poems, in which he encounters ghosts from his past, is as good as anything he has written. The final section of the book, which Gross finds somewhat obscure, shows us the poet following his own soundings. The book, however, will enhance Heaney's reputation.
    Reprinted 1985.73.

34 HARDY, BARBARA. "Meeting the Myth: *Station Island,*" in *The Art of Seamus Heaney*, edited and introduced by Tony Curtis (Bridgend: Poetry Wales Press; Chester Springs: Dufour Editions): 149–63.

Hardy points to the ambition of *Station Island* "in fortifying and intensifying personal experience through myth." The work has three sections, dealing respectively with the living, with the dead, and with a blending of these two. In *Station Island* we get a new structure in which Heaney recalls childhood experiences and shows a sense of political unease. The encounters with alternative selves, the personal recollections and confessions, are skillfully done. The sections involving other writers are not as lively as the pastoral and political poetry, and are the least imaginative. The "Sweeney Redivivus" section contains meditations on childhood, art, and politics. Individual poems such as "Sandstone Keepsake" deal with the poet's wonder and detachment "as he dares to contemplate the natural world at the frontier where history and politics overlook solitary meditation."

35 HARMON, MAURICE. "Seamus Justin Heaney," in *20th-Century Poetry* (Chicago and London: St. James Press): 219–20.

Reprint of 1983.21.

36 HEATH-STUBBS, JOHN. "Reviews," *Acumen* 1 (April): 95–97.

Review of *Station Island*. Heath-Stubbs notes that Heaney belongs to several traditions: as a rural realist, as an Ulsterman, and as a Catholic Ulsterman. These all give him "a painstaking truth to the realities of the observable world." This sense of things, however, militates against his prowess as a visionary. The visionary does take over in the "Station Island" sequence. The third section contains some of his best and most lyrical poems.

37 HOBSBAUM, PHILIP. "Craft and Technique in *Wintering Out*," in *The Art of Seamus Heaney*, edited and introduced by Tony Curtis (Bridgend: Poetry Wales Press; Chester Springs: Dufour Editions): 35–43.

Reprint of 1982.13.

38 INGERSOLL, EARL G. "[Book Review]," *Eire-Ireland* 20, 1 (Spring): 150–51.

A review of *Sweeney Astray*. The poem has its roots in Heaney's move from Belfast to Wicklow and his search for what it means to be a poet. His sympathy with the mad king is evident, as he himself tries to break the constraints imposed by the admirers and critics alike of his poetry. The violence in Northern Ireland confirmed in Heaney the search for what it means to be a writer.

1985

39   JOHN, BRIAN. "[Book Review]," *Canadian Journal of Irish Studies* 11, 2 (December): 89–91.

Reviews of *Sweeney Astray, Station Island,* and *Hailstones.* Heaney's achievement, as in the case of many modern Irish poets, is rooted in the Irish tradition. The bog for Heaney was a "fertile matrix" in the early seventies. The Sweeney myth may well serve him in a similar fashion in the future. The myth shows the dual nature of the creative process, bringing both pain and illumination. In *Station Island* he finds himself subject to tensions of place, language, and sectarianism. He faces accusations, in the final sequence, adopting the Sweeney persona, he achieves freedom for himself. In *Hailstones*, we find the familiar Heaney terrain and themes. John concludes, "there are few poets. . .who can match Heaney for mastery of theme and language."

40   JOHNSTON, DILLON. "Kavanagh & Heaney," in his *Irish Poetry after Joyce* (Notre Dame: University of Notre Dame Press): 121–66.

In his chapter on Kavanagh and Heaney, Johnston discusses the latter poet's work from *Death of a Naturalist* to *Station Island.* Kavanagh's influence on Heaney can be seen in Heaney's preoccupation with "radiant moments of ordinary rural life." Kavanagh had taught Heaney that this rural subject matter would possess "extraordinary nostalgic appeal." Although Johnston examines Heaney's volumes in chronological order, he concentrates on *North* and *Field Work.* Of *North*, Johnston argues that Part II of the volume is noticeably inferior to Part I; the critic sees Part II as Heaney's "dues paid to compatriots and a response to prodding from some Belfast poets." In *Field Work*, Johnston focuses upon many of the elegies, some of which he argues are too self-conscious in their appeal to tradition. The chapter ends with an analysis of *Station Island.* Johnston admires Heaney's experimentation in the volume, especially in relation to the "narrative complexity" of the book.

41   KENNER, HUGH. "An Irish Poet Masters His Trade," *Washington Post Book World* 108 (January 27): 1, 4.

Kenner, in his review of *Station Island*, compares the title sequence of poems to Yeats's "Cuchulain Comforted" and Eliot's "Little Gidding." He considers "Station Island" to be "as fine a long poem as we've been given in 50 years." The reviewer comments upon the continuity of imagery in Heaney's work from "Digging" to "First Gloss" in "Sweeney Redivivus."

42   KINNELL, GALWAY. "Galway Kinnell Introduces Seamus Heaney," *Envoy* 47 (April): 1.

Kinnell asserts that as Kavanagh is immersed in country life and Yeats is immersed in Irish mythology, so is Heaney immersed in both. His poetry is full of new words yet it is based on common speech. Rhyme, form, and music come naturally to him.

43 LANCHESTER, JOHN. "[Book Review]," *Oxford Poetry* 3: 58–61.
    Review of *Station Island*. Lanchester sees memory as the guiding motive of the first section of the book. Further on, the reviewer notes the self-examination and guilt which Heaney undergoes in meeting the ghosts of dead writers and friends. He is encouraged by the advice of James Joyce, the last ghost: "swim out on your own." In the third section, the "Sweeney Redivivus" series of poems, the influence of Yeats is seen in Sweeney as the figure of the artist. It is a revision of Yeats's "golden bird of art" in "Sailing to Byzantium"—Sweeney is both golden bird and scarecrow. The Sweeney figure "permits Heaney to retain conscience as well as the impulse to dare and to surprise."

44 LEHMAN, DAVID. "Pilgrim in Purgatory," *Newsweek* 105 (April 15): 92A.
    Review of *Station Island*. Lehman recalls the Bog Poems in *North* as a sign of Heaney's inability to escape the violence in Northern Ireland while he refuses to sentimentalize the tragedy. This refusal results in guilt, which is at the heart of *Station Island*. Ghosts from his past come to accuse him until the ghost of James Joyce advises him to forget all and sound his own work.

45 LLOYD, DAVID THOMAS. "Lyric Impulse and Epic Dimension in Heaney's North and Hill's Mercian Hymns." Ph.D. dissertation, Brown University.
    This dissertation examines two contemporary poetic sequences, Seamus Heaney's *North* and Geoffrey Hill's *Mercian Hymns*, to show ways in which the sequence fuses lyric and epic material. To sustain the large-scale cultural/historical exploration and the portrayal of a sophisticated consciousness, *North* and *Mercian Hymns* employ a complex and extended structure. These factors are responsible for the authority of voice Heaney and Hill achieve in their sequences, approaching the authority of a poet speaking for his or her people.

46 LLOYD, DAVID T. "Pap for the Dispossessed: Seamus Heaney and the Poetics of Identity," *Boundary* 2 13, 2–3 (Winter-Spring): 319–42.
    Lloyd's essay forms a highly critical approach to Heaney's work up to and including *Field Work*. He questions the assumptions of Heaney's work "as articulating important intuitions of Irish identity." For Lloyd, Heaney's treatment of the relation between politics and writing is superficial, as he resorts to metaphors which disregard the relation of writing with identity on many fronts. He reduces history to myth in positing a continuity between Iron Age human sacrifices and the killing which is taking place in Northern Ireland. Certainly, Heaney's poems in *Field Work* prove all the assumptions we make about good lyric poetry: they crystallize specific emotions and they express a unity of tone or feeling of a poetic voice. Nevertheless, Heaney's elevation "to a touchstone of contemporary taste. . .is. . .profoundly sympto-

1985

matic of the continuing meshing of Irish cultural nationalism with the imperial ideology which frames it."
    Reprinted 1992.32.

47   LONGLEY, EDNA. "*North*: 'Inner Emigré or 'Artful Voyeur'?," in *The Art of Seamus Heaney*, edited and introduced by Tony Curtis (Bridgend: Poetry Wales Press; Chester Springs: Dufour Editions): 65–95.
    Reprint of 1982.17. Reprinted 1986.35 (with additional material).

48   LONGLEY, EDNA. "Poetry and Politics in Northern Ireland," *Crane Bag* 9, 1: 26–41.
    This essay is not limited to Heaney. It is a discussion of the way in which the political situation in Northern Ireland has affected literature in general and Heaney's poems in particular.
    Reprinted, with additional material, 1986.36.

49   LOWERY, ROBERT. "Seamus Heaney: Warts and All," *Irish Literary Supplement* 4, 2 (Fall): 3.
    A casual account of the role gossip plays in shaping Irish-American literary careers—in this case, in the life of Heaney. The writer asks how someone like Heaney, who has met so many people and who is read by such diverse audiences, has managed to alienate so few. The article ends with one brief anecdote which testifies to Heaney's reputation for immense generosity.

50   LUCIE-SMITH, EDWARD. "Sweeney Agonistes," *Punch Books Extra* 288 (April 17): 7.
    Brief review of *Sweeney Astray*. Lucie-Smith states that Heaney is the "boss-poet" of the poetry groupies. He does not think that *Sweeney Astray* adds much to Heaney's reputation. Heaney is not speaking with his own voice, much less with the voice of the original Irish-language poet. Here he seems to be using the voice of Yeats—"the poetry is often too sweet and dimpled to be entirely convincing."

51   McCLATCHY, J. D. "Poetry Chronicle," *Hudson Review* 38, 1 (Spring): 170–76.
    Review of *Station Island* and several others. This is Heaney's sixth and most ambitious collection. McClatchy finds the poems of Part I "disappointing," and those in Part III "surprising" and "esoteric." The central sequence is a major accomplishment. Since *North,* Heaney has addressed the political situation in Ireland. Here, in this complex, demanding poem, "Station Island," he fully dramatizes the conflict but does not resolve it.

52 McCULLY, C. B. "Choosing Voices," *PN Review* 44 (11, 6): 36–41.

McCully reviews five books, including *Station Island* and *Sweeney Astray*. He asserts that in *Station Island* Heaney can be accused of political backsliding. To be free he must subject himself to the purgatory of *Station Island*, a religious setting where he meets political and artistic voices. He finds his freedom in Sweeney, who dominates the last section of *Station Island.*

53 McGOVERN KING, PATRICIA. "An Interview with Seamus Heaney," in *An Gael* 3, 1 (Summer): 2–4.

McGovern King explores with Heaney the connection between writing and history in Ireland. Irish identity is commented on. The need to use words that have their narrative reality is stressed, in the same way as the archaeological remains have a worth that is both conservative and renovative.

54 McMILLAN, PETER AIDAN JAMES. "Illuminations: Editing a Magazine of Contemporary Writing." Ph.D. dissertation, University of Southern California.

The volume reprints the first four numbers of *Illuminations,* a magazine designed to promote new writers by publishing their work with that of more established writers. Noted authors include Tom Stoppard, Susan Sontag, Seamus Heaney, Allen Tate, James Dickey, Thomas Kinsella, Padraic Fiacc, Stephen Spender, Craig Raine, Christopher Isherwood, Joseph Brodsky, W. H. Auden, Michael Hamburger, Peter Porter, Flannery O'Connor, Bin Ramke, Friederike Mayrocker, Charles Wright, and James Merrill. A short introduction includes the history of the magazine and an explanation of editorial principles. A brief discussion of the principles of free verse and their application in modern poetry ends the introduction.

55 MACRAE, ALASDAIR. "Seamus Heaney's New Voice in *Station Island,*" in *Irish Writers and Society at Large*, edited by Masaru Sekine (Gerrards Cross, Buckinghamshire: Smythe; Totowa, N.J.: Barnes & Noble): 122–28.

MacRae reads Heaney's *Sweeney Astray* and *Station Island* in light of T. S. Eliot's essay "The Three Voices of Poetry." MacRae concludes that in these two volumes Heaney adopts Eliot's "third voice," the dramatic voice, and thus relies less heavily upon the other two—quasi-dramatic and non-dramatic verse. The essay stresses not only a change in voice (almost the adoption of Yeatsian masks), but also a shift in structural assumptions. According to MacRae, "the scheme of the sequence allows Heaney to investigate from different angles questions of concern to him," which ultimately allows him "to speak in a more dramatic voice." The dramatic voice also provides Heaney with a means of approaching his past from more oblique angles and thus providing the artistic freedom he desires.

1985

56 "The Manuscript Drafts of the Poem 'North,'" in *The Art of Seamus Heaney*, 2d ed., edited and introduced by Tony Curtis (Bridgend: Poetry Wales Press; Chester Springs: Dufour Editions): 53–62.
    Reprint of 1982.21.

57 MATHIAS, ROLAND. *"Death of a Naturalist,"* in *The Art of Seamus Heaney*, 2d ed., edited and introduced by Tony Curtis (Bridgend: Poetry Wales Press; Chester Springs: Dufour Editions): 11–25.
    Reprint of 1982.22.

58 MATHEWS, AIDAN. "[Book Review]," *Poetry Ireland Review* 14 (Autumn): 81–85.
    Mathews, in his reviews of *Station Island* and *Sweeney Astray*, contrasts the favoritism shown to *Station Island* with the "few votive phrases" tossed to *Sweeney Astray*. He sees the two works as complementary—a journey between accusation and advocacy. In *Station Island* the poet is expiating his own guilt while he champions the innocent man, the scapegoat in *Sweeney Astray*. One is his self-confession; the other is his attempt to state his innocence, preferring "nature's pantry. . .to the salted fields of final enmity."

59 MOLDAW, CAROL. "[Book Review]," *Wilson Library Bulletin* 59, 8 (April): 566.
    Brief review of *Station Island*. Moldaw sees Heaney here facing the tension between the Irishman and the writer. In the "Station Island" sequence, the dead, some who have died in the violence in Northern Ireland, judge and advise the poet. The last voice is that of James Joyce, advising the poet to strike out in his own voice. Moldaw concludes, "This is a book of immense conscience and mastery."

60 MOLE, JOHN. "Responsibilities: Recent Poetry," *Encounter* 64, 2 (February): 47–48
    Review of *Station Island*, with notice of *Sweeney Astray*. Mole comments on the first sequence of six poems in *Station Island,* in which Heaney holds a dialogue with himself, showing himself as a poet who witnesses the importance of his feelings no matter how fugitive the source. He regards the "Station Island" sequence as important, though "written rather too much in the knowledge that it is so." The sequence is an exercise in expiation and self-accusation raising questions of responsibility. The closing series of "Sweeney Redivivus" is "caught between the instincts of section one. . .and the imperatives of section 2." Mole sees *Station Island* as an impressive book. His image of Heaney's poetry is "a deer caught in the thicket of circumstance."

61 MOORE, BRIAN. "[Book Review]," *Los Angeles Times: Book Review* (June 2): 1, 8.
    Review of *Station Island*. Moore outlines the basic themes and constructs of the work. He concludes that Heaney (the Irish Dante) avoids "satire" and takes the advice of Joyce at the end of the sequence when the poet flies off with Sweeney.

62 NYE, ROBERT. "An Irish Parnassian at work," *Times* (London, January 24): 11.
    In his review of *Station Island*, Nye describes Heaney as "a sad example of what Hopkins meant by [a] Parnassian" poet —a poet who wills his poems into existence instead of writing inspired verse. He finds the central sequence too rhetorical and formulaic. Nye also glances at *Sweeney Astray*, which he calls "Kerrygold verse." In general, the reviewer considers this period in Heaney's career as one marked by "an unpleasant excess of charm," which is manifest in his "linguistic self-caressing."

63 O'BRIEN, DARCY. "Poet Has Permanence," *Tulsa World* (January 20): 8
    Brief review of *Station Island*. O'Brien states that Heaney writes with the energy of youth and the wisdom of the ancients.

64 O'CONNELL, SEAN. "Heaney Agonistes: The Poet in Exile," *Boston Review* 10, 1 (February): 20–21.
    In his review of *Station Island*, O'Connell describes his trip to Heaney country guided by a rough map drawn by the poet himself. The review asserts that the poems of the "Sweeney Redivivus" section are "dramatic" as understood in the "Joyce-Stephen construct. . .detached"; and are in the voice of a persona. *Station Island* is more about the poetic life than the political life, according to O'Connell.

65 OXLEY, WILLIAM. "Reviews," *Acumen* 1 (April): 88.
    The principal concern here is an examination of the business of making poetry. Heaney delivers a series of penetrative meditations on the creative act and the forces that shape it. The writings are so clearly textured that one is hard put to find anything to criticize in them.

66 PETTINGELL, PHOEBE. "Poetry as Performance," *New Leader* 68 (April 8): 15–16.
    In this brief descriptive review of *Station Island*, the author identifies the volume's main themes of "separation and guilt," themes that are related to Heaney's divided past and nature.

1985

67   PINSKY, ROBERT. "Poet and Pilgrim," *New Republic* 192 (February 18): 37–39.
    Pinsky, in his review of *Station Island*, discovers several similarities between Heaney's poetry in this volume and that of modern and contemporary American poets. These similarities often appear in what the reviewer labels as the "postmodern" aspects of Heaney's writing. Pinsky speculates that Heaney must have at some point decided not to write an epic, even though the narrative is as strong as Frost's and reminiscent of Dante. The sequence's central theme is the past—a past that must be confronted despite its incomprehensibility and the potential suffering it holds.
    Reprinted 1985.73; 1986.49.

68   "Poet warns architects about 'profane' buildings," *Irish Times* (November 11): 11.
    Unsigned news report on Heaney's address to the annual conference of the Royal Institute of the Architects of Ireland in Templepatrick, Co. Antrim. In his speech, Heaney pleaded on behalf of the spirit, which should be cared for even in essentially utilitarian buildings. Even when bound by economic constraints, architects should keep faith with their artistic responsibilities.

69   QUINLAN, K. "[Book Review]," *World Literature Today* 60 (Winter): 102.
    Review of *Sweeney Astray*. Quinlan sees Heaney, like most Irish writers, interested in contemplating the ancient Irish past. This poem shows the traditional tension between Celtic and Christian Ireland. Sweeney can also be seen as the figure of the displaced and guilty artist.

70   REMNICK, DAVID. "The Bard from the Bogland—Seamus Heaney and His Passion for Place," *Washington Post* 108 (May 3): C1.
    In this interview Heaney talks about heavily covered issues: his youth and early reading, his move to Wicklow, and his teaching at Harvard. There are a few interesting comments. Heaney says he counters the stereotype of the Irish poet as "voluble Celt" by being a "strict and serious poet." He says that his poem "Chekhov on Sakalin" was written partially in reponse to the hunger strikes in 1981. He says his move from the North was informed by "the submerged politics" of not wanting to be "just an Ulster poet": "I wanted to be an Irish poet."

71   RUSS, LAWRENCE. "[Book Reviews]," *Parabola* 10, 4 (November): 100–103.
    Review of *Sweeney Astray* and of Dick Allen's *Overnight in the Guest House of the Mystic*. Heaney's translation of a poem written in the late Middle Ages tells of the tribulations of the warrior-king Sweeney and his redemption through his great suffering. Heaney's talent for rhythm and sound gives new life to the old story.

72   SCHMIDT, A. V. C. "'Darkness Echoing': Reflections on the Return of Mythopeia in Some Recent Poems of Geoffrey Hill and Seamus Heaney," *Review of English Studies* 36 (May): 199–225.

Schmidt's essay is essentially a critical analysis of Heaney's "The Toome Road" and "Sibyl," and of Hill's "Quaint Mazes" and "A Short History of British India (I)." The analysis is prefaced by an outline of literary theory and literary history as context. He finds that there is a real affinity underlying the work of the two poets, with Hill sacrificing some of the compassion which is at the center of Heaney's poetry. Each poet "questions the logic of practical reason. . .by withdrawing from the light of common day into the echoing darkness of myth."

73   "Seamus Heaney 1939–," in *Twentieth-Century British Literature* 2, edited by Harold Bloom (New York: Chelsea House): 1122–80.

The Chelsea House Library of Literary Criticism. Contents include reprints of essays by Francis X. Clines (1983.12), 1123–24; Robert Fitzgerald (1976.10), 1124–26; James Randall (1979.31), 1126–28; John Unterecker (1967.10), 1128; Jon Silkin (1967.9), 1128; John Press (1969.12), 1128–29; "Fear in a Tinful of Bait" (1969.5), 1129–30; George A. Brinton (1973.3), 1131–32; Robert B. Shaw (1970.11), 1132; Patricia Beer (1972.1), 1132–33; Douglas Dunn (1973.6), 1133; Jonathan Galassi (1973.8), 1133; Helen Vendler (1976.27), 1133–34; Richard Murphy (1976.19), 1134–36; Donald Hall (1977.11), 1136–37; Denis Donoghue (1979.7), 1137–39; A. Alvarez (1980.1), 1139–41; Daniel J. Casey (1980.11), 1141; Andrew Motion (1980.27), 1141–42; Robert Pinsky (1980.31), 1142–43; Marjorie Perloff (1981.31), 1143–44; Seamus Heaney. "Introduction to *Sweeney Astray*, 1144; Denis Donoghue (1984.11), 1144–45; Elizabeth Gaffney (1984.13), 1145–46; John Gross (1985.33), 1146; Robert Pinsky (1985.67), 1146–48; Richard Ellmann (1985:24), 1148–50; Benedict Kiely (1970.8), 1150–54; John Wilson Foster (1974.3), 1154–59; Arthur E. McGuinness (1978.5), 1159–63; Calvin Bedient (1979.2), 1164–47; Harold Bloom (1980.7), 1167–71; Jay Parini (1980.29), 1171–75; Blake Morrison (1982.24, chapter 5), 1175–80.

74   "Seamus Justin Heaney," in *Oxford Companion to English Literature*, 5th ed., edited by Margaret Drabble (Oxford: Oxford University Press): 445.

Brief biographical outline, followed by a chronology of his principal writings.

75   SHAW, ROBERT B. "Heaney's Purgatory," *Yale Review* 74, 4 (July): 581–87.

Review of *Station Island*. Shaw asserts that the readers of Heaney's volume experience "catharsis and purgation" by participating in the poet's own "efforts of self-understanding." He calls the title sequence poem "an epic

1985

katabasis." Although Shaw admires much of Heaney's pilgrimage, he finds the Joyce section flat and "wrong" for Heaney.

76 SMITH, DAVE. "Short Reviews," *Poetry* 147, 1 (October): 35–37.
In his review of *Station Island,* Smith notes that Heaney is a pastoral poet writing on natural beauty, love, and domestic relationships, but always in the context of sectarian violence. More than in his previous collections, there is autobiography here and re-imagining of the artist's life and purpose. The middle and title part of the book is a spiritual pilgrimage, while the final selection is a new "step into the depths of vision." While the last section disappoints by a general vagueness, *Station Island* is his best book.

77 SMITH, STAN. "Seamus Heaney," in *Contemporary Poets*, 4th ed. (New York: St. Martin's Press): 364–65.
Revision of 1980.37; 1991.66.

78 STEVENSON, ANNE. "The Peace Within Understanding: Looking at *Preoccupations,*" in *The Art of Seamus Heaney,* edited and introduced by Tony Curtis (Bridgend, Mid. Glamorgan: Poetry Wales Press); Chester Springs: Dufour Editions): 131–37.
Reprint of 1982.34.

79 STEVENSON, ANNE. "*Stations*: Seamus Heaney and the Sacred Sense of the Sensitive Self," in *The Art of Seamus Heaney*, edited by Tony Curtis (Brigend, Mid Glamorgan: Poetry Wales Press; Chester Springs: Dufour Editions): 48–51.
Reprint of 1982:35.

80 VENDLER, HELEN. "Echo Soundings, Searches, Probes," *New Yorker* 61, 31 (September 23): 108, 111–16.
Review of *Station Island*. Vendler considers Heaney's movement into "the space of writing"—a space that appears in response to Heaney's "uprooted life" and religious and aesthetic quest(ioning). She describes the self-portrait of Heaney that emerges as "full of Chaucerian irony and overpainted Dantesque earnestness." Much of the review is taken up with the argument that Heaney remakes his voice because "to attempt a new complexity of voice is to create future possibilities for one's past." She concludes the review with a glance at the "Sweeney Redivivus" section, which she feels achieves the "spareness and chill of the early Irish tonality."
Reprinted 1986.58; reprinted 1988.75, where it is combined with her 1981 essay, "The Music of What Happens," to form her essay, "Seamus Heaney."

81 WATER, DONNA A. VAN DE, and DANIEL C. O'CONNELL. "In and About the Poetic Line," *Bulletin of the Psychonomic Society* 23, 5 (September): 397–400.

The authors analyze Heaney's reading of nine of his poems in a scientific study which argues that punctuation is more significant in determining the duration of pauses than is lineation. They use the "Siemens Oscillomink L and F-J Fundamental Frequency Meter (Type FFM 6502)" to measure the duration of Heaney's pauses—"Any silence less than 130 msec was not considered to be a pause."

82 WATSON, GEORGE. "The Narrow Ground: Northern Poets and the Northern Ireland Crisis," in *Irish Writers and Society at Large*, edited by Masaru Sekine (Gerrards Cross: Colin Smythe; Totowa, N.J.: Barnes & Noble): 207–24.

Watson examines the work of four Northern Irish poets, two Catholic and two Protestant: Heaney, Montague, Mahon, and Paulin. Watson begins by noting the dominant aesthetic/religious stereotypes: Catholic writers are obsessed with ritual, whereas Protestant poets write out of a cultural vacuum which is manifested in an inferiority complex. Although there are notable exceptions to these stereotypes, there is much truth in them as well, Watson concludes. Of Heaney, Watson ponders how a poet of such immense poetic empathy cannot write more insightfully or compassionately about Protestants and their traditions. Referring to a handful of poems from various volumes, Watson argues that Heaney can "penetrate the corpses of the bogs" while ignoring or faltering "before living representatives of 'the other side.'" The section on Heaney concludes that the poet's "atavistic vision" is embodied in his "Catholic" mythmaking.

83 WESTLAKE, JOHN H. J. "Seamus Heaney's 'Punishment': An Interpretation," *Literatur in Wissenschaft und Unterricht* 18, 1: 49–58.

Heaney's "Punishment" has often been cited to illustrate his ambivalent attitude towards the IRA. Westlake maintains that when the entire poem is considered, a more complex picture emerges. The overall effect is that of puzzlement. Heaney sees the relevance of past history to what is happening in Northern Ireland today.

1986

1 ANDREWS, ELMER. "'All the Realms of a Whisper': The Poetry of Seamus Heaney," *Contemporary Review* 249 (November): 256–60.

Andrews argues that Heaney's poetry evokes the unconscious image which he follows to where his imagination leads. Some key poems recreate the past in order to reflect critically on the present. The distinguishing feature of his poetry is its inwardness which brings to light those facts of reality that we do not know—or do not want to know. His language is constantly leaving the local historical moment as it becomes the voice of the contemplative mind.

2   BARRY, KEVIN. "Antarctica and the North," *Irish Literary Supplement,* 5, 1 (Spring): 25.
    Review of Mahon's *Antarctica* and Heaney's *Place and Displacement: Recent Poetry of Northern Ireland.* Heaney's pamphlet deals mainly with Mahon, Longley, and Muldoon, in whom Heaney sees, according to Barry, "a technical preoccupation which, he proposes, has a political analogy." Heaney argues that the finished poem releases the poet from political extremism.

3   BEDFORD, WILLIAM. "To Set the Darkness Echoing," in *Seamus Heaney,* edited and with an introduction by Harold Bloom (New York: Chelsea House): 11–18.
    Reprint of 1977.1.

4   BEISCH, JUNE. "An Interview with Seamus Heaney," *Literary Review* 29, 2 (Winter), 161–69.
    Beisch introduces the interview with some general remarks on Heaney at Harvard, on his recent poetry, and on the themes in his poetry. In the interview Heaney comments on life at Harvard, on being a writer, and on *Sweeney Astray.* He also talks about working in poetic forms, poets breaking new ground, politically involved poetry, and the language of poetry.

5   BLOOM, HAROLD. "Introduction," in *Seamus Heaney,* edited by Harold Bloom (New York: Chelsea House): 1–10.
    Reprint of 1980.7, where it appeared under title "The Voice of Kinship;" reprinted 1983.4 (excerpts); 1985.73.

6   BROWN, TERENCE. "A Northern Voice," in *Seamus Heaney,* edited and with an introduction by Harold Bloom (New York: Chelsea House): 25–38.
    Reprint of 1975.8,where it appeared under title "Four New Voices: Poets of the Present"; reprinted 1977.4; 1983.9 (excerpts).

7   BURRIS, SIDNEY JOHNSON. "The Pastoral Art of Seamus Heaney." Ph.D. dissertation, University of Virginia.
    Seamus Heaney was born a Catholic in rural Northern Ireland, and his poetry matured as his country suffered the sustained sectarian violence and social upheaval of the late 1960s and early 1970s. Belfast, the city most affected by these changes, was intermittently home to Heaney from 1957 until 1972; and if Kermode is correct in suggesting that pastoral literature is essentially an urban product, a literature that deals with rural life from a distance,

then Heaney would seem well qualified to fashion such a poetry. Heaney's verse draws much of its imagery, subject matter, and dialectal rhythms from the countryside of County Derry, but it revives the genre's proclivity for social and political commentary by developing several characteristics central to the pastoral tradition.

8   CHRISTOPHER, NICHOLAS. "A Pilgrim in County Donegal," *Contemporary Literary Criticism* 37: 167–68.
        Reprint of 1985.13.

9   COBB, ANN VALENTINE. "Seamus Heaney: Poet in a Destitute Time." Ph.D. dissertation, Tufts University.
        A developmental study of the first twenty years of Heaney's poetry, 1966–1986, which includes a discussion of Heaney's early, unpublished version of *Buile Suibhne*, later rewritten and published under the title *Sweeney Astray*.

10   CORCORAN, NEIL. *Seamus Heaney* (London: Faber): 199 pp.
        This is a detailed look at the life and work of Seamus Heaney. He includes material from his conversations with the poet and shows the importance of names and places in Heaney's political and poetical landscape. Staying close to the poetry, he traces its development from *Death of a Naturalist* to *Station Island*. This is a reflective, not always laudatory, assessment of Heaney's career up to and including *Station Island*. He points to the significance of the work as a whole, and sees Heaney as a poet constantly remaking himself and his art. This is more than a "student guide," assuming, as it does at times, a high level of knowledge of contemporary poetry.

11   CONNER, LESTER. "Dr. Conner's Introduction," *Irish Edition* 6, 6 (June): 9.
        Presentation remarks on the occasion of the conferring of the honorary degree of Doctor of Humane Letters at Chestnut Hill College, Philadelphia on May 10, 1986.

12   DEANE, SEAMUS. "Contemporary Literature, 1940–80: Poetry," in *A Short History of Irish Literature* (London: Hutchinson): 227–49.
        Deane's look at modern Irish poetry surveys Heaney's work up to and including *Station Island*. He has moved far beyond "the regional territory opened by Kavanagh." There is still much to come from Heaney.

13   DI NICOLA, ROBERT. "Time and History in Seamus Heaney's 'In memoriam Francis Ledwidge,'" *Eire-Ireland* 21, 4 (Winter): 45–51.
        Di Nicola notes that critics have discussed Heaney's references and allusions to Ireland's history in his poetry. His poem on Francis Ledwidge, the young Irish poet killed in World War I, however, seems to have escaped com-

1986

ment in this regard. Di Nicola asserts that appreciation of this poem can be heightened by paying attention to "the historical significance of place-names and of other references." World War I, the Easter Rebellion, Thomas MacDonagh, Lord Dunsany, Robert Emmet, the Boyne Valley, passage graves, and Slane are among the allusions and references to be found in "In memoriam Francis Ledwidge."

14 DONOGHUE, DENIS. "Heaney's Sweeney," in his *We Irish: Essays on Irish Literature and Society* (New York: Knopf): 267–71.
      Reprint of 1984.11, where it appeared under title "A Mad Muse"; reprinted 1985.73.

15 DONOGHUE, DENIS. "[Untitled]," *Contemporary Literary Criticism* 37: 163.
      Reprint, in part, of 1984.11.

16 DUNN, DOUGLAS. "Heaney Agonistes," in *Seamus Heaney*, edited and with an introduction by Harold Bloom (New York: Chelsea House): 153–58.
      Reprint of 1984.12.

17 DURKAN, MICHAEL J. "Seamus Heaney: A Checklist for a Bibliography," *Irish University Review* 16, 1 (Spring): 48–76.
      A comprehensive listing of the books and pamphlets by Heaney, together with contributions to books, pamphlets and periodicals. Also added are listings of Interviews, Books and Essays about Heaney and His Work, and Reviews in English of each work.

18 EHRENPREIS, IRVIN. "[Untitled]," *Contemporary Literary Criticism* 37: 162–63.
      Reprint, in part, of 1981.14.

19 EINSPIELER, ULRIKE. "Neither True nor Beautiful," *Honest Ulsterman* 82 (Winter): 91–94.
      Review of *Ausgewahlte Gedichte: Selected Poems 1965–1975*, Englisch und Deutsch, Ubertragung und Nachwort von Henrietta Beese (Stuttgart, 1984).

20 ELLMANN, RICHARD. "Heaney Agonistes," in *Seamus Heaney*, edited and with an introduction by Harold Bloom (New York: Chelsea House): 159–66.
      Reprint of 1985.24; reprinted 1985.73.

21 FITZGERALD, ROBERT. "Seamus Heaney: An Appreciation," in *Seamus Heaney*, edited and with an introduction by Harold Bloom (New York: Chelsea House): 39–44.
      Reprint of 1976.10; reprinted 1985.73 (without the poems).

22   FOSTER, JOHN WILSON. "'A Lough Neagh Sequence': Sources and Motifs," in *Seamus Heaney*, edited by Harold Bloom (New York: Chelsea House): 45–50.
        Reprint, without footnotes, of 1977.10, where it appeared under title "Seamus Heaney's 'A Lough Neagh Sequence': Sources and Motifs."

23   GARRATT, ROBERT F. "The Poetry of Commitment: Seamus Heaney," in his *Modern Irish Poetry: Tradition and Continuity from Yeats to Heaney* (Berkeley: University of California Press): 230–58.
        Garratt points to Heaney's early success and the positive reception which has been shown to his writing. Despite this, there is in his recent work some self-doubt and an uncertainty about his place in Irish writing. This has resulted in a lessening of his treatment of rural life and "a more universal consideration of human nature." There is, too, the pressure concerning the public voice in conflict with self-expression. The struggle between the poet's public and private voices is seen clearly in *North* and *Field Work*, though the reaction to these works concentrated on the political aspects of the poetry.

24   GIBBONS, REGINALD. "Station Island," *TriQuarterly* 66 (Spring/ Summer): 201–21.
        A review of *Station Island,* along with works by James Fenton and Bruce Weigl, poets who Gibbons asserts have had close experience with war and violence. Gibbons sees Heaney as initially a poet of the domestic scene who is now trying to address Ireland's violent history. For Heaney, the poet has to face the competing claims of the physical world, the personal world, and the social sphere. Dante is present in the main sequence. While Dante portrayed sinners, Heaney portrays victims and failures, who in their turn reprimand and question the poet. In the final sequence, Heaney uses the voice of the solitary Sweeney to wrestle with the poet's relation to the world outside. This is Heaney's most disturbing book: those for whom he spoke in the two earlier parts are left behind, to be replaced by this figure who is alone and apart.

25   GREEN, CARLANDA. "The Feminine Principle in Seamus Heaney's Poetry," in *Seamus Heaney*, edited and with an introduction by Harold Bloom (New York: Chelsea House): 143–52.
        Reprint of 1983.20.

26   HOUSTON, DOUGLAS NORMAN. "Myths of Place: The Importance of Landscape in the Poetries of W. H. Auden and Seamus Heaney." Ph.D. dissertation, University of Hull.
        Numerous studies of landscape in the works of Wordsworth and his predecessors exist; very few books, however, are concerned with its significance in modern and contemporary poetry. Works on Auden and Heaney make ref-

1986

erence to local elements, but do not consider the overall and continuous importance of landscape in their writings. It is hoped that this study goes some way towards remedying these deficiencies.

The philosophical and imaginative cohesiveness of successive poems relating to single landscapes in the works of Auden and Heaney suggests the term "myth of place." In according landscape a central role in the major dialects of their poetries, Auden and Heaney make the most valuable contributions to the local mode since Wordsworth's advances beyond the picturesque.

27   HULSE, MICHAEL. "Sweeney Heaney: Seamus Heaney's 'Station Island,'" *Quadrant* 30, 5 (May): 72–75.

In what amounts to a discussion of Heaney's entire work, Hulse begins his essay by comparing "The Strand at Lough Beg" (*Field Work*) with part VIII of the "Station Island" sequence. He charges the poet with being more concerned with his own image than with the matter of the poems themselves. Hulse maintains that in *Station Island,* Heaney is "insistent on his own status." Much of his early work was borrowed from Hopkins, Dylan Thomas, and Ted Hughes. Nevertheless, as we read his work through *North* we take pleasure in his acoustic consonance and in the emerging of a plainer, more flexible, and carefully structured style. There is a heightened confidence. When we come to *Station Island,* we are aware of a new maturity in which his language is allowed to speak for itself. Hulse ends by suggesting that, in time, Heaney may become a great religious poet if his "attraction to a medieval wholeness of church and universe continues to gain power and persuasiveness."

28   INGERSOLL, EARL G. "[Book Reviews]," *Eire-Ireland* 21, 1 (Spring): 139–43.

Ingersoll takes us through the three sections of *Station Island* in order where Heaney records his own childhood and growing up and at the end identifies with the free-spirited Sweeney. The centerpiece is the "Station Island" sequence, where he encounters the spirits of the dead and receives advice, ending with Joyce's "Now strike your note."

29   JENNINGS, ELIZABETH. "The Spell-Binder," *Contemporary Literary Criticism* 37: 165–66.

Reprint of 1984.15.

30   JOLLY, ROSLYN. "Transformation of Caliban and Ariel: Imagination and Language in David Malouf, Margaret Atwood and Seamus Heaney," *World Literature Written in English* 26, 2 (Autumn): 295–330.

Caliban and Ariel are the greatest achievements in Shakespeare's *The Tempest.* The play is usually performed with the emphasis on romance and fantasy rather than on the New World discovery and on colonization. Caliban and Ariel, however, live under conditions which must be dealt with by modern colonial writers—usurpation of political power, expelled from the land, using an imposed language. Caliban's reaction to land and language recalls Atwood's showing of the European in Canada, Malouf's depiction of exile, and Heaney's close sympathies with the landscape. Ariel personifies the power of the imagination to which colonial writers may aspire in order to transcend their Caliban-like situation. Heaney's response is different from those of Malouf and Atwood because his land is not independent of England and is not part of the New World.

31 KEARNEY, RICHARD. "Poetry, Language and Identity: A Note on Seamus Heaney," *Studies* 75 (Winter): 552–63.
    There is a stereotyped portrait of Heaney as the poet of the national landscapes, "devoted to the recovery of national pieties." Kearney asserts that Heaney's poetry is not primarily about place; it is about transitions from one place to another. Heaney has been criticized by some for refusing to adopt a fixed position regarding Northern Ireland. Heaney, however, recognizes that poetry's primary fidelity is to language—he is not a party politician. In the early works he talks of home in terms of a search for self-identity; in his later works the sense of "home" is a more metaphysical preoccupation. His "bog poems"' are examples of both "homecoming" and "estrangement." The lost homeland is less an actual place than an entity which eludes the boundaries of a particular nation. This is not to say that Heaney has no concern for the plight of his native Northern Ireland. By tracing the current political and social mythologies back to their roots, he is exploring or exposing them. In *Station Island* the poet interprets the fascination with home in terms of tradition, ancestry, community, memory, etc. Memory, however, is racked with guilt. Heaney is faithful to the ambiguity of opposing demands and refuses to adopt a position which would permit the illusion of a final solution.
    Reprinted (in a longer version) 1988.33.

32 KELLY, Henry Ansgar. "Heaney's Sweeney: The Poet as Version-Maker," *Philological Quarterly* 65, 3 (Summer): 293–310.
    Kelly sets out to relate Heaney's *Sweeney Astray* to the original medieval tale as edited and translated by J. G. O'Keeffe. In his introduction, Heaney suggests a fairly close translation of the original Irish. Kelly maintains that a comparison shows otherwise and that Heaney's "version" means "adaptation." Heaney intended to produce a complete version but chose instead to abridge the work. Kelly chronicles the cuts and also points out the variations in the syllabic patterns. Heaney's use of "words that seem too learned for the context" are set against his use of "slangy clichés" in other places. The tone and content of Heaney's version are very different from that of O'Keeffe. Heaney again makes use of Sweeney in *Station Island,* but this latter Sweeney is a different character.

1986

33 KENNELLY, BRENDAN. "[Untitled]," *Contemporary Literary Criticism* 37: 163–64.
    Reprint of 1984.20, where it appeared under title "Soaring from the Treetops."

34 KING, P. R. "I Step through Origins," in *Seamus Heaney*, edited and with an introduction by Harold Bloom (New York: Chelsea House): 69–96.
    Reprint of 1979.18, where it appeared under title "'I Step through Origins': The Poetry of Seamus Heaney."

35 LONGLEY, EDNA. "'Inner Emigré' or 'Artful Voyeur'? Seamus Heaney's *North*," in her *Poetry in the Wars* (Newcastle upon Tyne: Bloodaxe Books), 140–69.
    Reprint (with additional material) of 1982.19; reprinted 1985.47.

36 LONGLEY, EDNA. "Poetry and Politics in Northern Ireland," in her *Poetry in the Wars* (Newcastle upon Tyne: Bloodaxe Books): 185–210.
    Reprint (with additional material) of 1985.48.

37 LYDON, CHRISTOPHER. "Derek Walcott, Seamus Heaney, and Christopher Lydon: Robert Penn Warren," *Partisan Review* 53, 4 (Fall): 606–12.
    This interview was conducted by Lydon for the Ten O'Clock News, WGBH-TV, Boston. Heaney sees Warren's choice as poet laureate an excellent one because of Warren's poetry and its history content. Poetry has always been challenged to take on public and historical matters, and Warren is one of those who accepted that challenge. Poets should be the alternative government. Warren has that epic quality, but he can also show "the lyric, intimate moment," as in his poem "Tell Me a Story."

38 McGUINN, NICHOLAS. *Seamus Heaney: A Guide to the Selected Poems 1965–1975* (Leeds: Arnold-Wheaton): 126 pp.
    McGuinn's approach is thematic. He argues that each volume represents a particular stage in Heaney's development, from his early poems about nature and childhood to his explorations of political history and mythology. He also includes a series of glossaries, historical and political notes, and a reading list.

39 MAGUIRE, AISLING. *Seamus Heaney: Selected Poems* (York Notes) (Harlow: Longman). 79 pp.
    This work deals with the texts as found in the *Selected Poems 1965–1975*. Maguire's study includes the biographical and historical background. This is followed by summaries and a section of commentary under

the headings of themes, imagery, symbolism, versification, and diction. There are also "Hints for Study" and a brief bibliography.

40 MARSH, FABIENNE. "Seamus Heaney at Harvard," *Poetry Review* 75, 4 (February): 27–28.
    Marsh's account of Heaney's poetry class for undergraduate and graduate students presents the poet as an amiable and obviously knowledgeable teacher. Heaney often quotes from "the masters," notes Marsh, who gives the example of Heaney reciting Robert Graves's "Dance of Words." She also mentions that Heaney referred to Michael McLaverty's advice to "Listen. Go your own way. Do your own work," which Marsh observes is echoed in "Station Island."

41 MAXWELL, D. E. S. "Heaney's Poetic Landscape," in *Seamus Heaney*, edited and with an introduction by Harold Bloom (New York: Chelsea House): 19–24.
    Reprint of 1975.25, pp. 171–75, where it appeared as part of a larger essay under title: "Contemporary Poetry in the North of Ireland."

42 MAY, DERWENT. "One Feels the Iron Swerving Out of Control," *Contemporary Literary Criticism* 37: 166–67.
    Reprint of 1984.33.

43 MOLLOY, F. C. "From Personal to Public: The Poetry of Seamus Heaney," *The Teaching of English* (Sydney), 51 (September): 22–30.
    Molloy introduces the basic biographical details before proceeding to an examination of Heaney's poetry up to and including *North*. He discusses the rural background, creativity, craft, and technique in *Death of a Naturalist*. In *Door into the Dark,* language is used to deal with the sources of inspiration. For Heaney the most potent part of the landscape was the bog, which provided a means of commenting on the violence in Northern Ireland in *Wintering Out* and in *North*. Molloy sees Heaney acquiring a maturity and "proceeding like Yeats towards a voice that can make statements."

44 MORRISON, BLAKE. "The Hedge-School: *Field Work,*" in *Seamus Heaney*, edited and with an introduction by Harold Bloom (New York: Chelsea House): 127–42.
    Reprint of Chapter 5 of 1982.24; 1985.73.

45 MULDOON, PAUL. "Sweeney Peregraine," *Contemporary Literary Criticism* 37: 164–65.
    Reprint of 1984.37.

1986

46   NIEL, RUTH. "Digging into History: A Reading of Brian Friel's *Volunteers* and Seamus Heaney's 'Viking Dublin: Trial Pieces,'" *Irish University Review* 16, 1 (Spring): 35–47.

    Niel argues that the play and the poem of the essay's title shed light on each other. Two-thirds of the essay is devoted to Friel's play, while the remaining third discusses Heaney's use of "digging" in relation to the bog poems of *North*. Niel, like the other critics she cites, sees Heaney's digging as a way of connecting the past and the present.

47   O'CALLAGHAN, KATE. "Seamus Heaney—A Poet of His People," *Irish America* (May): 24–30.

    The place of the poet and poetry in America, as well as his own experiences in this country, are the interview's major topics. Heaney also covers familiar facts related to his youth, education, and poetic apprenticeship. He mentions Hopkins as the first "influence," and then alludes to Ted Hughes and Kavanagh. His first published poem was "Tractors." The move from Belfast to Wicklow, Heaney reflects, was in part influenced by the desire "to get out of the gang life." Talking about the bog, Heaney says: "When you go there, as a child, you go with older people. It's the only place I ever saw my father actually lighting a fire. . . ." The poet also compares his bog poems to "worrybeads." There is a lengthy analysis of Daniel Corkery's *Hidden Ireland* by Heaney. The Irish language as used by his family is also touched upon, as well as the roots of *Anahorish*. Heaney declares that he never looks up a word in a dictionary to use in a poem. In response to a question regarding the hunger strikes, Heaney confides: "It was a critical moment for everybody. I think we all failed; I failed; through fastidiousness." Talking about guilt, Heaney agrees that its an Irish thing, and what he likes about America is the permission it gives one. But, "the worst thing about this country [America] is the greed of the first person singular." Heaney wraps up the interview by describing the organicism of the poetic process: "My notion of poetry is that it grows like moss inside you and then at certain times you start picking it off."

48   PARINI, JAY. "The Ground Possessed," in *Seamus Heaney*, edited and with an introduction by Harold Bloom (New York: Chelsea House): 97–120.

    Reprint of 1980.29, where it appeared under title "Seamus Heaney: The Ground Possessed"; reprinted 1983.30.

49   PINSKY, ROBERT. "Poet and Pilgrim," *Contemporary Literary Criticism* 37: 167.

    Reprint of 1985.67; reprinted 1985.73.

50   QUINLAN, KIERAN. "Verse," *World Literature Today* 60, 2 (Spring): 312.
Quinlan, in his short review of *Station Island,* argues that the three sections of the book can be seen as the poet's escape to freedom as well as a recapitulation of his artistic development, beginning with *Death of a Naturalist.* Though the syntax in some of the poems is obscure, Quinlan finds *Station Island* well worth visiting.

51   *Seamus Heaney,* edited and with an introduction by Harold Bloom (New Haven, New York, Philadelphia: Chelsea House): 199 pp.
Modern Critical Views series. Contents: "Editor's Note," vii–viii. "Introduction" by Harold Bloom, 1–10; "To Set the Darkness Echoing" by William Bedford, 11–18; "Heaney's Poetic Landscape" by D. E. S. Maxwell, 19–24; "A Northern Voice" by Terence Brown, 25–38; "Seamus Heaney: An Appreciation" by Robert Fitzgerald, 39–44; "'A Lough Neagh Sequence': Sources and Motifs" by John Wilson Foster, 45–50; "The Matter of Ireland and the Poetry of Seamus Heaney" by Rita Zoutenbier, 51–68; "I Step through Origins" by P. R. King, 69–96; "The Ground Possessed" by Jay Parini, 97–120; "The Hiding Places of Power" by Anthony Thwaite, 121–26; "The Hedge-School: Field Work" by Blake Morrison, 127–42; "The Feminine Principle in Seamus Heaney's Poetry" by Carlanda Greene, 143–52; "Heaney Agonistes" by Douglas Dunn, 153–58; "Heaney Agonistes" by Richard Ellmann, 159–66; "Echo Soundings, Searches, Probes" by Helen Vendler, 167–80.

52   STEWART, JAMES. "Sweeney Among the Fighting Gaels: Aspects of the Matter of Ireland in the Work of Seamus Heaney," *Angles on the English Speaking World* 1 (Autumn): 7–37.
Stewart focuses on selections from Heaney's work that deal with "the matter of Ireland." He looks at certain poems: "Bog Queen," "Nerthus," "The Grauballe Man," "The Scribes," "The Cleric," "The Given Note," "Maighdean Mara," and "Shelagh na Gig." For each poem Stewart gives the poet's inspirational or written source in some detail.

53   TAPSCOTT, STEPHEN. "Poetry and Trouble: Seamus Heaney's Purgatorio," *Southwest Review* 71 (Autumn): 519–35.
As a background for his argument, Tapscott provides a lengthy discussion of Yeatsian and Joycean aesthetics as they relate to culture and class. Heaney's sense of the ironies of Irish history (young romantics with guns), combined with his treatment of rural topography and class, connects him with both Joyce and Yeats. Focusing on *Station Island* and *Sweeney Astray,* Tapscott explores Heaney's conception of Joycean playfulness and the contemporary poet's struggle to maintain "the dignity of the old Irish" tradition. Tapscott concludes that in *Station Island* Heaney "heals" the split between Yeats's "peasant and the aristocratic strands."

1986

54 THOMSON, GEDDES. "Seamus Heaney," in *Hardy to Heaney: Twentieth Century Poets, Introductions and Explanations,* edited by John Blackburn (Edinburgh: Oliver & Boyd): 189–99.

   In this brief overview of Heaney's career, themes, and images written for readers unfamiliar with Heaney's poetry, Thomson discusses "Digging," "Shore Woman," "Docker," "Strange Fruit," "Punishment," and "Casualty." The essay emphasizes the importance of autobiographical materials and the strong sense of ambivalence which informs the poetry.

55 THWAITE, ANTHONY. "The Hiding Places of Power," in *Seamus Heaney,* edited and with an introduction by Harold Bloom (New York: Chelsea House): 121–27.

   Reprint of 1980.40; 1983.42.

56 TONER, MICHAEL. "A Conversation with Seamus Heaney," *Irish Edition* (June).

   In this lengthy and rambling interview, Heaney talks about issues and events which are central to, and familiar in his work. The poet comments upon the civil rights movement in the 1960s and 1970s in Northern Ireland. He argues that the Troubles were not the source of the creative energy that appeared during the time, but that the increase in political and artistic activity arose out of more ancient forces, the "same internalized pressures." Heaney refers to similar situations faced by Caribbean poets and the relationship between language (as dialect), national identity, and colonialism. In this regard, Heaney comments that many Black American writers who use dialect have become "too exclusive." Heaney goes over some recognizable information related to his childhood and academic career and recalls that the day students from Belfast considered the "boarders" at St. Columb's to be "rednecks." The interview ends with a discussion of *Sweeney Astray*: "Many people relate to Sweeney, because he wants gregariousness but can't stand people."

57 VENDLER, HELEN. "Echo Soundings, Searches, Probes," in *Seamus Heaney,* edited and with an introduction by Harold Bloom (New York: Chelsea House): 167–80.

   Reprint of 1985.80; reprinted 1988.75, where it is combined with her 1981 essay "The Music of What Happens" (1981.35), to form her essay "Seamus Heaney."

58 WALSHE, JOHN. "Heaney enthrals young fans," *Irish Independent* (December 4): 9.

Walshe describes Heaney's visit to St. Pius X school in Templeogue, where he read selections from his poetry.

59   ZOUTENBIER, RITA. "The Matter of Ireland and the Poetry of Seamus Heaney," in *Seamus Heaney*, edited and with an introduction by Harold Bloom (New York: Chelsea House): 51–68.
Reprint of 1979.41.

1987

1   BEHAN, DOMINIC. "The forgettable fire," *Evening Herald* (July 10): 18.
Behan, in his discursive review of *The Haw Lantern*, has little that is good to say about the work. He discounts the comparisons with Yeats and bemoans the fact that Heaney seems to have lost his early fire. Behan finds the primary element in Heaney's poetry is enjoyment while it lacks the political note of resistance.

2   BLAKE, JAMES J. "Mad Sweeney: Madness in Irish Literature," *Nassau Review* 5, 3: 40–47.
This essay deals with the character of Sweeney as "a metaphor for the human tendency to let mental processes lead us astray." A summary of the medieval Irish poem is given, followed by a concentration on three incidents from the poem which illustrate the theme of marginalization in Irish literature. Quotations from Heaney's *Sweeney Astray* and from Cathal O' Searcaigh's *Súile Shuibhne* illustrate modern interpretations of the Sweeney story.

3   BRIHAULT, JEAN. "Le Temps dans la poesie de Seamus Heaney," in *Studies on Seamus Heaney*, collected by Jacqueline Genet (Centre des publications de l'Université de Caen): 109–21.

4   BURNHAM, ANNE MULLIN. "Seamus Heaney: 'The Liberating, Appeasing Gift of Utterance. . .,'" *International Poetry Forum Anniversary Season 1966–1986* (Pittsburgh, February 4): 4–15.
Overview of Heaney's work up to *Station Island*. His craft is more that of the sculptor than the builder. In his latest work he is moving towards realizing his view of poetry "as divination, as restoration of the Culture itself."

5   CAHILL, EILEEN MARY. "An Intentional Echo: Translation in the Poetry of Medieval Lyricists, William Wordsworth, and Seamus Heaney (England; Ireland)." Ph.D. dissertation, State University of New York at Buffalo.
This study examines the motif of translation as both an interlingual process and an intralingual theme, beginning with the medieval English lyri-

cists, extending to William Wordsworth, and climaxing with Seamus Heaney. Language, for Heaney, Wordsworth, and their medieval predecessors, is an affirmation and enactment of the imagination. Ideally, then, this process of translation would express the inexpressible.

6   CAHILL, EILEEN MARY. "A Silent Voice: Seamus Heaney and Ulster Politics," *Critical Quarterly* 29, 3 (Autumn): 55–70.
    Cahill examines Heaney's poetry up to and including *Station Island*. She concentrates on the poetry as it expresses the poet's experience of the political situation in Northern Ireland. In responding to the problem, the poet uses various strategems, submerging protest and imposing a silence both internal and external. With *Station Island,* however, he shows a verbal confidence, finds his voice, and allows political concerns to surface in his poetry.

7   CAREY, JOHN. "The Stain of Words," *Sunday Times* (London, June 21): 56.
    Review of *The Haw Lantern* and of Paul Muldoon's *Meeting with the British*. Carey sees in Heaney's new poems an attempt to return us from words to things. He constructs a series of fictional countries, parables of silence in his reaction to Ireland's troubled past and present. The silence and emptiness are enriched by bereavements for a dead friend and for the poet's mother. The ideal object against which we should measure ourselves is "the wintry haw hanging on its thorn."

8   CASEY, PHILIP. "The development of a poet's mind," *Sunday Press* (July 19): 16.
    Casey asserts in his review of *The Haw Lantern,* that Heaney is not a modernist poet but a "lyric poet of the traditionalist school." The reviewer finds many of the poems too familiar. Casey singles out "From the Land of the Unspoken" as an example of Heaney at his best.

9   CLAMPITT, AMY. "Seamus Heaney and the Matter of Ireland," *Boston Globe* (October 18): 10.
    Review of *The Haw Lantern*. Ireland and its history is here, as in his other books. So also is the hawthorn, which Clampitt calls "one of the landmarks throughout Heaney territory." There is also a different, distrustful attitude towards language, suggesting that Heaney is close to Beckett.
    Reprinted 1991.17.

10   CLARKE, ROGER. "Heading for Disaster," *Spectator* 258 (June 27): 35–36.
    Review of *The Haw Lantern*. This is a radical departure from his previous work. The natural is giving way to the cerebral; real places are being usurped by metaphysical countries. Heaney is going mainstream and living in his head, which is the worst place for him to be. He can do much better than he appears in this book, though there are some fine poems in it.

11 CORCORAN, NEIL. "From the Frontier of Writing," *Times Literary Supplement* (June 26): 681–82.

In his review of *The Haw Lantern,* Corcoran speaks of some less than felicitous moments of repetition, comparing "A Postcard from Iceland" with the lovely "Polder" in *Field Work.* The "Clearances" sequence on his relationship with his mother "are perhaps a little tired with their own facility." However, the best of the book is demanding, spare, and assured.

Reprinted 1993.9.

12 CORCORAN, NEIL. "Seamus Heaney and the Art of the Exemplary," *Yearbook of English Studies* 17: 117–27.

Corcoran reflects on Heaney's use of the word "exemplary" in his discussion of Yeats and other writers. It is both a moral and an aesthetic judgment. Heaney uses it also as a "bolstering imaginative system of self-instruction." Heaney sees the need for a modern "exemplar" for Irish poets. The political violence in the North demands a cultural reappraisal, and this has become an "informing presence" in his poetry. In his earlier poetry, the exemplary is dedicated labor in the service of the comunity. His later poetry finds the exemplary figures drawn from the community's history. Further on, the exemplary figure embodies the commitment to art itself. This is realized in its fullest in *Station Island* where the final exemplary presence is that of James Joyce. The "Sweeney Redivivus" mask allows the poet "to interiorize the exemplar to the point where the voices of poet and exemplar are inextricably one."

13 D'EVELYN, THOMAS. "[Book Review]," *Christian Science Monitor* (October 28): 19.

D'Evelyn, in his review of *The Haw Lantern,* comments on Heaney's conversational style and imagery. He compares the poetry to wood, planed and polished to a high luster. Ireland has brilliant, sophisticated, and exciting poets, but none "uses the language more effectively than Seamus Heaney."

14 DODSWORTH, MARTIN. "Rivers in the Trees," *Guardian* (July 17): 13.

In this review of *The Haw Lantern,* among other books, Dodsworth concludes that Heaney is "protected by his own lack of certainty" from becoming predictable. "The Stone Grinder" is cited as an example of Heaney's ability to write poems that "refuse to describe what they are doing it while they are doing it."

15 DUNN, DOUGLAS. "Luminous Verse," *Punch* (June 24): 62.

Dunn's review of *The Haw Lantern* considers it less substantial than *Station Island,* but nevertheless praises its excellence. Much of the book is concerned with self-examination, which Heaney accomplishes in poetry full of beautiful phrases and cadences. Commenting on a poem in the sequence

"Clearances" about the poet's mother, Dunn says it reveals the "geographical and class origins of the best contemporary poetry."

16 ERLANGER, STEVEN. "How Gracious and Generous Grows Ireland's Poet," *The Boston Globe* (July 3): 24.

The occasion of the article is a reading of poems from *The Haw Lantern* by Heaney in Dublin. The article includes several interesting quotations from Heaney's introductions to individual poems. For example, he explains the context of the opening poem of the "Clearances" sequence.

17 FORBES, PETER. "The Growth of a Poet's Mind," *Listener* (July 9): 29–30.

In his review of *The Haw Lantern*, Forbes argues that Heaney is still writing about his main theme, "the growth of a poet's mind." Forbes points out the strong presence of Auden in the volume. According to the reviewer, it appears as if Heaney's most difficult task is to avoid repeating himself or forcing his "breathy" voice on to the ten-syllable line. Forbes believes the title poem to be among the best in the book.

18 GENET, JACQUELINE. "Heaney et l'homme des tourbières," in *Studies on Seamus Heaney*, collected by Jacqueline Genet (Caen: Centre des publications de l'Université de Caen): 123–47.

19 GENET, JACQUELINE. *Studies on Seamus Heaney*. Collected by Jacqueline Genet. (Caen: Centre des Recherches de Litterature, Civilisation et Linguistique des Pays de Langue Anglaise), 147 pp.

A collection of eight essays on his work: Claude Fiérobe, "Signes et Signatures dans la poésie de Heaney." Adolphe Haberer, "The ways of the possible: A textual analysis of *Gifts of Rain* by Seamus Heaney." Maurice Harmon, "'We pine for ceremony': Ritual and reality in the poetry of Seamus Heaney (1965–1975)." Caroline MacDonough, "Seamus Heaney: The makings of the poet." Patrick Rafroidi, "The sense of place in Seamus Heaney's poetry." Colin Meir, "Grammars of Feeling: syntax and subject in the poetry of Seamus Heaney." Jean Brihault, "Le Temps dans le poésie de Seamus Heaney." Jacqueline Genet, "Heaney et l'homme des tourbières."

20 GOWRIE, GREY. "The Burden of Literacy," *Harpers and Queen* 87, 7 (July): 41–42.

In this review of *The Haw Lantern*, Gowrie states that a new work by Heaney "is an event in one's own life." The reviewer argues that Heaney has been affected by late twentieth-century "classicism" and pessimism. Heaney's poems in this volume are too literary and knowing, according to Gowrie.

21 HABERER, ADOLPHE. "The Ways of the Possible: A Textual Analysis of "Gifts of Rain" by Seamus Heaney," in *Studies on Seamus Heaney*, collected

by Jacqueline Genet (Caen: Centre des publications de l'Université de Caen): 27–45.

Haberer begins his examination of "Gifts of Rain" by asserting that meaning is not the first purpose of poetry but rather the after-effect of reading or listening. He initially uses what he terms "the formal approach." He finds that the first section of the poem has a "phonological cohesiveness," to which each of the following sections is related with end-rhymes, parallels, and repetitions. He examines the semantic structure of the poem, and affirms that this structure is one of progress or gain, with "the rain as the referential agent of that progress."

22 HABERSTROH, PATRICIA BOYLE. "Poet and Artist in Seamus Heaney's North," *Colby Library Quarterly* 23, 4 (December): 206–15.

Heaney's work is generally autobiographical, but in *North* he turns to social problems. Instead of focusing on the poet as persona, he examines the role of the poet/artist in social crisis. His major theme is that art and life are bound together.

23 HAFFENDEN, JOHN. "Seamus Heaney and the Feminine Sensibility," *Yearbook of English Studies* 17: 89–116.

Haffenden examines the commentary on Heaney, both positive and negative. "The Tollund Man" of *Wintering Out* emphasizes the feminine bog receiving the male body. In *North*, some poems explore the theme of the mother country, the female landscape, Mother Earth. There is in Heaney a duality in the act of writing: intellectual design and lyric impulse; masculine forging and feminine incubation. A poem which probably best marries the masculine and feminine modes is "Punishment." The love of the mother country is Heaney's essential subject. He also sees the distinction between masculine and feminine modes in the dualism between English and Irish traditions. This dualism also forms the poet's struggle within himself: the tension between "creative nature" and the "deliberated poetic effort." Finally, in *Station Island* Heaney rises above current religious and political troubles and chooses to go the way of Joyce, using the English language "to embrace the internationalist examples of Dante, Mandelstam and Joyce."

24 HAMILTON, IAN. "Excusez-moi," *London Review of Books* 9, 17 (October 1) 10–11.

Hamilton in this review of *The Haw Lantern* looks at the entire body of Heaney's poetry and sees in the early work a rebellion against the autobiographical "I." Since the Troubles erupted, Heaney has tried to reconcile the writing of poetry with "the duties of the tribal bard." With *Field Work,* the personal is felt and expressed, as friends and relatives are being killed. In *Station Island* he returns again to the role of the poet assisted by other artists: Dante and Joyce. *The Haw Lantern* shows a sense of silence and emptiness as

well as weariness. Heaney has been arraigned both by himself and by others' expectations of him as he attempts to cross "the frontier of writing."
Reprinted 1993.15.

25 HARMON, MAURICE. "'We pine for ceremony': Ritual and Reality in the Poetry of Seamus Heaney," in *Studies on Seamus Heaney*, collected by Jacqueline Genet (Caen: Centre des publications de l'Université de Caen): 47–64.

Harmon traces Heaney's poetry in book form up to and including *North*. *Death of a Naturalist* gives us realistic portrayals of customary events. *Door into the Dark* contains, on the whole, descriptive, one-dimensional poems. In *Wintering Out* he connects and identifies with people and objects. *North* is a book concerned with the violence in Northern Ireland. Heaney's response to the violence is communal and ceremonial: "Horror is subsumed in the account of past atrocity and becomes an object of beauty."
Reprinted 1992.22.

26 HART, HENRY. "Pastoral and Anti-Pastoral Attitudes in Seamus Heaney's Early Poems," *Southern Review* 23, 3 (Summer): 569–88.

Heaney turns away from Acadian pastoral when he discovers the anti-pastoral elements of his home ground. He seizes on myth quite early, taking the Genesis story as his basis. Before constructing a new pastoral faithful to his own view of rural life, he would "have to strip the historical model to its bones." His early, uncollected "Pastoral" elegizes the pastoral tradition itself.

27 HART, HENRY. "Seamus Heaney's Poetry of Meditation: *Door into the Dark*," *Twentieth Century Literature* 33, 1 (Spring): 1–17.

Door into the Dark is a significant psychological advance—dark and light are now associated with speech and writing. Hart presents "the forge" as the best example of Heaney's meditative style and examines it in detail. For Heaney, writing "derives from a natural urge to reproduce life out of life." The doors of the dark past open to the present, which has strong links with the past. Heaney's renunciations in *Door into the Dark* "give to the old forms a new complexity and an attractive personal finish."

28 HEBERT, HUGH. "Heaney's Popularity Tells Us About Ourselves. . .," *Guardian* (June 25): 12.

Hebert uses the occasion of the publication of *The Haw Lantern* to discuss Heaney's work. He quotes English and Irish poets on Heaney's reputation as a poet, and then goes on to give us some details of the poet's life and achievement. He ends with further evaluations of Heaney and his poetry by Andrew Motion and Philip Hobsbaum.

29 HILDEBIDLE, JOHN. "A Decade of Seamus Heaney's Poetry," *Massachusetts Review* 28, 3 (Autumn): 393–409.

In the ten-year span of *North* (1975), *Field Work* (1979), *Sweeney Astray* (1984), and *Station Island* (1984), Heaney has tested many stances: to find meaning in the past; to look at various histories; to solve the problem of writing after separation from one's roots; and to escape from sectarian entanglements. He is hardly finished with the question: How to be a poet in a violent, divided, contentious Ireland.

Reprinted 1993.16.

30 HOFFERT, BARBARA. "[Book Review]," *Library Journal* 112, 17 (October 15): 83.

In her brief review of *The Haw Lantern*, Hoffert sees Heaney in a more melancholic, introspective mood. He compares writing to a tense passage through a blockade and sees himself as a stone grinder or the bearer of the haw lantern's wintry light. For Hoffert, Heaney is no small light, and she longs "fleetingly for the poet's own release."

31 HOWARD, BEN. "The Pressed Melodeon," *Kenyon Review* 9, 1 (Winter): 33–49.

This is a general assessment of modern Irish poetry, which Howard asserts has the capacity "to contain and transform [Ireland's] melancholy past." The Irish poet has to choose "between two languages, two cultures, two allegiances." Heaney insists on his Irish identity, Hewitt writes of Protestant Ulster, while Mahon has gone outside to take as his models Auden and MacNeice. Irish poets try to grapple with Irish history. Heaney looks for "symbols adequate to our predicament" and finds these emblems of the political violence in Danish bogs. Is this "sober, elegaic attitude" an appropriate response to eight hundred years of conflict? Irish poets cannot ignore their country's sorrow.

32 HOWARD, PHILIP. "Writing a book with the head," *Time* (November 4): 24.

Howard comments on the nominees for the Whitbread Book of the Year award. Among the five nominated is *The Haw Lantern,* in which "Heaney sets sail into new imaginative territory." Heaney explores the theme of loss and meditates on the conscience of the writer. The Troubles are also there, "but Heaney has become more introspective and more universal."

33 HUNTER, CHARLES. "Seamus Heaney: Keeping a steady watch," *Irish Times Weekend* (June 20): Weekend 9.

Heaney's popularity has been matched with awards and appointments. In spite of this, he remains friendly and open. The Northern Ireland crisis has kept him at center stage, and he has dealt with it in his poetry. This raises the question of the poet's "self." Heaney is concerned with this in the prose collection *Preoccupations.* In *Station Island* and in *The Haw Lantern,* he continues to keep a steady watch on himself.

34 HUNTER, JEFFERSON. "Bog Photographs and Bog Poems," in his *Image and Word: The Interaction of Twentieth-Century Photographs and Texts* (Cambridge: Harvard University Press): 183–95.

> The poems Heaney wrote in response to the photographs in P. V. Glob's *The Bog People* benefit in a special measure from a comparison with the actual pictures. Even before he had read Glob, some of his poetry had been inspired by archaeology. With other poets and photographers, the matching of poem and photograph is not as felicitous as it is with Heaney. Heaney looks on the photographs as "social artifacts in need of interpretation."

35 JOHNSTON, CONOR. "Seamus Heaney, Sweeney and *Station Island,*" *Eire-Ireland* 22, 2 (Summer): 70–95.

> The concern for the community is central to Heaney's work, as is his emphasis on the poetic vocation. Both themes are central to *Sweeney Astray* and *Station Island.*

36 JOHNSTON, FRED. "Poet's Lantern," *Irish Times* (July 4): 5.

> Review of *The Haw Lantern.* MacNeice died in 1963, two years before Heaney's first book of poems was published. The similarities between the two are interesting. Heaney has accepted the task of defining an identity for Northern poetry. *The Haw Lantern* confirms this role for him as poet of a displaced tribe. The art with which he does this carries with it a responsibility.

37 KAVANAGH, P. J. "Ambassador for life," *Spectator* (July 18): 34.

> Heaney is concerned with the problem of the poet's role in society. The popular idea of poetry is that it is a young man's game. Heaney lives in a time when celebrities are made instantly, and he himself is one. He has declared himself and is seen as the representative of the poetic conscience in our time—it is a difficult position.

38 KEMP, PETER. "The Tools of the Trade," *The Independent* (June 24): 13.

> Kemp weaves a number of quotations from Heaney into this review of *The Haw Lantern.* Kemp mentions the influence of East European poets on the volume. Talking about his writing in general, Heaney says that he wrote "The Bog Queen" on his first day at his Glanmore cottage.

39 KERRIGAN, JOHN. "From Parable Island to Steel City," *Poetry Durham* 17 (Winter 1987/8): 31–49.

> The argument about poetry and politics is still being waged in Ireland. In this essay Kerrigan reviews *The Haw Lantern* in addition to works by Edna Longley, Tom Paulin, Douglas Oliver, and Paul Muldoon. There is a degree

of self-awareness in Heaney; nevertheless, Kerrigan argues that "certain attitudes and strategies lie outside his range." There is something of critical theory in this book. Heaney's creative and critical idioms are coming together:
"his verse is being foddered on abstractions."

40   KILLEEN, TERRENCE, "Seamus Heaney—Shedding New Light," *Irish
Press* (July 18): 8.
      Killeen, in his review of *The Haw Lantern*, argues that the continuity of
life and language are central to Heaney's poetics. Although Killeen admires
"The Mud Vision," he finds Heaney's allegorical poems problematic, either
too universal or not universal enough.

41   LAW, PAMELA. "Seamus Heaney," *Sydney Studies in English* 12 (1986–87):
92–100.
      Law begins by stating that while Heaney's poetry is accessible, it is also
deceptively simple. There is an emphasis on voice—though it was not until
North that he found his own voice. For Heaney, poetry is self-revelation.
Among his greatest strengths is that of listening to voices and allowing them
to speak as fully as they can. In the relation between place, ancestors, and
symbol, Heaney has come to find his own technique, his own voice.

42   McCLATCHY, J. D. "The Exile's Song," *New Republic* 197, 25 (December
21): 36–39.
      Review of *The Haw Lantern*. McClatchy opens with a succinct summa-
ry of Heaney's career, which he asserts has been successful because Heaney
has continually "flown the nets of their [readers'] expectations." He describes
Heaney as "a poet of the body." Although the reviewer senses that some readers may find *The Haw Lantern* "disappointing," he speculates that Heaney
may be intentionally working in a minor key. McClatchy is attracted to the
book's "exhilirating variety"—for him the heart of the book is "elegaic."
      Reprinted 1993.21.

43   MACDONOGH, CAROLINE. "Seamus Heaney: The Makings of the Poet,"
in *Studies on Seamus Heaney*, collected by Jacqueline Genet (Caen: Centre
des publications de l'Université de Caen): 65–78.
      MacDonogh sets out to explore the origins of the sensory poetic voice.
Heaney's "Digging" is his analogy for the writing process. MacDonogh sees
parallels between Heaney's childhood and that of Montague. *Death of a
Naturalist* puts an end to his encounter with nature. *Door into the Dark* goes
beyond this and sets him off on his poetic mission. *North* is a significant
exchange between language and place. The sense of place is essential to Irish
writers. This sense of place is either illiterate and unconscious or learned and
conscious. The cultural, political heritage also contributes to the making of the
poet.

1987

44   McMILLAN, PETER. "On the frontier of writing: the poetry of Seamus Heaney," *Japan Times* (August 24): 10.
     The article was written during Heaney's week-long visit to Japan. McMillan writes in his overview of Heaney's career that the poet often transforms the fears of childhood into "an adult's sense of pragmatic husbandry."

45   MAY, DERWENT. "Beauty at the Border," *Sunday Telegraph* (July 5): 16.
     In this review of *The Haw Lantern*, May observes that Heaney has had difficulty writing about The Troubles, but so have other poets from the North. The reviewer begins with an anecdote about meeting Heaney in New York, the moral of which is that Heaney is not a violent man. May mentions as particularly good poems "Postcard from Iceland," "The Haw Lantern," and "From the Frontier of Writing."

46   MEIR, COLIN. "Grammars of Feeling: Syntax and Subject in the Poetry of Seamus Heaney," in *Studies on Seamus Heaney*, collected by Jacqueline Genet (Caen: Centre de publications de l'Université de Caen): 89–107.
     Meir argues that by failing "to discriminate between feeling getting into words and words turning to feeling," Heaney sets out the poetics behind *Selected Poems: 1965–1975*. In *Death of a Naturalist*, feeling is given form through what is perceived and how it is expressed. There are also mythmaking images which are far from the closeness of reality and language. In *Wintering Out*, the list of subjects widens while his forms become less flexible. The touchstone is always the quality of the emotion rather than ideas and imagery. After the publication of *North*, Heaney distinguishes between two kinds of language for poetry—the instinctual (female) and the rational (masculine). The way forward is a syntax which expresses personal feeling.

47   MEZEY, ROBERT. "A Partial Indulgence," *Los Angeles Times Book Review* (October 25): 6.
     In his review of *The Haw Lantern*, Mezey notes that there is much to admire in this book, which will be welcomed by Heaney's many readers. Its virtues are considerable: a rich and varied vocabulary; a delight in its shapes and sounds; and a gift for the accurate and vivid phrase. He enjoys the power of rhyme and meter and he is capable of using them.

48   MOLINO, MICHAEL R. "Heaney's 'Singing School': A Portrait of the Artist," *Journal of Irish Literature* 16, 3 (September): 12–17.
     Molino examines Heaney's sequence from *North*, "Singing School," through a close reading of the individual poems. The six poems in the sequence chart "the development of a young Irish poet as he struggles for his identity as an artist." Molino compares the sequence to Wordsworth's *Prelude* and Joyce's *Portrait of the Artist*. Even though "Singing School" is

implicitly autobiographical, the author also sees it as representative of "an Irish artist's growth" ultimately inscribed by politics.

49 MORRISON, BLAKE. "Clearing the Old Ground," *Observer* (June 28): 23.
    In his brief review of *The Haw Lantern,* Morrison comments that the volume "feels like a book between bigger books, its new poetic style still struggling to work itself out." The reviewer points out that the image of "frontier" is related to the "symbolic judgment place" and is manifest in Heaney's exploration of the concept of "clearance."

50 MURRAY, LES. "A Music of Indirection," *The Australian* (August): 20.
    Murray in his review of *The Haw Lantern* speaks of Heaney's guardedness and attributes it to his Ulster upbringing. The realities of the violence in Northern Ireland are not prominent but are nevertheless there in this short but varied and quite experimental collection. There are the usual vivid couplets and the poems of observation. Murray finds less poetic emotion in the semi-allegorical poems, which he terms "intriguing rather than exciting." He admits that these poems are the poet's way to reinvent poetry and have a legitimate place in the book which is well worth getting.
    Reprinted 1992.40.

51 NYE, ROBERT. "Master manner or fine frenzy," *Times* (London, October 22): 21.
    Review of *The Haw Lantern* and of *The Moon Disposes* by Peter Redgrove. Nye comments on Heaney's recognizable style, which has problems inasmuch as it could prevent him from taking risks. However, he is not negative about Heaney's poetry. He finds much to commend in this book, especially the sonnet sequence about the poet's mother.

52 O'BRIEN, SEAN. "From Woolly to Wiry," *Honest Ulsterman* 84 (Winter): 57–59.
    Review of *The Haw Lantern*. O'Brien finds the volume uneven but still the most interesting book by Heaney since *Wintering Out*. The book's "streamlined economy" appeals to the reviewer, especially in "Alphabets," which he compares to "Among School Children." O'Brien disagrees with those who describe the more abstract poems as "allegories." Instead, he sees them as a "move into international fabulism" and as poems that require the reader to meet the poet at the border of language and meaning itself.

53 O'NEILL, CHARLES LEE. "Circumventing Yeats: Austin Clarke, Thomas Kinsella, Seamus Heaney." Ph.D. dissertation, New York University.
    Yeats's poetry has fostered the myths of the Celtic Twilight and that of the Anglo-Irish "intellectual tradition." Irish poets after Yeats have challenged these myths. Heaney's Ireland is a pastoral one, in which violence and ritual sacrifice are commonplace.

1987

54 PARKINSON, THOMAS. "Serious Work: The Poetry and Prose of Seamus Heaney," in his *Poets, Poems, Movements* (Ann Arbor: U.M.I. Research Press): 153–65.
    Reprint of 1982.28.

55 "Poet wearing the mantle of Yeats," *Observer* (June 21): 7.
    Heaney is a popular poet both in England and the United States, and influential critics praise him. While surprised at this celebrity status, the poet keeps part of himself in reserve. His post at Harvard has brought him into contact with other major poets. He is not a political animal. Born and reared in Northern Ireland, he moved in 1972 to the Republic for practical as well as "emblematic" reasons. He keeps his links with the North. He is aware of the difficult relationship between art and politics and has insisted on his right to separate the two and write.

56 "[Radio appearances]," *Listener* 118 (July 23): 13.
    This brief account of Heaney's appearances on radio in connection with the publication of *The Haw Lantern* quotes from interviews on "Kaleidoscope" (R4) and "Bookshelf" (R4).

57 RAFROIDI, PATRICK. "The Sense of Place in Seamus Heaney's Poetry," in *Studies on Seamus Heaney*, collected by Jacqueline Genet (Caen: Centre des publications de l'Université de Caen): 79–88.
    Rafroidi bases his essay on Heaney's 1977 lecture "The Sense of Place." The link between landscape and the creative imagination has been a constant in Ireland. Heaney's interest in places has to do with dispossession and with the political desire to repossess. To counter the danger of excessive regionalism, Irish writers stress the universality of the local. The landscape is limited on the horizontal surface but not vertically in depth, where the bog introduces an archeological dimension.

58 REGAL, MARTIN. "Buried World, Severed Head: The Image of the Dead Man in the Works of Seamus Heaney," *Proceedings of the Third Nordic Conference for English Studies, Stockholm Studies in English* 73: 727–39.
    Heaney's work has shown his strong interest in archaeology. This sense of digging and uncovering layers of meaning informs his writing. His Bog Poems put special emphasis on the head. Regal quotes Derrida as saying that in the writing process, the writer has to commit a "literary suicide." By standing outside himself he becomes "a dead man."

59 RUDMAN, MARK. "Voluptaries and Maximalists," *New York Times Book Review* 92 (December 20): 12.
    Review of *The Haw Lantern* and of works by Amy Clampitt and Derek Walcott. Rudman finds Heaney's previous concern for "origins" still present

in this volume. He likes the "Clearances" sequence, but he finds Heaney's allegories lacking in his "usual lyric intensity." Rudman describes Heaney as a poet of "excision," a poet who knows what to cut out.

60   SCAMMELL, WILLIAM. "The Singing Robes of Art," *Poetry Review* 77, 3 (Autumn): 42–44.

Scammell's perceptive review-essay focuses upon *The Haw Lantern*. In this thoughtful piece, the reviewer praises and criticizes Heaney's work from many perspectives, arguing that he is a "tender" poet (not sentimental) and not a "toughie." He writes that Heaney "finds unsanctimonious sanctity" in the ordinary, and that the poet turns everything into Mass. However, unlike Joyce, Heaney "remains boy-size" and is a "watchful acolyte rather than priest." Scammell does not like Heaney's "self-communings and admonitions," and he particularly does not like the "preacher" in Heaney. The "Station Island" sequence is hampered by the big names (Eliot, Dante, Joyce) and by the noisy machinery. The reviewer prefers Heaney's playful allusions over the pretentious ones, and he is not impressed by the allegories of *The Haw Lantern*.

61   SMITH, DAVE. "Irish bard Heaney shines brightly in 'Haw Lantern,'" *Atlanta Constitution* (December 27): F10.

"The will to love" fuels Heaney's *The Haw Lantern*, Smith argues in his review of the book. Smith describes Heaney's social-awareness as "non-accusative" even while acknowledging the "war zones." As in other of his volumes, "Heaney has venerated, validated, and praised the zeitgeist of survivorship." In his poetry, Heaney meditates on speech, silence, and the dutiful life.

62   SWANN, JOSEPH. "The Poet as Critic: Seamus Heaney's Reading of Wordsworth, Hopkins and Yeats," in *Literary Interrelations: Ireland, England, and the World, 2: Comparison and Impact*, edited by Wolfgang Zach and Heinz Kosok (Tubingen: Narr): 361–70.

Concentrating on Heaney's critical writings related to the poets listed in the essay's title, Swann examines Heaney's misreading of these poets. Swann sees Heaney as defending his own poetry while attempting to avoid the nets of influence. Heaney's tendency to create mutually exclusive categories, such as masculine and feminine, active and passive, in his metaphoric readings of these poets is one aspect of Heaney's misreading. Swann describes the critical situation as that of the "feminine poet becoming a masculine critic." Heaney is a "listener," and his success as a critic, according to Swann, "rests in the completeness of his response to the physical sense of language."

1988

63   WATSON, GEORGE. *"The Haw Lantern," Irish Literary Supplement* 6, 2
      (Fall): 35.
             The motifs of vanishings and absences are seen throughout *The Haw
      Lantern* in poems about death and bereavement. Yet this is not a gloomy
      book. It is not innovative as *North* and *Station Island,* but in it we find a more
      relaxed Heaney.

64   WICHT, WOLFGANG. "Seamus Heaney's Field Work: The Politics of
      Poetry," *Zeitschrift fur Anglistik und Amerikanistik* 35, 4: 299–300.
             Wicht uses poems from *Field Work* to support his discussion of the pol-
      itics of form and metaphor in Heaney's poetry: "Verbal form and structure
      are message." Wicht also discusses some basic tensions in Heaney's work,
      such as the exchange between subjective experience and public events. The
      essay concludes with a brief discussion of the material presence of the poems
      and Heaney's manipulation of it: "The letters and words on the page . . . [are]
      phenomena for the eye *and* for the ear."

65   YOUNG, AUGUSTUS. "Poet without a safety net," *Fortnight* (September
      25): 18–19.
             Review of *The Haw Lantern* and of Paul Muldoon's *Meeting the
      British.* In the late 1950s and early 1960s, there was much talk of internation-
      alism, of a united Europe rather than of a united Ireland. There was much sur-
      prise, therefore, when a group of Northern poets began to emerge for whom
      Kavanagh was the inspiration. Their work was appreciated more in England
      than within the Republic of Ireland. Heaney's popularity abroad was not
      shared at home until *North* and finally *Station Island* showed the doubters that
      there was powerful writing here. *The Haw Lantern* is his most ambitious and
      also his most inconsistent book. There are some strong, longish poems in
      which he becomes more himself. There are also some sub-standard pieces
      which should have been reworked or omitted. However, *The Haw Lantern* in
      part signals Heaney's "brave release from everybody's expectations."

1988

1   ALLEN, MICHAEL. "'Holding Course': *The Haw Lantern* and Its Place in
     Heaney's Development," *Irish Review* 3: 108–18.
             Allen finds the Heaney of *The Haw Lantern* to be "an astute and subtle
     craftsman" meditating on power, philosophy, and art. Heaney is conducting a
     self-evaluative, backward look. He is laying down his burden of guilt. Since
     the publication of *North*, the problem "has been to reconcile wide appeal. . .with
     the 'fit audience though few' assumed by most poets and poetry-lovers." The
     best poems in *The Haw Lantern* are the elegies, but outside of these there is a

concern with the poet's past performances, image, and audience, presented with skillful, literary artifice.

Reprinted 1992.1.

2   ALLISON, JONATHAN. "Community and Individualism in the Poetry of W. B. Yeats and Seamus Heaney." Ph.D. dissertation, University of Michigan.

This dissertation examines the tension between individual vision and communal affiliation informing the poetry of W. B. Yeats and Seamus Heaney. Yeats served as an example for post-war poets of the possibility of addressing the question of nationalism and the violent world of Irish politics without becoming consumed by partisan rhetoric and popular cliché. The last two chapters show how Heaney appropriates Yeats's tropes and phrases, especially in his prose, and how his poetry reproduces the tension Yeats's work expressed between individualism and community.

3   ANDERSON, NATHALIE. "Queasy Proximity: Seamus Heaney's Mythical Method," *Eire-Ireland* 23, 4 (Winter): 103–13.

Anderson argues that Heaney's "mystical method" in *North* is foreshadowed in his early work. In *Death of a Naturalist* the images show an undercurrent of revulsion and sexuality. This metaphoric management is explored again in *Door into the Dark*. In *Wintering Out* the landscape is infused with sexual potency, and Heaney has moved from revulsion and control to a conscious use of sexual tension in a political context. In *North* the poet endows these ambivalencies with political significance to convey the profound ambivalencies at the heart of the bond with Ireland.

4   ANDREWS, ELMER. *The Poetry of Seamus Heaney: All the Realms of Whisper.* New York: St. Martin's Press, 219 pp.

A chronological examination of Heaney's work up to 1987 and excluding *The Haw Lantern*. The study discusses the central issues (e.g., the conflict between the free imagination and the claims of social responsibility). Andrews provides an analysis of the major themes in Heaney's work. He suggests that a male universe can be found coinciding with a female approach. Andrews is a fair commentator, discussing Heaney's weaknesses when he sees them. He is better on the later works, *Sweeney Astray* and *Station Island*. However, his study is governed by chronology and explication rather than by concept.

5   BALAKIAN, PETER. "Seamus Heaney's New Landscapes," *Literary Review* 31, 4 (Summer): 501–5.

Balakian, in his review of *The Haw Lantern*, says that the book shows Heaney's continuing ability to move in new directions without abandoning his core. The poems to his mother remind us of his lyricism. They are accompanied by poems which establish a completely new idiom, and which are sometimes set in surreal, modern landscapes far removed from his rural world. These landscapes also provide new ways for him to state his fundamental values.

6   "[Book Review]," *Publisher's Weekly* (November): 57.
    Brief review of *The Government of the Tongue*. The reviewer mentions Heaney's charting of the "emergence of the poet as witness" in the twentieth century. Heaney asserts that poetry has political energy since it heals the self, which then produces cultural change. Heaney sees some poets, such as Lowell, Plath, and Auden, as spiritual antennae, and thus they speak for the age.

7   BRANDES, RAND. "Seamus Heaney: An Interview," *Salmagundi* 80 (Fall): 4–21.
    In this interview Heaney comments upon a range of topics and poets. The interview is constructed around *The Haw Lantern* and *The Government of the Tongue*. In relation to the former, Heaney discusses the importance of Eastern European poets, such as Milosz—especially in terms of his catholicism. In addition, Heaney not only looks to these poets as examples, but also finds their use of parable and fable liberating. Heaney talks about major poems in the volume; there are extended references to "Alphabets," "Mud Vision," and "Clearances." Heaney responds to questions about *The Government of the Tongue*. There is a lengthy passage on Kavanagh and the importance of "absence" to his poetic vision. Heaney elaborates upon his understanding and practice of translation: "You just want the standards that usually operate; you want a certain decorum, chastity, and integrity of language to be maintained." American poetry and poets are a central part of the interview. The Irish poet suggests what he finds unsatisfying about American poetry. In contrast, he also mentions the poets he admires, such as Wallace Stevens, Ashbery, Merrill, and Elizabeth Bishop. T. S. Eliot also occupies a large segment of the exchange. Finally, Heaney defines what he means when he quotes "the end of art is peace."

8   BROWN, TERENCE. "A Northern Renaissance: Poets from the North of Ireland, 1965–1980," in his *Ireland's Literature: Selected Essays* (Mullingar: Lilliput Press; Totowa, N.J.: Barnes & Noble): 203–22.
    Brown points out that in Northern Ireland since the sixties, the well-made poem could exist and thrive by accommodating an unfamiliar language, such as that employed by Heaney and Montague. The journey poem made it possible for the poets to widen their horizons without great risk, as Heaney does in "Whatever You Say, Say Nothing," "The Tollund Man," "Westering," and "Night Drive." Brown cites examples from Mahon, Longley, Montague, Ormsby, Muldoon, and Carson.

9 BROWN, TERENCE. "The Witnessing Eye," *Poetry Ireland Review* 21 (Spring): 59–62.

A review of *The Haw Lantern* and of *Seamus Heaney* by Neil Corcoran. Brown sees Heaney in *The Haw Lantern* dealing with the accusing eye of the public. This accusation and the "desire for exoneration and release" has implications for the sequence "Clearances." In the political parables of imaginary places, such as "From the Republic of Conscience," the spark of necessity is lacking. "The Mud Vision," however, shows that "the poet is ready to accept the public's gaze." As was the case with *Wintering Out*, there is the sense that *The Haw Lantern* is a transitional work.

10 BYRON, CATHERINE. "'Incertus' Takes the Helm," *Linen Hall Review* 5, 3: 23.

In her review of *The Government of the Tongue*, Byron accuses Heaney of being "too tinged with certainty" and of having become too attached to the "mainly white and male international canon of poetry." He is good in his treatment of dissident Soviet bloc poets, but she is disappointed that he seems deaf to the many eloquent and radical new voices now appearing.

11 CAREY, JOHN. "The most sensuous poet to use English since Keats," *Sunday Times* (London, April 3): G8–9.

Among the factors that have made Heaney a best-selling poet is his avoidance of obscurity. His subject matter and his sensuous use of language help him to feel his way past words to things. While he believes that poetry cannot be converted into a political platform, he nevertheless asserts that "it must make its way in a world that is public and brutal." He is also a poet who constantly innovates, as he shows in some of the poems in *The Haw Lantern*.

12 CAREY, JOHN. "A Plea for Poetry in Our Time," *Sunday Times: Books* (London, June 12): 1–2.

Carey in his review of *The Government of the Tongue* sees Heaney giving an overview of the possibilities for poetry at this time. For Heaney, the poetic gift is beyond the evils of this world, and he would warn that otherwise it will be exploited by those professing one dogma or another. Among the important poets in his view are some Eastern bloc writers who work in the face of great deprivation. Heaney seeks a function for poetry, knowing that "any function will destroy its self-validating singularity."

13 COULTER, CAROL. "Yeats's personifications 'put Irishwomen in a straitjacket,'" *Irish Times* (August 9): 5.

Coulter's report on the opening sessions of the Yeats Summer School in Sligo focuses on Professor Butler-Cullingford's lecture. She reports Butler-Cullingford's asserting that the personification of Ireland as a woman by Yeats,

1988

Pearse, and Heaney "has helped imprison Irish women in a straitjacket of purity and passivity." Heaney, she says, has associated Irish republicanism with a female goddess.

14 CUNNINGHAM, FRANCINE. "A modern martyrology," *Fortnight* 264 (July/August): 19–20.

In her review of *The Government of the Tongue,* Cunningham sees Heaney guiding a tour of international poetry. The efficacy of poetry in the present troubles is raised again. Poets must fight for poetic integrity, and today that fight is taking place in Eastern Europe. Poets are the guardians of the cultural and folk memories of the country. Heaney believes in the redemptive power of art. There is a danger, however, that the poet may be "inclined to sing for his supper." Even in his critical writings, Heaney is a towering figure.

15 DAVIE, DONALD. "Responsibilities of *Station Island,*" *Salmagundi* 80 (Fall): 58–65.

The sequence *Station Island* is structured, like much of Dante's *Divine Comedy,* in its discussion between the poet and the spirits of some of the dead. This ambition, signalled in *Field Work,* was not entirely vindicated in *Station Island* because Heaney's verses "were too permissively various" to bear the strong authority of the Dante line. Dante was a politically partisan poet; Heaney is under continued pressure to declare himself politically. In *Station Island* Heaney declares how impossible this is for him. In the "Sweeney Redivivus" section Sweeney becomes a symbol of the past who soars over the Irish factions locked in conflict. The poet's duty, as Heaney sees it, is to resist political persuasion.

16 DOCHERTY, THOMAS. "The Sign of the Cross," *Irish Review* 5: 112–16.

In his review Docherty examines two threads which run through *The Government of the Tongue*: "ethics" and the "political dialectic. . .of Identity and Difference." He sees Heaney's politicization of aesthetics, which assumes the role of "conscience," as a notable limitation of the essays. Heaney attempts to compensate for this limitation, according to the reviewer, "through the ghostly presence of a theology."

17 DREXEL, JOHN. "Haw Lantern," *Partisan Review* 55, 3 (Summer): 500–505.

Review of *The Haw Lantern.* From the beginning of his career Heaney used digging as a metaphor for writing. This phase ended with *North.* In *Field Work* and in *Station Island,* he is far less absorbed with the archaeological past. *The Haw Lantern* opens up new territory with some difficult, abstract, allegorical poems. Heaney's refusal to endorse those who would manipulate language to achieve power is very evident in this book. The heart of the work is the sequence "Clearances," in memory of his mother. Drexel sums up: "*The*

Haw Lantern is not necessarily the book we would have expected, ten years ago, from Heaney, but it is what might have been hoped for."

18 DUFFY, CHARLES F. "Heaney's DIGGING," *Explicator* 46, 4 (Summer): 44–45.

Duffy points to the importance of the digging image in Heaney's work. He suggests an additional Biblical stratum to broaden the poem's Irish dimensions.

19 DUNN, DOUGLAS. "Power of the Poet," *Glasgow Herald* (June 11): Weekender 2.

Dunn, in his review of *The Government of the Tongue*, comments on the innately "subjective" aspect of critical prose written about poetry by a poet. Consequently, Heaney presents a book in which "he worries passionately at themes close to his own life of writing." Dunn appears to sympathize with the basic tensions between "beauty" and "truth," art and life, which inform many of the essays. Dunn briefly alludes to the fact that several of Heaney's arguments relating to Irish poetry in an English context could be applied to Scottish poetry.

20 FAHEY, WILLIAM A. "Heaney's FIELD WORK," *Explicator* 46, 2 (Winter): 47–49.

Fahey sees in "Field Work" not alone the work of the farmer—ploughing, herding, digging—but also the transformation of those tasks and the landscape into images that are echoed throughout the "Field Work" sequence in the book.

21 FIEROBE, CLAUDE. "La Tourbiere comme memoire et mythe dans la poesie de Seamus Heaney," *Etudes irlandaises* 13, 1: 127–38.

Fierobe examines the role of the bog in Heaney's poetry. The pivotal poem in *Selected Poems* is "Bogland." The bog is Heaney's mythopoetic purgation.

22 FILKINS, PETER. "[Review]," *Iowa Review* 18, 2 (Spring, Summer): 184–206.

Review of *The Haw Lantern* together with works by Derek Walcott and Peter Viereck. Here we are shown a poet reassessing his art at mid-career. Language is what has brought him to what he has now become. This work shows us a vision gained through the handling of abstractions, thought, and consciousness as if they were entities. This is a poetry of ideas grounded in vibrant language. The book includes four poems which address the nature of conscience or consciousness. The duties of a poet are pressing and vital, the best of humankind will somehow continue to flourish. Poetry can increase its impact over time.

1988

23 FRENCH, SEAN. "A call to Action," *New Statesman* 1, 2 (June 17): 41–42.
    In his review of *The Government of the Tongue,* French sees Heaney's generosity—of appreciation, of critical method. In these essays he is aware of himself as a poet in an oppressive political situation bound by an alien literary tradition. Poetry must "escape the genteel English tradition."

24 FRY, AUGUST J. "Confronting Seamus Heaney: A Personal Reading of His Early Poetry," *Dutch Quarterly Review* 18, 3: 242–55.
    Fry sets out to become acquainted with Heaney's beginnings as a poet in his first four books. This involves consideration of the role of the father, the Northern Ireland countryside, the writing of poetry, civil war, and religious differences. In *North* the bog, which had appeared in Heaney's poetry only incidentally, is now seen as the center from which his poetry rises: "The poet stands firmly in Ireland in the midst of new troubles."

25 GOLDENSOHN, BARRY. "The Recantation of Beauty," *Salmagundi* 80 (Fall): 76–82.
    Goldensohn examines Heaney's poem "The Strand at Lough Beg," on the sectarian killing of his cousin, and his return to the same event in Section VIII of *Station Island.* In the *Station Island* poem, he calls his earlier work to account, recognizing "that the world of death and violence does not obey the reconciling gestures of poetry."

26 GRAHAM, KEITH. "Seamus Heaney's poetic pen conveys 'the good, the true,'" *Atlanta Constitution* (April 15): E1, E4.
    Graham's article surveys Heaney's life and his career as a poet. His first poem appeared in 1962 and began his expression of his rural experience. Later, with the increasing violence in Northern Ireland, he began to move into more complex levels. Pressure to become more political in his poetry was resisted by him. He developed an anthropological approach which culminates in a sense of outrage at the violence done to victims. He is the most respected poet in Ireland, yet he is unmoved by his fame. He feels an obligation to his talent: as Heaney himself says, "You speak the reality as truly as you can."

27 HABERSTROH, PATRICIA BOYLE. "Poet, Poetry, Painting and Artist in Seamus Heaney's *North*," *Eire-Ireland* 23, 4 (Winter): 124–33.
    Haberstroh takes the two dedicatory poems in *North*, "Sunlight" and "The Seed Cutters," to show how they connect Heaney to painters and painting and illustrate his belief in the value of the artist to society. Throughout *North* he gives us images of violence and hostility drawn from his own experience as well as from art and artifacts of history. As do Breughel, Shakespeare, Baudelaire, Goya, and Yeats, so also Heaney combines "the 'beauty of art' with the 'mess of the actual.'"

28 HART, HENRY. "Ghostly Colloquies: Seamus Heaney's 'Station Island,'" *Irish University Review* 18, 2 (Autumn): 233–50.

A study of the poem, the text, and the debt to Dante and to T. S. Eliot. Despite the private nature of his poetry Heaney's "final direction is always to the community" of Ireland and its troubles.

29 "Heaney inaugurates Ellmann lectures," *Emory Magazine* (August): 8–9.

The article contains a few quotations by Heaney about Richard Ellmann. Heaney also talks about his desire to "go back into the unworded, prereflective world."

30 HYWEL, ELIN AP. "Diogenes in Doubt: Seamus Heaney's *The Haw Lantern,*" *Text & Context* 3 (Autumn): 133–40.

Hywel discusses the significance of "absence" in Heaney's *The Haw Lantern.* This absence is related to Heaney's ambivalence over taking an active role, which leads to an impasse that even Heaney can not overcome. Hywell also mentions that Heaney's use of the Irish language is often onomatopoeic.

31 "Irish poet to inaugurate Ellman Lectures in Modern Literature," *Emory Wheel* (April 5): 9.

Notice of the forthcoming visit of Seamus Heaney to Emory University to deliver the first series of the Richard Ellmann Lectures in Modern Literature. Heaney will deliver three lectures and will read from his own poetry. A video of Heaney and Ellmann discussing modern poetry will also be shown.

32 JOHN, BRIAN. "Contemporary Irish Poetry and the Matter of Ireland: Thomas Kinsella, John Montague and Seamus Heaney," in *Medieval and Modern Ireland,* edited by Richard Wall (Totowa, N.J.: Barnes & Noble): 34–59.

John's intention is to show that Kinsella, Montague, and Heaney draw upon the Irish tradition both to link themselves to the Irish past as well as to explore the self and the contemporary world. For Heaney, the Irish tradition is central and indispensable to a full appreciation of his work. His *An Open Letter, Sweeney Astray,* and *Station Island* point to the case. Sweeney's continuing attraction for Heaney has many explanations: his love of the Sweeney territory familiar to him throughout his life; the nature poetry and descriptions of his rural childhood; and the mystery of the creative process. In *Station Island* the Sweeney myth has affected his work and has liberated his imagination to express deep-seated personal experience. Love, transformation, Ireland, and poetry all come together through his involvement in the Irish tradition.

33 KEARNEY, RICHARD. "Heaney and Homecoming," in his *Transitions: Narratives in Modern Irish Culture* (Manchester University Press): 101–12; with Appendix: "Heaney, Heidegger and Freud—The Paradox of the Homely": 113–22.

Heaney's poetry is seen by many as inspired by place, as a returning to forgotten origins. Kearney sets out to show that the cultural theme of homecoming in Heaney has little to do with "insular notions of parochial *pietas*." He aims to show that Heaney's treatment of homecoming is an unresolved debate between the claims of home and homelessness. He argues that Heaney's poems are about transitions from place to place—for Heaney, homecoming is never the actuality of an event but the possibility of an advent. Some of the poems in *North* deal explicitly with this theme. There is always a delicate balance between belonging to a home and being exiled from this home, which is similar to Heaney's own predicament. Heaney is faithful to the ambiguity of opposing demands. One of the strengths of *Station Island* is the refusal to choose between Heaney or Sweeney, between the "pilgrim of history or the carefree émigré of the imagination."

In the appendix, Kearney shows that Heaney's poetic concerns are not only Irish but international and universal. Heaney's ambivalent attitude to homecoming resembles Heidegger's search for Being as a passage towards "home" through the "unhomely." This corresponds also to Freud's identification of the unconscious with the "homely unhomely" paradox.

Reprint, in a fuller version, of 1986.31.

34 KELTERS, SEAMUS. "Waiter turned poet returns and inspires," *Irish News* (September 19): 8.

Kelters reports on the first Newcastle Poetry Festival. Among those present was Seamus Heaney, who conducted a workshop. Heaney spoke of his desire at one time to demystify poetry and his shift from that position.

35 KIBERD, DECLAN. "The War Against the Past," in *The Uses of the Past: Essays on Irish Culture*, edited by Audrey S. Eyler and Robert F. Garrett (University of Delaware Press): 24–54.

Kiberd traces the Irish obsession with history in the work of Joyce, Pearse, Synge, Yeats, O'Casey, Friel, and Heaney. The Irish writers, victims of their own literary history, live in a cycle of repetitions.

36 KINZIE, MARY. "Deeper than Declared: On Seamus Heaney," *Salmagundi* 80 (Fall): 22–57.

Kinzie concentrates on Heaney's *North* and *Station Island* and maintains that Heaney was ill-prepared "to write the large-scale politico-religious work." We see this ambivalence of theme and tone in the "Station Island" sequence of *Station Island*. In the first section of *Station Island*, "The Mind Vision" is "a style-piece that may lead to greater things." In *Sweeney Astray* and in the Sweeney poems of *Station Island*, Heaney has moved forward "in his ability to frame a political statement." There we find a material style unhampered by peculiarities of diction or rhythm. This technique has been evident in his prose but seldom in his verse.

Reprinted 1993.20.

37 LOGAN, S. "Not a Thinking Voice," *Spectator* 261 (November 5): 46–47.

In his review of *The Government of the Tongue*, Logan sees Heaney's use of metaphor in his criticism as sometimes apt, while at other times it adds superfluous detail. He also accuses the poet of grandiloquence. Using Heaney's own words, he asserts that the root of the trouble lies in the fact that the poet's voice "is not an abstract thinking voice at all." Heaney's attempt to encompass the rival tasks of controlling and obeying the forces inherent in language may serve a poet well, "but for the critic it is reckless to pretend that such claims are evenly balanced."

38 LOJKINE-MORELEC, MONIQUE. "Memoire et desir dans la poesie de S. Heaney," *Etudes Irlandaises* 13, 2: 61–79.

Examines the place of memory and sexual desire as a means of confronting current problems in Heaney's work.

39 LONGLEY, EDNA. "Putting on the International Style," *Irish Review* 5 (Autumn): 75–81.

Heaney has a strong interest in Eastern European poetry, which is shown in *The Government of the Tongue*. This, however, leads him away not only from the Internationalism he desires but also from his own national roots, the source of his inspiration.

40 LONGLEY, EDNA. "When Did You Last See Your Father," in *Cultural Contexts and Literary Idioms in Contemporary Irish Literature*, edited by Michael Kenneally (New York: Barnes & Noble): 88–112.

In the work of Montague, Heaney, Friel, and Bernard MacLaverty, the most pervasive theme is the burden of history, which has been accorded the status of myth and is therefore "deterministic." Muldoon, however, questions that history by employing techniques which "sabotage all kinds of certainty."

41 LUFTIG, VICTOR, and STEVEN REESE. "Haw Lantern," *Georgia Review* 42, 3: 645–48.

This review of *The Haw Lantern*, in which the poet conveys his sense of the public relevance of poetry, sees it as a quieter book than its predecessors. There was more direct confrontation with public reality in *Field Work* and in *Station Island*. The reviewers give space to a discussion of "A Peacock's Feather" and see it as a sign that Heaney has achieved for himself an assured and independent public stance. Overall, *The Haw Lantern* shows a confidence in the place and purpose of poetry and announces its newly achieved political force.

42   McCORMACK, W. J. "Holy Sinner," *Krino* 6 (Autumn): 65–69.
      Review of *The Government of the Tongue*. While the essays are individually excellent, including the splendid essay on Sylvia Plath, one feels uncomfortable with the occasionalness of some of them. The lack of an essay on Yeats in a collection concerned with the relationship between poetry and violent politics is regrettable.

43   McCURRY, JACQUELINE. "The Female in Seamus Heaney's Prose, Poetics and the Poetry of *The Haw Lantern*," *Eire-Ireland* 23, 4 (Winter): 114–24.
      McCurry identifies what she considers to be the female element of Heaney's "androgynous" poetics, in part by using the poet's own understanding of the female. She finds this element in *The Haw Lantern* in the "circularity in movement and imagery," the "evocative language," "fluidity," and the elements of earth and water. McCurry asserts that in many of Heaney's poems that adopt a female voice, "Heaney's female personae are direct, un-self-conscious, believable." She employs some secondary feminist theory in her essay. She mentions that one of Heaney's working titles for *The Haw Lantern* was *Hard Water*.

44   McKENDRICK, JAMIE. "Poetry's Governing Power," *Poetry Durham* 20 (Winter 1988/89): 34–38.
      Review of *The Government of the Tongue*. McKendrick finds Heaney's use of personal anecdotes an effective compliment to the poet's resourceful "generous intelligence." Although he admires the majority of the essays, McKendrick finds the volume's title essay, the piece on Auden, and the commentary on Larkin flawed.

45   McLOUGHLIN, DEBORAH. "Heaney's WINTERING OUT," *Explicator* 47, 1 (Fall): 52–55.
      Focusing upon four poems from *Wintering Out* ("Limbo," "Bye-Child," "Maighdean Mara," and "Servant Boy"), the author concludes that despite early reviews to the contrary, Heaney writes about the "suffering of his country" obliquely by using a variety of emblems. The author interprets the "warm eggs" of "Servant Boy" as possibly "poems" that Heaney gives to a "British publishing house."

46   MAHON, DEREK. "The need to sing," *Irish Times* (June 18): Weekend 9.
      In his review, Mahon observes that unlike *Preoccupations, The Government of the Tongue* is informed by a "unity of purpose." However,

while the latter book is highly studied and academic, the former is "fresh and frank." Consequently, Mahon feels that *The Government of the Tongue* is "excessively professional."

47 MARIUS, RICHARD. "[Book Review]," *Erato/Harvard Book Review* 11–12 (Winter and Spring): 13.

Review of *The Government of the Tongue*. Marius says Heaney writes brilliantly about poetry he loves, as well as about poetry itself. These essays reflect the values which Heaney writes into his own work. He discusses a great range of poets—one of the loveliest of his essays is on Elizabeth Bishop. As with his poetry, his prose is both accessible and profound.

48 MARTIN, AUGUSTINE. "In defence of the poet," *Sunday Press* (Dublin, July 31): *Living* 8.

Review of *The Government of the Tongue*. Martin claims that Heaney is the best poet-critic since Auden and perhaps since Eliot: "Heaney is a better critic than Auden because his ear is more sensitive to the poem's unheard melodies and when his intelligence closes with that of his subject it is always a moment of true recognition." Martin writes that critics looking for an ideological charge from the essays will be disappointed, but he notes that those looking for fine prose and assistance with their reading will enjoy the essays. Heaney's re-evaluation of Kavanagh in the book is a significant point in Heaney's career, according to Martin.

49 MENDELSON, EDWARD. "Poetry as fate and faith," *Times Literary Supplement* (July 1–7): 726.

In his review of *The Government of the Tongue*, Mendelson gives the essays a tough and skeptical reading. He calls the collection an apology not only for poetry, but also more specifically an apology for the "subjects and silences of Heaney's poems." Like other critics, Mendelson challenges Heaney's assertion that the "note of crisis has disappeared from British poetry," and the reviewer states that a "double standard seems to apply to poets of Britain and Ireland and the poets of Poland and Russia" in Heaney's book. The reviewer also finds Heaney's celebration of the moment of inspiration "romanticized" and limited, since it does not account for the post-inspiration labor of editing and revising. Finally, Mendelson declares that Heaney's treatment of Nero in the book's opening essay is based upon an "unexamined cliché," which a few minutes with Gibbon would correct. It is not clear whether Mendelson condemns Heaney in the end or sympathizes with the position of his writing: "this book points insistently towards the essential loneliness of Heaney's work."

1988

50 MILBURN, MICHAEL. "[Book Review]," *Harvard Book Review* 7 and 8 (Winter and Spring): 1.
    The Haw Lantern's centerpiece, "Clearances," contains some of the best poems Heaney has written. In the allegorical poems he seems to be testing his horizons while still holding on to clarity and pace. He has written here "a significant number of poems which do full justice to his art."

51 "Modern Poetry. To speak, to dream," *Economist* 308, (July 30): 86–87.
    Review of *The Government of the Tongue*. In times of horror, most poets wonder whether or not poetry does any good. The Northern Ireland violence gives Heaney the experience of living in the presence of danger. He has sympathy also for the difficulties under which Eastern European poets, such as Holub, Herbert, and Milosz, write. The reviewer finds the real delight of the book to be in Heaney's eye for an image.

52 MOTION, ANDREW. "Power of Words in the Darkest Hour," *Independent* (June 16): 23.
    Review of *The Government of the Tongue*. Motion's review argues in part against Heaney's description in the essays of contemporary British poetry as plagued by genteel self-absorption. Instead, Motion makes a case that his contemporaries are writing with political awareness and integrity when writing about "unemployment, racism. . . ." The remaining part of the review is descriptive and asserts that Heaney's work "demonstrates. . .a capacity to make value useful and to ease the tension between song and suffering."

53 MOTION, ANDREW. *Harpers and Queens* (London) 88, 12 (December): 46.
    Motion selects his favorite books of the year, which include *The Government of the Tongue*. Motion says that "the piece on Plath is one of the masterpieces of modern criticism."

54 NEILL, EDWARD. "A Truant Romantic," *Times Educational Supplement* 3773 (October 21): 27.
    In this review of *The Government of the Tongue*, Neill comments upon the "Jungian depths" of Heaney's verse as well as the "thick-textured metaphoric phrasing" of the poet's essays.

55 NÍ CHUILLEANÁIN, EILÉAN. "Reviews," *Poetry Ireland* 24 (Winter): 56–60.
    Heaney's *The Government of the Tongue* is one several books examined in this review. Ní Chuilleanáin finds Heaney's essays traditional and shaped by the formalities of their occasions and the seriousness of their subjects. She argues that Heaney's concentration on the poets' style and language causes him to overlook important aspects of the poems' "intellectual and political" content. One major problem with Heaney's discussion of the Eastern-European

poets, according to the reviewer, is Heaney's faith in translators to reproduce the truth. Thus, as with his poetry, Heaney comes to few conclusions.

56 O'BRIEN, DARCY. "Piety and Modernism: Seamus Heaney's Station Island," *James Joyce Quarterly* 26, 1 (Fall): 51–65.
       O'Brien concentrates upon the issue of faith or belief as it is worked out and not worked out in the "Station Island" sequence. O'Brien argues that Heaney's aesthetic and religious position is closer to Carelton than Joyce; but that unlike the earlier writers, Heaney is not interested in the "angry role." O'Brien mentions that Heaney made the pilgrimage to Lough Derg four times in his youth. The author relates the fact that the Irish can be strongly anti-clerical and still be Catholic. This idea is connected to the religious dimension of Heaney's poem and to his modernist aesthetic.

57 O'BRIEN, EDNA. "Books of the Year," *Observer* (December 4): 20.
       O'Brien notes that Heaney's *Government of the Tongue* reminds us "that poetry is the only thing left to us."

58 O'NEILL, CHARLES. "From the Land of the Unspoken," *Spirit* 54 (Spring-Summer): 46–50.
       Review of *The Government of the Tongue* and of *The Haw Lantern*. The poems in *The Haw Lantern* are those of a lyric poet in mid-career attempting to honor both beauty and truth. The essays in the other volume also deal with this tension. The poet's duty is to keep his poetry alive, as the Eastern European poets have done through times of great difficulty. These concerns have also exercised the minds of earlier poets. The visionary also has a claim on Heaney; he sounds the silences and articulates the demands of truth and beauty.

59 O'TOOLE, FINTAN. "Public v. Private Property," *Sunday Tribune* (Dublin, June 12): 21.
       O'Toole, in his review of *The Government of the Tongue*, considers Heaney more of a celebrant who scrutinizes the lives of other poets than a crit-ic who dissects their work. In this regard, he says, Heaney "is looking for moments in the lives and works of others that will vindicate his own practice and his own dilemma." O'Toole finds it interesting that Heaney chooses to write on the lyrical, mystical, and rapturous aspects of Kavanagh's and Larkin's poetry and not on the social and historical elements.

60 O'TOOLE, FINTAN. "Seamus Heaney: Beyond the Normal Niceties," *Colour Tribune* (April 10): 2.
       This biographical sketch of Heaney is built around the poet's political comments made while receiving *The Sunday Times* writing award in England after which some in the audience called "rubbish." O'Toole's article contains several interesting quotations from Heaney and a few from his wife.

1988

61 PARINI, JAY. "The Co-opted and Obliterated Echo: On Heaney's 'Clearances,'" *Salmagundi* 80 (Fall): 71–75.

Much as the "Glanmore Sonnets" were to *Field Work*, so does the sonnet sequence "Clearances" lie at the center of *The Haw Lantern*. The poet's mother is present with her son throughout the sequence, until the father replaces the son at the mother's deathbed. Her absence or "clearance" is felt in the final sonnet, where she has become "a bright nowhere."

62 PARKIN, ANDREW T. L. "Public and Private Voices in the Poetry of Yeats, Montague and Heaney," *AAA: Arbeiten aus Anglistik und Amerikanistik* 13, 1: 29–38.

W. B. Yeats was pleased that Archibald MacLeish praised the "public voice" in his verse above that of other modern poets. Yeats's public voice, however, works in conjunction with a personal, private voice. A similar play of voices can be found in works by Seamus Heaney and John Montague. Heaney's poetry uncovers Ireland through his close observation of the jobs and trades of the country. In *North* he finds the historical mythology to hold together Irish and Northern European culture.

63 QUINLAN, KIERAN. "Verse," *World Literature Today* 62, 3 (Summer): 459.

Quinlan, in this brief review of *The Haw Lantern*, notes Heaney building on his earlier work without repeating himself. There is a confidence in his voice; nevertheless the private sentiment remains private while being offered to us.

64 ROBERTS-BURKE, ROBIN J. "The Country of the Mind: Homeland Symbolism in Twentieth-Century Hebrew and Irish Poetry (Greenberg, Kavanagh, Ratosh, Heaney)." Ph.D. dissertation, University of California–Los Angeles.

Treating a literature of the homeland as a topos of human experience with mythological sources, this study of nationalistic poetry uncovers common elements in the narratives of two diverse cultures, the Jewish and the Irish. In particular, this study examines the poet's role in articulating the collective experience in a national mythos whose structure and rhetoric share a universal paradigm based on the Oedipus complex.

65 ROBINSON, ALAN. "Seamus Heaney: The Free State of Image and Allusion," in his *Instabilities in Contemporary British Poetry* (London: Macmillan Press): 123–60.

Robinson focuses his discussion on Heaney's *Station Island* and *The Haw Lantern*. Using Heaney's references to Eastern European poets as a starting point, the author examines the tension he finds in Heaney's work between the imaginative life and the historical life. Robinson also talks about the role of religion in *Station Island* and Heaney's political response to the Troubles. Heaney's quest for primal fulfillment in *The Haw Lantern* (which is often frustrated) is one form of his attempt to establish the autonomy of art in a hostile political world.

66 SCAMMELL, WILLIAM. "The children of art and life," *Guardian* (June 17): 27.

In his review of *The Government of the Tongue,* Scammell praises the book, but he wishes for a more autobiographical ending to the opening essay (instead of referring to Jung) and feels that Lowell is a lesser poet than Heaney makes him out to be.

67 SCRUTON, JAMES ALBERT. "A Vocable Ground: The Poetry of Seamus Heaney." Ph.D. dissertation, University of Tennessee.

Seamus Heaney's consistent reliance upon earthy metaphors for language and consciousness is indicative of what he calls a poet's real "technique," his "stance towards life, a definition of his own reality." Through his eight volumes of poetry to date, Heaney has continually enlarged the symbolic and thematic dimensions of his landscape, his ground made vocable.

68 "Seamus Justin Heaney," in *Cambridge Guide to Literature in English,* edited by Ian Ousby (Cambridge: Cambridge University Press): 445.

Brief biographical outline, followed by a chronology of his principal writings.

69 SIMPSON, LOUIS. "The Poet's Theme," *Hudson Review* 41, 1 (Spring): 93–142.

The essay considers the work of, among others, Yeats, Frost, W. C. Williams, Spender, Patrick Kavanagh, Eliot, and Heaney. Simpson briefly (pp. 125–26) refers to Heaney's poem "A Constable Calls" from the "Singing School" sequence as an example of a poetry of "real events." Simpson suggests that this is Heaney's theme, and that any poet worthy of the name works with and is chosen by a theme. Simpson concludes: "Theme is an expression of consistent thinking, an expression of character."

70 SINNER, ALAIN THOMAS YVON. "'Protective Colouring': The Political Commitment in the Poetry of Seamus Heaney (Northern Ireland)." Ph.D. dissertation, University of Hull.

There is a tension in Seamus Heaney's poetry between his desire to escape from the Northern Troubles into a private domestic world, and the political responsibilities he has toward his Catholic community. He tries to reconcile the demands of politics and art by concealing his political message below the protective coloring of analogy, metaphor, and parable.

1988

71 SPEIRS, LOGAN. "Current Literature 1987: 1. 'New Writing: Drama and Poetry,'" *English Studies* 69, 5 (October): 421–32.

In the course of his survey, Speirs cites *The Haw Lantern* and comments briefly on Heaney's precision and his divided consciousness, which is a result of living in Ireland.

72 STANFIELD, PAUL SCOTT. "Facing *North* Again: Polyphony, Contention," *Eire-Ireland* 23, 4 (Winter): 133–44.

Stanfield studies *North* to examine Heaney's hovering between the wish to perfect his art and the obligation to speak for his community. Stanfield bases his arguments on a detailed examination of the poems "Punishment" and "Viking Dublin." He argues that the poet's identification with the crowd in "Punishment" does not negate his identification with the victim. In the same way, he contends that in "Viking Dublin" the fascination with the power and violence that created the past does not cancel the poet's wish to be free of that past by understanding it, knowing it, and naming it.

73 THOMSON, DERICK. "Heaney's Law," *Cencrastus* 31 (Autumn): 51.

In his review of *The Government of the Tongue*, Thomson remarks on the fact that very few of the poets discussed are English. Part of Heaney's thesis is that English poetry needed energizing by these non-English writers and not the least by the Eastern bloc poets. He is insistent that poetry to survive, must "put poetic considerations first." He is most successful when he is closest to the poetry. The unity of the collection is not as coherent as he wished; still, it is a very positive achievement.

74 TROTTER, DAVID. "Troubles," *London Review of Books* 10 (June 23): 11–12.

In his review of *The Government of the Tongue,* Trotter asserts that the main theme of the essays is the difficult relationship between art and life. This is especially so when he contemplates the East European poets, who according to Heaney have re-invigorated British poetry. Heaney's argument on Auden and others is weak because he refuses "to admit that lyric action involves relation rather than transcendance, and can therefore be analyzed." Heaney's essays in this collection show the dichotomy between art and life. Some are "deferential to academic expectation," and critical discourse is avoided. We must admire Heaney's constant awareness of the problems of being a writer "in a place and at a time of trouble."

75 VENDLER, HELEN. "On three poems by Seamus Heaney," *Salmagundi* 80, (Fall): 66–70.

Vendler examines Heaney's "Canton of Expectation," "The Haw Lantern," and "Alphabets" in terms of territorial, ethical, and linguistic issues. She sees changes in Heaney's poetry in relation to the "evolution of the widened gaze," whereby the poet moves "beyond the private concerns of the self" and "from geography into allegory."

Reprinted 1993.32.

76 VENDLER, HELEN. "Seamus Heaney," in her *The Music of What Happens: Poems, Poets, Critics* (Cambridge: Harvard University Press): 149–65.

Reprint of two earlier published pieces: "Echo Soundings, Searches, Probes" (1985.80) and "The Music of What Happens" (1981.35).

77 VENDLER, HELEN. "Second Thoughts," *New York Review of Books* 35, 7 (April 28): 41–45.

In her review of *The Haw Lantern,* Vendler finds it a book of second thoughts, full of parables, allegories, and satires of Irish life. It is also concerned with the "bleakness of loss," as the poet sifts through and discards old pieties and rules. There are, however, strong presences in this book such as the hawthorn berry which flames throughout the bleak winter. The alphabet is another which can last and open up the world to both the humanist and the scientist.

78 WATERS, MAUREEN. "Heaney, Carleton and Joyce on the Road to Lough Derg." *Canadian Journal of Irish Studies* 14, 1 (July): 55–65.

The "Station Island" sequence of twelve poems in *Station Island* gives the poet the opportunity to confront spirits of the dead, among them the powerful personalities of the nineteenth-century Irish novelist William Carleton and of James Joyce. Both were alienated from their fellow Irishmen; both were concerned with problems of language which still trouble the Irish writer; neither provides final answers.

1989

1 ADAIR, TOM. "Calling the Tune," *Linen Hall Review* 6, 2 (Autumn): 5–8.

Seamus Heaney, interviewed by Tom Adair, discusses his move to the Republic in 1972, Ulster in the fifties, life as a teacher, family background, life at college, and his work and its future. He concludes with a discussion of current poems—the desire for a lighter approach, the self-reflexive character of these poems, and their stylistic changes.

2 BATTERSBY, EILEEN. "Oxford poetry post for Heaney likely," *Irish Times* (June 3): 5.

Heaney's election prospects are championed by Peter Levi and John Montague. Heaney himself is diffident, though acceding to the "gentle pressure" to take the post.

1989

3   BATTERSBY, EILEEN. "Stirring the cultural pot with a wooden spoon," *Irish Times* (June 5): 5.

    Battersby reports on Heaney's election as Professor of Poetry at Oxford University, and his reaction to the appointment.

4   BAYLEY, JOHN. "Living in and Living out: The Poet's Location for the Poetry," *Agenda* 27, 1 (Spring): 32–36.

    Bayley contends that while poetry has difficulty in dealing with the horrors of contemporary life, Heaney's handling of the problem shows his real strength. He achieves this with true humility and delicacy and by thinking before he writes. Houseman claims that "poetry was different from the things the poet was saying," and Heaney's poetry makes this distinction.

    Reprinted 1993.2.

5   BEDFORD, WILLIAM. "Seamus Heaney, The Government of the Tongue," *Agenda* 27, 1 (Spring): 72–78.

    Review of *The Government of the Tongue*. Bedford sees in this work the contention between the creative imagination and the pressures of political and other obligations. The best essays are those devoted to criticism. This work is required reading for those who would try to assess the directions of Heaney's reecent poetry. In Heaney's preoccupation with political conflict, there is no evasion; there is, however, "assuagement."

6   BILLEN, ANDREW. "Time to put a pig in the bacon factory," *Observer* (May 7): 45.

    Billen provides an account of the front-runners for the Oxford Poetry Professorship (Heaney is one of three) and a society-page description of the politics and history behind the professorship.

7   BORUCH, MARIANNE. "Comment: Thresholds," *American Poetry Review* 18, 6 (November-December): 21–23.

    Review of *The Government of the Tongue,* along with works by other poets. Boruch concentrates on Heaney's essay on Sylvia Plath and commends his sane and passionate argument. Heaney examines the poet at the moment of creation alone with the poems themselves. The poetic voice gradually turning inward and intensifying over the years is a recurring point of wonder for Heaney.

8   CORCORAN, NEIL. "Heaney's Joyce, Eliot's Yeats," *Agenda* 27, 1 (Spring): 37–47.

    Corcoran states that no Irish writer can avoid Joyce. Heaney's encounter with Joyce in *Station Island* is on a par with T. S. Eliot's meeting in *Little Gidding* with his compound ghost, who is taken to be Yeats. In *Station Island* Heaney is saying farewell to the restrictions of Irish Catholicism.

Joyce's great act of rebellion was the rejection of Catholic Ireland, while Heaney's rejection of the British State of Northern Ireland involved a turning toward Catholic Ireland. In *Station Island* Heaney realizes that collusion is not the way for the creative artist. This is the lesson he takes from Joyce. Eliot in his poem makes his Yeatsian figure indicate that his partner ("I, and another saved them") was also the shade of Joyce.

9   CROWDER, ASHBY BLAND. "Heaney's 'Elegy for a Still-Born Child,'" *Explicator* 47, 2 (Winter): 51–52.
        Heaney uses oxymorons to provide a paradoxical view of life. The oxymorons gain in power and gravity with each section of the poem, until the imagery of ultimate loss is presented in the final two stanzas. The final image is that of the pregnant woman full of hope yet reminding us of the sorrow that overtakes her and her husband.

10 DAVIE, DONALD. "Seamus Heaney's Station Island," in his *Under Briggflatts: A History of Poetry in Great Britain, 1960–1988* (Chicago: University of Chicago Press): 245–51.
        In *Station Island,* the "Station Island" sequence of poems is structured, as is much of Dante's *Divine Comedy*, around a dialogue between the poet and the ghosts of some people whom he admired. Dante was a politically partisan poet; Heaney tries to avoid such a stance. Heaney is here responding, with some equivocation, to the pressure from some of his readers who expect him to make a political statement on Northern Ireland. In the "Sweeney Redivivus" section, he uses Sweeney as a symbol of the poet who is above the factions in the Irish conflict. This refusal to endorse one faction over another is Heaney's civic duty as a poet.

11 DAWE, GERALD. "Of Tact and Fidelity," *Honest Ulsterman* 86 (Spring/Summer): 43–48.
        Heaney's collection of prose *The Government of the Tongue* is much more personal than his *Preoccupations*. He is concerned with detecting trends. His examples of the problems of cultural identity could be found closer to home, say in Scotland, than in Eastern Europe, though the relationship between poet and state in the latter is quite distinctive. Heaney's voice in this book is a moderate voice—an apolitical poet interested more in poetic ideas.

12 DI PIERO, W. S. "Digs: On Seamus Heaney," *Memory and Enthusiasm: Essays 1975–1985* (Princeton: Princeton University Press): 108–15.
        Reprint of 1981.14; reprinted 1983.14.

13 DOCHERTY, THOMAS. "The Sign of the Cross," *Irish Review* 5: 112–16.
        Review of *The Government of the Tongue.* Heaney's criticism has two threads: a concern with ethics and a concern with politics. You see the role of

the poet as conscience: one who wakens us to our capacity to know the same thing together.

14   FOSTER, THOMAS C. *Seamus Heaney* (Boston: Twayne; Dublin: O'Brien). 219 pp.

In addition to explicating the poetry and charting the development of the poet, Foster also details Heaney's relationship to other Irish, British, and American poets. He also deals with the politics of Heaney's poetry. Foster notes the influences on Heaney, the historical circumstances which shaped the earlier work, and the later trends. Included at the end is a substantial excerpt from an unpublished interview with Heaney conducted in 1987.

15   HABERSTROH, PATRICIA BOYLE. "Poet, Poetry, Painting and Artist in Seamus Heaney's *North,*" *Eire-Ireland* 23, 4 (Winter): 124–33.

What is the value of art in addressing social problems? This is a significant problem for Heaney. He raises the problem throughout *North* where he decides to confront the political situation and the violence in Ireland. He does not confine himself to literature and moves beyond it to the visual arts. There are questions and doubts throughout, but the poet "combines the 'beauty of art' with the 'mess of the actual.'"

16   HALPIN, TOM. "Heaney on the Demands of Art and Community," *ALPHA* (November 23): 18.

In his review of *The Place of Writing*, Halpin comments on Heaney's essay on Yeats, noting that Heaney "recognizes how the paradoxical fears and despairs" of Yeats's poems are the source of their power. Halpin finds Heaney's essay on MacNeice, Mahon, and Longley "subversive." The reviewer praises Heaney's evaluation of Kinsella in the book's final pages.

17   HART, HENRY. "Crossing Divisions and Differences: Seamus Heaney's Prose Poems," *The Southern Review* 25, 4 (Autumn): 803–21.

Hart discusses Heaney's *Stations,* in which his debt to Bly and Snyder, as well as the technical examples of the symbolists and the modernists, is shown. Other strong influences were Wordsworth, Geoffrey Hill, Joyce, and Theodore Roethke. Heaney's sympathies are crossed between Northern Irish Catholic and Protestant factions, between American free verse and Anglo-Irish formalism. Heaney investigates the bond between self and nature, between private concerns and political and cultural ones.

18   HART, HENRY. "History, Myth, and Apocalypse in Seamus Heaney's *North,*" *Contemporary Literature* 30, 3 (Fall): 387–411.

Heaney examines the mortuary of the past together with the myths that motivate or sanction the acts that lead to violence and death. He protests the violence which begets more violence and the deaths of the innocents who are compromised by the myths.

19 HART, HENRY. "Poetymologies in Seamus Heaney's *Wintering Out*," *Twentieth Century Literature* 35, 2 (Summer): 204–31.
    Hart looks at the allegorical wordscapes which Heaney uses to unite the poetic and the political in this book and finds there a recreation of a ritual bond between "word and root, place name and sacred oath." He is giving us another view of "the bloody cycles of attack and revenge" of Irish history.

20 HART, HENRY. "Seamus Heaney's Anxiety of Trust in *Field Work*," *Chicago Review* 36, 3–4: 87–108.
    Hart sees Heaney's work as a series of surges and counter-surges. In *Field Work,* he wavers between trust and distrust in his new community in the Republic of Ireland, the move to which was a flight to freedom as well as a return to old responsibilities and anxieties. Contrary forces form the fundamental tension in *Field Work*—poetic freedom and tribal demands. Hart sees the major influence in *Field Work* as not Dante but rather Robert Lowell. As with other artists memorialized there he becomes Heaney's ambiguous double, dramatizing his own confusions. Poetic quarrels with real and artistic fathers recognize the conflict which is at the root of creation. His marriage poems, with their separations, reunions, and squabbles, arise from the poles of trust and distrust. Trust and doubt are also seen in the political poems in *Field Work.* There is intense self-scrutiny in this work, as Heaney tests his poetic accomplishments with self-questionings and self-accusations.

21 HART, HENRY. "Seamus Heaney's *The Government of the Tongue*," *Verse* 6, 2: 65–71.
    This collection of essays continues the theoretical enterprise begun in Heaney's first collection of critical prose, *Preoccupations.* Here again, he emphasizes his freedom from critical orthodoxies and the poet's need to establish and protect his freedom. The poet transcends all governments, and, as Heaney asserts, poetry is a government unto itself. He repeatedly argues that the poet should stand up for his own artistic principles, for language loses its freedom to enchant when the civil tongue is granted too much authority. He explores the art that has to suffer to assert itself under totalitarian oppression. He keeps asking "What is poetry and what should its role in the world of society and politics be?"

22 "Heaney speaks of Irish awareness," *Irish Times* (March 3): 14.
    On the Radio Ulster interview in which Heaney explained why he had signed the March 2 worldwide statement in defense of Salman Rushdie and of freedom of expression.

1989

23 HOGAN, KATHERINE M. "The Political Poetry of Seamus Heaney: An Explication of Poetic Strategies." Ph.D. dissertation, New York University.

Seamus Heaney, a Catholic poet born and raised in Northern Ireland, writes political poetry which represents the viewpoint of an oppressed group of people. This political poetry to date has not been fully explicated. The purpose of this dissertation is to identify, describe, and analyze the aesthetic strategies used by Heaney in his political poetry.

24 HOWARD, BEN. "Places and Losses," *Poetry* 154, 6 (September): 340–42.

Heaney's *The Haw Lantern* is one of several books reviewed. Howard sees this as a pivotal collection for Heaney, since it marks the poet's move into "the poet's mind" and the "lightness of touch" and away from the weight of the world—a weight often rooted in the poet's childhood memories. The reviewer finds the allegories and parables which dominate the volume "flat." This flatness is related to the "seminar" voice and intellectual orientation of the poems.

25 HOWARD, RICHARD. "Heaney explores the poet's craft," *Boston Globe* (February 26): 12.

Review of *The Government of the Tongue*. Howard notes that Heaney's book is chiefly concerned with Irish matters and with poets of Eastern and Central Europe. Heaney is genuinely concerned here with matters of poetry and the poet's responsibility to the craft.

26 HUEY, MICHAEL. "The Home Forum," *Christian Science Monitor* (January 9): 16–17.

In this interview, Heaney responds to questions about the teaching of poetry and creative writing classes. He says that poetry involves the freedom (and seriousness) of play. Heaney feels that a poet becomes necessarily more self-conscious the longer he or she writes. He also reflects on the relationship between writing poetry and earning a living.

27 HUNTER, JEFFERSON. "The Cart-Track Voice," *Threepenny Review* 36 (Winter): 16–18.

Review of *The Haw Lantern*. There is much familiar material in this book: the landscape, the people, childhood memories. There is also the dilemma of the poet expected to take a political stance. Heaney is outspoken in poems such as "From the Canton of Expectation" but there is no political commitment.

28 JOHNSON, ANNE JANNETTE. "Seamus (Justin) Heaney, 1939– ," in *Contemporary Authors: New Revision Series*, edited by Hal May and Deborah A. Straub (Detroit: Gale): 193–98.

Johnson looks at Heaney's life and work through the eyes of selected critics and commentators. A listing of the principal works by Heaney precedes the essay, and a bibliography of secondary works is appended at the end.

29   KERLEY, GARY. "Insightful Collection Studies Poetry Function," *Atlanta Constitution* (June 25): 10.

Review of *The Government of the Tongue*. Kerley sees the function of the poet and poetry itself at the heart of Heaney's new book. Heaney's American experience and his readings of English and European poetry give him an insight into what poetry can achieve even when faced with indifference or political violence. In these essays Heaney tells of his own poetic growth and makes a strong case for poetry as "a necessary and fundamental" act of freedom. His best essays are concerned with the problem of poetry in a society which is indifferent or hostile to it. Heaney sees poetry as the "antenna or conscience of humanity," shown in these dangerous times by the Eastern European poets. Kerley salutes the work as "an examination of our ethics and morals and how we create truth."

30   KIBERD, DECLAN. "Culture and Barbarism: Heaney's Poetry and its Recent Critics," *Poetry Ireland Review* 27 (Autumn): 29–37.

Heaney's first book was an attempt to translate violence into culture. Since that time, poetry and violence has always been one of his preoccupations. His bog poems distance the violence while at the same time they emphasize that there are no easy solutions to the Northern Ireland problem. In *Station Island* all Northern voices are heard, sometimes accusing the poet. Heaney is one of the few modern poets to give a full and subtle account of the relation between poetry and violence in Ireland.

31   LERNOUT, GEERT. "The Dantean Paradigm: Thomas Kinsella and Seamus Heaney," in *The Clash of Ireland: Literary Contrasts and Connections*, edited by C. C. Barfoot and Theo D'Haen (Amsterdam: Rodopi): 248–64.

Lernout notes the great influence of Dante on Irish literature in general. He goes on to maintain that the importance of Dante for Kinsella and Heaney lies in his blending of the personal and the political, the lyrical and the narrative.

32   LYSAGHT, SEAN. "Heaney vs. Praeger: Contrasting Natures," *Irish Review* 7: 68–74.

Lysaght's essay originates in Heaney's complaint concerning Robert Lloyd Praeger's dismissive comments on the Tyrone countryside in Praeger's book *The Way that I Went*. Lysaght states that Heaney's view of the landscape and our sense of place are conditioned historically. Praeger's relationship with the landscape is mediated and illustrated by nomenclature derived from botany and geology. Praeger's landscape is also characterized by its emphasis on labour, education, and order, as emphasized also by John Hewitt. Heaney reminds us that when considering the story of Ireland it is from the land itself one must start.

33 McDIARMID, LUCY. "Joyce, Heaney, and 'that subject people stuff,'" in *James Joyce and His Contemporaries*, edited by Diana A. Ben-Merre and Maureen Murphy (Westport, CT: Greenwood Press): 131–39.

Focusing on poem XII of the "Station Island" sequence (which first appeared as "A Familiar Ghost"), McDiarmid argues that Heaney calls on Joyce to "define himself." She asserts that at one level, the poem's dominant voice is an older Heaney addressing a younger Heaney. McDiarmid also examines Heaney's "Ocean's Love to Ireland" and "Act of Union" in terms of the "subject people stuff," and she concludes that "A Familiar Ghost" marks the end of this stance since Heaney has turned toward a European literary tradition.

34 McDIARMID, LUCY. "Solidarity with the Doomed," *New York Times Book Review* 94 (March 5): 25.

Review of *The Government of the Tongue*. McDiarmid finds Heaney's second book of prose "remarkably idealistic." The book, she argues, is arranged according to political intensity. She focuses upon Heaney's ambiguous handling of T. S. Eliot, but considers "The Impact of Translation" to be the best essay. She concludes that Heaney's conception of poetry is not founded upon "texts" but upon "a society of writing men and women."

35 McLOUGHLIN, DEBORAH. "'An Ear to the Line': Modes of Receptivity in Seamus Heaney's Glanmore Sonnets," *Papers on Language & Literature* 25, 2 (Spring): 201–15.

Heaney's "Glanmore Sonnets" speak of personal and national stress. The ambivalent identity of the past is affected by the tension between English and Irish culture and language. He is receptive to literary antecedents with whom he feels his situation to be analogous. Images and emotions of childhood are clarified and articulated.

36 MARIUS, RICHARD. "[Book Review]," *Erato, Harvard Book Review* (Winter and Spring): 13.

Marius argues in his brief review of *The Government of the Tongue* that the essays reflect the same values one can observe in Heaney's own poetry. Marius particularly appreciates Heaney's essay on Elizabeth Bishop.

37 MARSDEN, PETER H. "Book Reviews," *Irish University Review* 19, 1 (Spring): 168–70.

In his review of *The Haw Lantern*, Marsden is struck by the increased confidence and resonance in Heaney's poetry. While he continues to celebrate the world of childhood, there are new variations on old themes. We are shown glimpses of "Irelands of the mind" in poems such as "Parable Island," "From the Republic of Conscience," "From the Land of the Unspoken," and others. Marsden sees the poem "Alphabets" as holding the same key position in this work as "Digging" did in *Death of a Naturalist*. "For the poetic mind, no sign is arbitrary."

38 MATTHEWS, STEVEN. "'When Centres Cease to Hold': 'Locale' and 'Utterance' in Some Modern British and Irish Poets." Ph.D. dissertation, University of York.

In this thesis Matthews seeks to explore a different history of modern British and Irish poetry to that put forward by Donald Davie, prime propagandist for the so-called Movement poets. He discusses a group of poets who unlike the Movement have proved both responsive to the poetic and cultural visions of the "International Modernists" Pound, Eliot, and Joyce, and conversely have sought to tune in to indigenous "native" "roots" or traditions in specific regions of Britain and Ireland. Heaney's career to date has followed a path from Wordsworthian poet of locale to (in *Station Island* and *The Haw Lantern*) a poet openly seeking European models for his work. That path provides almost a paradigm of the divergent local and international affinities which are discussed in the thesis.

39 MEYER, CAROLYN. "Orthodoxy, Independence and Influence in *Station Island*," *Agenda* 27, 1 (Spring): 48–61.

Meyer states that Heaney's poetry shows his preoccupation with commitment. He resists being politicized and must decide if he is "to strike his own note." In *Station Island* he appropriates the structure of Dante's *Purgatorio*. He is caught between the claims of politics and religion on one side and those of artistic independence on the other. Images of bondage and incarceration, as well as those of flight or migration, are prevalent throughout the work. Heaney dramatizes his own struggle to assert the independent voice of the artist.

40 MOLONEY, KAREN MARGUERITE. "Praying at the Water's Edge: Seamus Heaney and the 'Feis' of Tara." Ph.D. dissertation, University of California, Los Angeles.

This study explores the ways in which an ancient Celtic motif, once associated with the inauguration rites of early Irish kings, serves in the poetry of Seamus Heaney as an important metaphor for the contemporary need to reinstate and honor archetypal feminine and Dionysian principles.

1989

41 MORGAN, GEORGE. "Seamus Heaney and the Alchemy of Earth," *Etudes Irlandaises* 14, 1 (Juin): 127–36.

Morgan reads Heaney's poetry up to and including *North* in terms of traditional alchemical symbolism, transformations, and sexual tropes. He examines in particular "Churning Day," "In Gallarus Oratory," and the bog poems of *North*. He describes Heaney's work in terms of the alchemical quest for unity.

42 O'DONOGHUE, BERNARD. "Weight to the Lighter Scale," *Poetry Review* 79, 4 (Winter 1989/90): 5–7.

In his report on Heaney's first two lectures as Oxford Professor of Poetry, "The Redress of Poetry" and "Above the Brim," O'Donoghue comments upon Heaney's "place" in the history of the lectures. The reporter outlines the lectures, mentioning that two-thirds of the first address was concerned with "poetic duty." The second lecture focused on Robert Frost.

43 RICHMAN, ROBERT. "At the Intersection of Art and Life," *New Criterion* 7, 10 (June): 68–73.

Review of *The Government of the Tongue* and of Robert Pinsky's *Poetry and the World*. Richman admires Heaney's writing in *The Government of the Tongue* and claims that Heaney has written one of the best sentences ever on Philip Larkin: "a repining for a more crystalline reality to which he might give allegiance." According to the reviewer, Heaney's main theme in the essays is the tension between life and art. Life is predominantly embodied in politics, which often attempts to distract or suffocate the poet. In *The Government of the Tongue,* we are in a world of transitions between the "uncanny and the real."

44 ROE, NICHOLAS. "'Wordsworth at the Flax-dam': An Early Poem by Seamus Heaney," in *Critical Approaches to Anglo-Irish Literature*, edited by Michael Allen and Angela Wilcox (Gerrards Cross, Buckinghamshire: Colin Smythe): 166–70.

Roe notes that Heaney's poem "Death of a Naturalist," according to the poet, derives its "grunting consonantal music" from his reading of Anglo-Saxon poetry and the work of Gerard Manley Hopkins. Another literary background is Wordsworth's *Prelude,* where the past resurfaces with a power to quicken the poet's imaginative life.

45 SACKS, PETER. "Unleashing the Lyric," *Upstream* 7, 4: 61–66.

In his review essay on *The Government of the Tongue*, Sacks notes the urgency of the essays. Sacks argues: "This counter-government in the free state of Song. . .is the true subject of Heaney's book." The reviewer agrees with Heaney's claims for the free state of poetry, but he points out the possible political costs of such a position—pessimism, isolationism, and egocentrism.

Reprinted 1990.62.

46   SCHUCHARD, RONALD. "Introduction," in *The Place of Writing* by Seamus Heaney (Atlanta: Scholars Press): 2–16.

Heaney has been preoccupied with the unstable role of place in the creative process. He sees Kavanagh and Montague creating a "country of the mind." Hewitt, from the Unionist tradition, is also deeply concerned with place. For Mahon, Muldoon, and Longley, place has come to mean a conflict between the ideal Ulster and the current Ulster. Heaney himself has identified with poets from the Eastern bloc and others who "proclaim the autocracy of art" in "The Republic of Conscience." The role of leader in this Republic is assigned to Dante and Yeats. Heaney has refused to allow poetry to become a supporter of political stances. Joyce advises him to abandon political claims and assume the obligations of his own art. In the lectures in this book, Heaney "continues to probe the creative tensions and political challenges in the writing of his countrymen."

47   SINNER, ALAIN. "A Note on Seamus Heaney's *An Open Letter,*" *ESL* 144: 53.

Sinner comments on Heaney's response to the inclusion of his work in *The Penguin Book of Contemporary British Poetry.* He stresses the fact that his poetry is not British but Irish.

48   SLEIGH, TOM. "In Rough Waters," *Boston Review* 14, 4 (August): 16–17.

Sleigh's review of *The Government of the Tongue* concentrates on the "moral intelligence" that informs the essays. Sleigh approves of the "rolled-sleeve alertness" and recklessness of Heaney's methodology, which reminds him of Hazlitt or Lamb. Much of Heaney's political resistance is lost on American readers, according to Sleigh. He is wary of Heaney's historical hindsight, which can become idealistic and abstract, especially when discussing Eastern European poets.

49   SMITH, KEVIN. "Regionalism a cloak for unionism says Heaney," *Irish Times* (August 8): 6.

Brief report on the John Hewitt Summer School session during which Tom Clark examined the historical context of Hewitt's regionalism. During the symposium that followed, Smith reports, Heaney suggested that Hewitt's regionalism was perhaps "another cloak for not-an-inch."

1989

50 STEWART, JACK. "Heaney Discusses Irish Literary Tradition," *Voice* (Emory University) 8, 6 (February 15): 10.

In this interview with Heaney, the poet "reads" modern Irish writers with a "mischievous political intent." Consequently, Joyce is the "literary equivalent of a Sinn Fein movement;" Joyce "broke the link with Britain aesthetically," and thus he created an image of Ireland which showed the Irish their "possibilities and deviousnesses." Heaney also says that he "'would like to write poetry that's more like parable—there's more universal truth in it.'" Heaney draws an analogy between the Ulster situation and the history of native Americans. The poet also answers questions about his bog poems.

51 TAMPLIN, RONALD. *Seamus Heaney* (Milton Keynes; Philadelphia: Open University Press). 128 pp.

Tamplin's book is designed for students who are unaccustomed to reading and discussing poetry and/or who are unfamiliar with Heaney's poetry. The book is built upon a number of selective close readings of poems which include references to Irish history and politics. Tamplin also mentions significant literary influences and points out relevant similarities between Heaney and other modern and contemporary poets. The book discusses Heaney's work in chronological order up to and including *The Haw Lantern*.

52 TOIBIN, COLM. "Special Award: Seamus Heaney, Poet's Progress," *Sunday Independent, Irish Life Arts Awards Supplement* (London, January 8): 7.

Toibin comments on the tendency in modern Irish poetry to define territory. Both Dermot Bolger and Heaney see a need to redefine poetry, to move it away from the emotions of a divided self. In *The Government of the Tongue,* Heaney treats of being an Irish writer, of dealing with a tradition and experience locked in combat. His achievement is to be an Irish voice within the English lyric tradition. He also writes a new poetry in which he invents countries and customs as he would wish them to be. For the past twenty years Heaney has been an important presence in Irish writing.

53 VENDLER, HELEN. "A Wounded Man Falling Towards Me," *New Yorker* 65, 4 (March 13): 102–7.

Review of *The Government of the Tongue*. Half of the book belongs chiefly to Life, half chiefly to Art. By "life" Vendler means that Heaney writes about those poets who have displayed "exceptional moral courage" under oppressive political constraints. By "art," Vendler refers to Heaney's consideration of poets who are "exemplary in their aesthetic practice" and who are "more responsible to the morality of style" than those who are responsible to the "lived life." Heaney pays tribute to the work involved in gaining the competence and freshness that is the necessary preparation for writing poetry.

Reprinted 1993.31.

54 WADE, STEPHEN. "Creating the Nubbed Treasure (*Station Island*)," *Agenda*, 27, 1 (Spring): 62–71.

Station Island sets out to present a unified sequence of poems with con-frontations and reiterations, as in Dante. Heaney uses the long poem to explore and probe. There is a commitment to self-centred ideals along with themes of conflict. The concerns of man and place, and continuity and sensi-tivity to language are well explored by Heaney. "The coherence and unity of his corpus to date has shown the mark of a poet who carries the creative bur-den of tradition 'and the individual talent.'"

Reprinted in 1993.33, under title "Self-Knowledge and Pastures New: The Station Island Sequence."

55 WATERMAN, ANDREW. "Keep it in the six counties, Heaney!" *PN Review* 16, 6: 37–41.

Review of *The Haw Lantern*. In this witty imaginary dialogue between the reviewer and a Belfast local, Waterman provides an excellent back-handed appraisal of Heaney's *The Haw Lantern*. Perhaps because of its satiric struc-ture, but perhaps not, the review adopts contradictory positions which leave the reader guessing over the author's reading of the volume. After deferring to negative evaluations of *The Haw Lantern* by "certain readers" who find the book, "flawed, self-indulgent. . .substituting a poetry of facile cerebration, loose expression, for his previously imaginative realizations of lived experi-ence," the reviewer finds the volume's "experimentation bracing." The vol-ume, however, lacks "imaginative *frisson*." The reviewer also argues that British reviewers have been too easy on Heaney, unlike this review.

56 WELCH, ROBERT. "Poetic Wisdom and Freedom," *Irish Literary Supplement* 8, 2 (Fall): 27.

Welch reviews *The Government of the Tongue* and *The Poetry of Seamus Heaney* by Elmer Andrews. Heaney's book is concerned with what poetry tells us. The human tongue can govern itself and its own freedom. Poetry is a place where "life happens at a 'higher level.'"

57 WHITE, BARRY. "Heaney talks to Barry White: What is wrong with life in the North, whatever side you are on," *Belfast Telegraph* (June 29): 9.

White questions Heaney on his election to the Oxford Chair of Poetry. Heaney comments that his election was a victory over racism: "My point was that the Oxford graduates had voted without regard for this kind of—and I used as violent a word as I could—racism." Heaney has not yet located a theme but foresees that the lectures will have to do with poetry. He talks at length about life in Northern Ireland, and concludes that the people of Northern Ireland are "hampered by their suspiciousness." Heaney also says that he "wouldn't have a clue" as to what young people in the North were

1990

about today. Heaney concludes with a few comments about his father, who was above politics: "He was very aristocratic."

58 WILMER, CLIVE. "Jubilation and Truancy," *PN Review* 15, 6: 63–64.
Review of *Government of the Tongue*. Although he admires Heaney's collection of essays, Wilmer chooses to focus upon the volume's shortcomings. Wilmer asserts that Heaney's view of contemporary poetry is "conventional," particularly in his tendency to "mystify" poetry. This mystification is the result of Heaney's uncritical "Romantic" assumptions. Wilmer is suspicious of Heaney's essays which find poetry not written under political oppression as inferior. In the end, Heaney's premises are "not sufficiently questioned."

59 ZWIER, JOSEPH R. "Stephen Spender Remembers Three Irish Poets: MacNeice, Yeats, Heaney," *Irish Literary Supplement* 8, 1 (Spring): 22–23.
Zwier interviewed Spender at the University of Connecticut, October 20, 1987. He discusses the distinction between Irish and British poetry, the oral tradition, and the dominance of Yeats. Most of the interview centers on Yeats: he speaks briefly of Heaney's need to exorcise Yeats and his importance in English poetry.

1990

1 ALMQVIST, BO. "Of Mermaids and Marriages: Seamus Heaney's 'Maighdean Mara' and Nuala Ní Dhomhnaill's 'An Mhaighdean Mhara' in the Light of Folk Tradition," *Bealoideas* 58: 1–74.
Almqvist in this long essay on the legend of the union between a mermaid and a man from the land discusses the various versions of the story and its treatment in the poems by Seamus Heaney and Nuala Ní Dhomhnaill. He is concerned with how the poets have handled their sources, the character of oral narrative, and the nature of artistic creativity. The poems have much in common but the differences are also marked. In his comparison of the literary creations and the sources which inspired them, Almqvist gives the texts of the poems together with the actual narratives on which they were based. Also included are transcripts of interviews with the two poets.

2 ARKINS, BRIAN and PATRICK SHEERAN. "Coloniser and Colonised: The Myth of Hercules and Antaeus in Seamus Heaney's *North*," *Classical and Modern Literature* 10, 2 (Winter): 127–34.
The first section of *North* begins and ends with the myth of Hercules and Antaeus—in between there are sixteen poems, which treat of the conquest of Ireland. The book deals with the complex relationships between England (Hercules) and Ireland (Antaeus)—the colonized through treachery helping in

its own subjugation. The analogy between Roman and British imperialism points to the contemporary sectarian conflict in Northern Ireland.

3   ATFIELD, JOY ROSEMARY. "'The end of art is peace': A study of creative Tensions in the Poetry of Seamus Heaney." Ph.D. dissertation, University of Sussex.

Atfield explores the "central preoccupying questions" Heaney poses, and the constant presence of the tensions created in his response to them. What is his relationship to his own voice, to his own place, to his literary heritage, to his contemporary world, and to the use of myth? These insistent questions project the poet into continual dilemmas. Atfield in this thesis considers how Heaney confronts, evades, resolves, or assimilates these tensions, which become more acute in his later collections, but are present even in the earliest.

4   BATTERSBY, EILEEN. "Sometimes a Great Notion," *Irish Times* (September 29): Weekend 5.

In her review of *The Cure at Troy*, Battersby draws on several quotations from Heaney. In the context of discussing the play, he says that he has been interviewed so many times that "I don't believe I was born on a farm in Derry anymore." He says that the play was influenced by the optimism flowing through Europe at the time the play was being translated.

5   BEAVER, HAROLD. "Seamus Heaney: Prospero or Ariel?" *Parnassus: Poetry in Review* 16, 1 (July): 104–13.

Review essay on *Sweeney Astray, Station Island, The Haw Lantern*, and *The Government of the Tongue*. Heaney's ear is well tuned to the rhythms and language of Northern Ireland. Yet as a spokesman for poetry, Beaver finds that he always advocates exuberance. The question remains: what is the function of the poet in a time of political upheaval? Heaney looks to the poets of Central and Eastern Europe for an answer. Two things are needed: a fidelity to native speech and some kind of authentic commitment. Beaver prefers Heaney as a critic who will not choose nostalgia—"he is too much in love with poetry that paints the world 'in a thick linguistic pigment.'"

6   BURRIS, SIDNEY. *The Poetry of Resistance: Seamus Heaney and the Pastoral Tradition* (Athens: Ohio University Press). 165 pp.

Burris sets Heaney's poetry beside that of literary ancestors such as Spenser, Crabbe, and Clare, locating it within the pastoral tradition although it nevertheless represents a radical revitilization of the genre. He poses the problem for Heaney: What is the responsibility of the writer towards the political and social problems of his community? He argues that while Heaney's poetry is sensitive to Ireland's political situation, at the same time Heaney's pastoral world is one continually subject to violation and invasion, and that his poetry depends for its effect on that realization.

1990

7   CLAMPITT, AMY. "What Comes Up out of the Ground: On Budenz, Heaney, Ashbery, and Others," in *Conversant Essays: Contemporary Poets on Poetry*, edited by James McCorkle (Detroit: Wayne State University Press): 264–68.

    With each new book Heaney has gone deeper into Ireland, the subject of his writing. In addition, his handling of the hoard of past experience is fixed in the Irish landscape. Like all of those who care about poetry, he is "embedded in the literature of the past."

8   COSGROVE, BRIAN. "Inner Freedom and Political Obligation: Seamus Heaney and the Claims of Irish Nationalism," *Studies* 79 (Autumn): 268–80.

    Cosgrove discusses the tension between artistic freedom and political engagement in Heaney's poetry. The author refers to several essays from *Government of the Tongue* and to poems from *Station Island*. Cosgrove suggests that even though Heaney attempts to adopt a Neo-Romantic position of the privileged individual imagination, the poet is ultimately shaped by Northern Irish politics, which in the end cannot be totally repressed.

9   COVENEY, MICHAEL. "Tragedy Replays in Fast Forward," *Observer Review* (October 7): 40.

    Coveney, in his review of the Derry Guildhall production of Heaney's *The Cure at Troy* (among others), applauds both the performance and the text. He comments upon the clarity and simplicity of Heaney's language, as well as its ability to express Heaney's complex ambiguities.

10   COYLE, JANE. "Seamus Heaney's first play opens in Derry," *Irish Times* (October 2): 8.

    Coyle finds *The Cure at Troy* scholarly. She asserts that perhaps the text is too close to the original. The performance needs more dramatic tension, according to the review.

11   COYLE, JANE. "The Trojan Warrior," *stet* 2 (Autumn): 17.

    In this inteview Heaney discusses *The Cure at Troy*. He says that he wrote the play in an idiom that would be appropriate "in the context of the Guildhall or the Parish Hall." Heaney says that the most interesting character is Neoptemus. Heaney was aware of Yeats's "verse medium" when writing the play. He also talks about the moment he decided to translate the play.

12   CROTTY, PATRICK. "Vocal Visions," *Irish Review* 9: 102–6.

    In his review of *Daddy, Daddy* by Paul Durcan and of Heaney's *New Selected Poems 1966–1987*, Crotty astutely discusses Heaney's ambiguous treatment of, and ambivalent relation to, "vision." Crotty argues that "vanishings are the central concern of all his [Heaney's] work." Crotty also points out that there are many revised poems in the volume. The reviewer does not like Heaney's use of "bald declarations of perceptive or affective stance." Crotty concludes by stating that he is uncomfortable with Heaney's "rituling *schema*" in relation to Ulster violence, but he finds the Sweeney mask in "Sweeney Redivivus" successful in managing the voice.

13 CULLINGFORD, ELIZABETH. "'Thinking of Her. . .as. . .Ireland': Yeats, Pearse and Heaney," *Textual Practice* 4, 1 (Spring): 1–21.
    The identification of Ireland with a woman is commonly accepted. Cullingford argues that this identification has helped to confine women to a secondary and passive role, and places the Irish people "in a debilitating stereotype."

14 DAWE, GERALD. "Shifting Ground," *Fortnight* 285 (June): 23–24.
    Review of *New Selected Poems 1966–1987*. Dawe considers this work to be celebratory evidence of Heaney's arrival on the English poetry scene. Heaney is not a political figure, and his writing is well within the mainstream of English poetry. Dawe's response to the early and middle sections of the book is enthusiastic, though less so with the later section. His final observation is that Heaney can show "the voice, the dramatic skill and the humanity we want to hear."

15 DEANE, SEAMUS. "Powers of Earth and Visions of Air," *Times Literary Supplement* (March 16–22): 275–76.
    Review of *New and Selected Poems 1966–1987* and of *The Place of Writing*. Also included are brief notices of *Seamus Heaney* by Thomas Foster (1989.12) and of *Seamus Heaney* by Ronald Tamplin (1989.50). Heaney's poetry has changed. His early work has a large vocabulary for earth, divisions of land, geography, and history. In the early poetry he found a way to make the ground speak in a human voice. In his later poetry he tries to get away from the ground of history to his ultimate home, which is not Ireland but "The Disappearing Island," the visionary. In *The Place of Writing* he searches for the place of the writer. In Ireland that place has political concerns—the struggle to be a writer rather than an Irish writer. You cannot be one without the other.

16 D'EVELYN, THOMAS. "Sounds Link Lines and Meaning," *Christian Science Monitor* (October 5): 10.
    D'Evelyn looks at Heaney and some other poets and finds that Heaney is partial to rhyme. Though he does not always use end rhymes, "he has integrated rhyme into his concept of poetic order." See also Ratiner, 1990.57.

17 DILLON, JOHN. "Choruses from the rock," *Times Literary Supplement* (October 12–18): 1101.

Review of the Field Day Company production of *The Cure at Troy*. In his play *Philoctetes*, Sophocles treated the problem of intransigence whereby a wrong bites so deeply that the sufferer cannot forgive or forget even when it is in his own best interest to do so. Heaney in his "translation" has this also in mind with the added reference to Northern Ireland. His play succeeds with a fine cast. His feel for language allows poetry to be poetry without interfering with the flow of dialogue.

18 DIXON, FRANCES. "Gathering Impressions in Heaney's *Wintering Out*," *Critical Review* 30: 91–111.

For some critics, Heaney's early reputation was that of a poet who had a way with words, but had nothing important to say. Dixon maintains that on the contrary Heaney had been concerned with more than using words for their own sake: that in addition he explores the timeless connections between mankind and the world it inhabits. She sees Heaney's *Wintering Out* as an important example of the complementary impulses to explore and define that intuition. It also suggests the richness of the earlier works and is a bridge to the later volumes.

19 DUNN, DOUGLAS. *The Topical Muse on Contemporary Poetry*, The Kenneth Allott Lectures, no. 6, delivered on 22 March 1990 (Liverpool: *Liverpool Classical Monthly*).

Dunn chooses Heaney (along with Tony Harrison, Derek Mahon, and Craig Raine) as one of his major reference points in his Allott lecture on Modernism and Post-Modernism. Dunn cites "Broagh," "Anahorish," "Gifts of Rain," and "Whatever You Say, Say Nothing." Dunn says of Heaney that his poetry gravitates "towards the local" and away from "international amor-phousness."

20 DUNNE, SEAN. "Unphased Heaney, a Poet who remains true to his roots," *Cork Examiner* (November 30): 8.

This profile of Heaney was written upon the occasion of his reading in Cork. Dunne reconfirms what many suspect, that Heaney is assaulted from all sides and that more ink is being spent on the Irish poet than any other. Dunne also notes that Heaney has not only avoided the post-modern hype, but also that he has ignored much of the cyber-bliss that technology has to offer. In other words, Heaney still uses words such as "wireless" and "oilcloth."

21 GIFFORD, TERRY. "Saccharine or Echo Soundings? Notions of Nature in Seamus Heaney's Station Island," *New Welsh Review* 3, 2 (Autumn): 12–17.

Gifford argues that for Heaney there can be no deliverance from political and religious struggles. He also asserts that *Station Island* is concerned with Heaney's pastoral use of the English language to explore these struggles.

22   GOODHEART, ADAM K. "Seamus Heaney's Poetry: Excavating His Irish Roots," *Harvard Crimson* (September 28): 2.
      This review of *Selected Poems, 1966–1987* includes glimpses of how Heaney is perceived by Harvard students.

23   GRENNAN, EAMON. "Illuminations," *Agni* 31/32: 292–95.
      Review of *The Government of the Tongue* and of John Montague's *The Figure in the Cave*. Grennan says that while Heaney's first collection of essays, *Preoccupations*, had some biographical efforts, this book is more concerned with literary and critical issues. Whatever subject Heaney treats, he is inevitably involved with language. At the center of many of these essays is the position of the poet as he faces political reality. There is also the search for what makes the poet himself or herself.

24   HARMON, MAURICE. "Poetry," *Linen Hall Review* 7, 3/4 : 32.
      Review of *The Tree Clock*. Heaney pretends to casualness, and in the ensuing apparent, ordinary poetry we find evocative and thoughtful work. When we recognize a particular mode in his work we should not underestimate its real achievement. There is no agonizing in this book over the demands of poetry as against those of public and politics. He is the confident spokesman for what he knows to be true.

25   HARRIS, T. J. G. "Sources and Soundings," *PN Review* 17, 1 (September/October): 57–59.
      Harris in his review of *New Selected Poems 1966–1987* states that Heaney more than most poets constantly reappraises his own poetry. He examines at some length the two poems "Anahorish" (*Wintering Out*) and "Sunlight" (*North*) and finds in them the subtlety of Heaney's genius. He examines the charges that the Northern crisis had given Heaney's poetry undeserved publicity and that he has also been too obviously influenced by other poets. Harris concludes that Heaney is his own man; and if occasionally he moves beyond the range of his readers, "that is a risk which must be taken."

26   HART, HENRY. "Heaney Among the Deconstructionists," *Journal of Modern Literature* 16, 4 (Spring): 461–92.
      Hart looks at the reviews of *The Haw Lantern* and finds that some of the critics speak of a disappointment in the work. They note its lack of grandeur, of music, and of the fullness of the sensual life. Among the poets

who helped him formulate his new philosophical style are Yeats, Wallace Stevens, and Zbigniew Herbert. His landscapes are now more psychological than geographical, and this he owes to Patrick Kavanagh and Philip Larkin. Some critics have been aware of Heaney's deconstructionist slant from the beginning. His self-conscious poetry is full of self-perpetuating energies. He dismantles past words and poems, and these become the substance of his new poems.

27   HART, HENRY. "Heaney's Sweeney," *Graham House Review* 13: 111–38.
     Hart speaks of the debate concerning imitation and originality in poetry. Heaney's *Sweeney Astray* and *Station Island* go to medieval legends for much of their material. The "Sweeney Redivivus" of *Station Island* is a self-portrait of Heaney, the artist devoted to art for its own sake. The Sweeney of *Sweeney Astray* is the prototype of the Irish exile who cannot quite escape the forces that set him in motion. These Sweeneys allow Heaney new ways to explore the dilemmas of the artist; to shift between comedy, tragedy, and farce; and to bring myth into contemporary Irish history. Heaney's Sweeney, reflects some of himself, some of Sweeney, and some of us.

28   HART, HENRY. "Seamus Heaney's Places of Writing," *Contemporary Literature* 31, 3 (Fall): 383–91.
     Hart's review of *The Place of Writing* begins with a look at some of the criticisms of Heaney and his poetry. The three lectures were delivered at Emory University in April 1988 to honor Richard Ellmann. He sees *The Place of Writing* focusing on the debate between the self and the competing factions of politics, religion, etc. Hart comments on Heaney's willingness to adopt modern critical theories and apply them confidently in his own way. In the final essay, Heaney pays tribute to Richard Ellmann's mode of inquiry. The essays mark a significant development in Heaney's work as a critic. Making use of old and new methodologies, his criticism grows more sophisticated as it deals with the place of poetry in a world that presents serious threats to it.

29   HUGHES, EAMONN. "Representation in Modern Irish Poetry," in *Aspects of Irish Studies*, edited by M. Hill and S. Barber (Belfast: Institute of Irish Studies): 55–64, 146–47.
     Applying current critical theories of language and culture to Part II of *North* (particularly "Singing School"), Hughes explores issues related to intertextuality in Heaney's poetry. Irish poetry is most fully comprehended in terms of "nativist" and "external influences" and how they relate to representation, according to Hughes. The author offers provocative new readings of Heaney's volume often by debunking the received wisdom of previous critics.

30 KEMP, PETER. "The wound and the show," *The Independent* (September 29): 30.

Heaney's comments on *The Cure at Troy* run throughout this article. Heaney mentions "the many potential political allegories" and comments that he had first considered translating Aeschylus's *Oresteia*. The article identifies one of the translations of Philocetes which shaped his own version. Kemp approves of Heaney's scraping off of any "antiquated veneer."

31 KENNAN, P. A. "Seamus Heaney: Bogs and Bodies, Myths and Metaphors," in *Annali dell'Istituto di Lingue e Letterature Germaniche* (Parma), edited by G. Caliumi (Roma: Bulzoni): 161–75.

Taking four poems—"Bog Queen," "Tollund Man," "Grauballe Man," and "Punishment"—he shows that "their imagery marks key points along the path of Heaney's questing into Irish and individual consciousness." Digging into the past can be a painful act, especially for public figures, while for the poet it can endanger the art of writing.

32 KEYES, JOHN. "A dramatic conversation," *Fortnight* 288 (October): 25.

Keyes talks to Heaney about the forthcoming Field Day production of his *The Cure at Troy*. A play and a poem demand different skills from the artist as well as different approaches from the reader. Heaney believes the differences are fundamental and have rarely been bridged. In a poem we listen to the poet himself. While *The Cure at Troy* has some relevance to the situation in Northern Ireland, it presents choices not solutions. Heaney says that a work of art must be itself: "It has to come through from the condition of the artist, as a thing out there having its own shape and vitality."

33 KINZIE, MARY. "A Poet of Upheaval: Seamus Heaney: Unofficial, and uneasy, laureate of Northern Ireland," *Chicago Tribune Books* (November 25): 5.

The turbulent history of Ireland has become the subject of much of Heaney's work since *North*. At his best, in such poems as "From the Canton of Expectation," he envies the unruly zeal of the young, and also delights in their minds "brightened and unmannerly as crowbars."

34 LAWRENCE, VINCENT. "Heaney Goes Greek," *Sunday Press* (Dublin, October 7): 11.

The Cure at Troy is the centerpiece of this article and interview with Heaney. Heaney, in retrospect, talks about the dangers that went along with living in the North in the early 1970s. He also talks about polishing the "small voice" of the poetry. Relating to the play, Heaney mentions the importance of reading an essay on Philoctetes, Edmund Wilson's "The Wound and the Bow." This is a jovial article.

1990

35   LEPKOWSKI, FRANK. "[Book Review]," *Library Journal* 115 (November 1): 93.
     Review of *Selected Poems 1966–1987*. Here we have a good selection of the poetry of one of the best of our contemporary poets. It has much of his recent work, but it does not include any new poems. His vocabulary, his line, and his distinctive music are to be noted. He deals with Ireland in themes and symbols that have universal application.

36   "The Line in the Sand," *Babele: Esperimenti Creativi in Lingue Diverse* (Italy) 1: 10–12.
     In this interview (in English) with Heaney, the poet explains what he wanted to accomplish in sections VI and VII in the "Station Island" sequence. He also discusses his approach to Dante, and he answers questions related to the language issue: "The sonnet is part of my deformation of my ear."

37   LYNDON, NEIL. "Seamus Heaney lectured here," *Independent* (May 7): 12.
     Lyndon records the reactions to Heaney and his third lecture as Oxford's Professor of Poetry. Heaney spoke on Yeats and Larkin and the differences in their attitudes toward death, and the proper place and function of poetry.

38   McCRACKEN, KATHLEEN. "Madness or Inspiration? The Poet and Poetry in Seamus Heaney's *Sweeney Astray*," *Notes on Modern Irish Literature* 2: 42–51.
     McCracken examines the Sweeney story and, using sources from medieval Ireland, concludes that though Sweeney is deemed a madman, he has the ability to see things differently. Living on the fringes of society, he is in a situation both physical and psychological which can give rise to poetry.

39   McDONALD, PETER. "The Liabilities of Integrity," *Irish Times* (March 24): Weekend 9.
     McDonald, reviewing *New Selected Poems 1966–1987*, comments that the work after *North* accounts for almost two-thirds of this book. The first three collections have been severely pruned. Heaney is too much of a self-critic, particularly in *Station Island*. His self-consciousness conditions a good deal of his writing in the 1980s. His preoccupation with Sweeney might not delight some of his readers. The centre of gravity for the collection is *Field Work* (1979), in which he speaks with an authentic, elegaic, and musical voice. Subsequent work has been less successful. Some good poems are missing from this selection while some useful additions are included, such as the prose-poems from *Stations*. Revisions he has made are seldom an improvement. This is a good bringing together of his work, but Heaney would do well to consider that "serious poetry is not always the same as a poet being serious."

40 McDOWELL, EDWIN. "6 Authors are given $35,000 in arts foundation awards," *New York Times* (September 16): 17, 33.

Brief notice which lists Heaney (along with Derek Mahon) as one of the winners of the awards given by the Lannan Foundation, based in Los Angeles.

41 McGUINNESS, A. E. "Politics and Irish Poetry: Seamus Heaney's Declaration of Independence," *Etudes Irlandais* 15, 2 (Decembre): 75–82.

The essay examines Heaney's appropriation of the "English line," his loyalty to the Irish language and affinity for traditional Gaelic prosody, and the general history of English and Irish in Ireland. McGuinness looks at Heaney's early short-line poems as well as stylistic changes in *Field Work* and the advice of Joyce's ghost in *Station Island*. The author provides a detailed reading of "Stations of the West" and "The Harvest Bow."

42 MARIANI, PAUL. "Ten on Ten: The Ecco Essential Poets," *The New England Review and Bread Loaf Quarterly* 12, 3 (Spring): 313–15.

The review covers Ecco Press's "essential" series, of which Heaney's *The Essential Wordsworth* is one. Mariani points out that T. S. Eliot taught us that it is important to watch whom contemporary poets are reading, since their reading will tell us something about our own age. The review approves of Heaney's introduction to the volume even though it finds the distant tone somewhat regrettable. Mariani makes a direct connection between Heaney's introduction and his writing in *Station Island* and *The Haw Lantern*.

43 MATTHIAS, JOHN. "Not for Sale in USA: Inside History and Outside History: Seamus Heaney, Eavan Boland and Contemporary Irish Poetry," *ACM: Another Chicago Magazine* 22: 212–27.

Review of *The Redress of Poetry, The Government of the Tongue* and *The Place of Writing* by Heaney together, with a review of *A Kind of Scar, The Journey and Other Poems, Selected Poems,* and *Outside History* by Eavan Boland. Matthias finds that Heaney's redress of poetry is a recognition of poetry's potential which is continually threatened by political and social circumstances. In *The Government of the Tongue,* Heaney proposes that because of poetry's relish of its own "pleasuring strain," it learns to govern its tongue. He also believes that poetry is its own reality and that the ultimate fidelity must be to the artistic event. His essays concern themselves with the issue of political and other tensions in the work of some Eastern European poets, among others. When the political issue is Irish nationalism, Heaney, in an essay in *The Place of Writing*, uses the figure of a lever moving the writer's historical/biographical experience. He comments on the extreme caution on the part of some recent Irish poets to avoid "any idiom that might possibly be construed as nationalistic." Because of the troubles in Northern Ireland, Heaney asserts that it is increasingly difficult for writers to express "fidelity to the ideals of the Irish Literary Revival."

Reprinted 1992.39.

1990

44 MEIR, COLIN. "Theatre: Colin Meir Reviews Heaney's *The Cure at Troy*," *Linen Hall Review* 7, 3/4: 12–13.

   Meir sees two kinds of anguish, mental and physical, which are dealt with in the play. Words take precedence over action; consequently, this production, at Belfast's Lyric Theatre, emphasizes simplicity of set and costume. The dialogue is colloquial and contemporary, spoken in Northern Irish accents. The pivotal performance is that of Des McAleer as Philoctetes. The overt references to Northern Ireland, in Meir's words, "constitute an artistic imbalance which is both untoward and unnecessary." The speeches of the Chorus offer limpid, evocative poetry which is true to the spirit of the play.

45 NOWLAN, DAVID. "Field Day with first play by Seamus Heaney," *Irish Times* (November 9): 6.

   A review of the Field Day production of *The Cure at Troy* at the Abbey Theatre, Dublin. The play, written in clear, seemingly casual verse, has resonances for today's Ireland. Nowlan sees it as "a serious dramatic tract for these times on this island." It has problems as a piece of theatre, dramatic impetus is lacking, it often seems more a homily than an engagement with emotions and ideas. It, however, puts forward "telling insights with impeccable sentiment."

46 NYE, ROBERT. "Artifice over Art," *Times* (London, June 16): 36.

   In his review of *New Selected Poems, 1966–1987*, Nye sees Heaney's decision to revise an awkward line from a poem in *North* as representative of the poet's tendency to produce "Kerrygold verse." Nye feels that Heaney should "ignore the curse of fame."

47 O'DOMHNAILL, AISLING. "Seamus Heaney and Other Poets," *Irish Edition* 10, 3 (March): 30.

   Review of *The Haw Lantern*. Many of the best poems here center around the writing life. He is at his best when writing about home.

48 O'DONNELL, MARY. "Heaney debut an ill-judged choice," *Sunday Tribune* (London, October 7): 27.

   O'Donnell's review of the performance and text of Heaney's *The Cure at Troy* finds the play lacking in many areas. The play's tone is "general and pedantic"; the central action of Philoctetes rejoining the tribe is "limp"; the play lacks power because it "falls between the stools of poetry and drama." Finally, the reviewer feels that Heaney's ending is simply a "softly-contoured political allegory."

49 O'DONOGHUE, BERNARD. "Word-Weaver," *Oxford Today* 2, 2 (Hillary Issue): 2.

Report on Heaney's inaugural lecture as Professor of Poetry on October 24. Heaney paid tribute to his predecessors and especially to those, like Peter Levi, whose concern has been with poets and poetry. Heaney's address indicated his intention to keep to this course with his own emphasis on the artist's duty to society in conflict with the wish for freedom of the imagination. O'Donoghue concludes with a comment on the eager crowd which was present and his happiness that poetry can command such attention these days.

50 O'DONOGHUE, BERNARD. "Weight to the Lighter Scale," *Poetry Review* 79, 4 (Winter 1989/90): 5–7.
A report on Heaney's first two lectures as Professor of Poetry at Oxford in October 1990. It was familiar material from Heaney—the duty of the artist to affect society; poetry must be a model of "the active consciousness." In the second lecture, on Robert Frost, he emphasized counterbalance as the essence of Frost's most successful poems. Frost's language, its "deliquescent backwash," is present despite the tightness of his forms.

51 O'GRADY, THOMAS B. "At a Potato Digging: Seamus Heaney's Great Hunger," *Canadian Journal of Irish Studies* 16, 1 (July): 48–58.
O'Grady examines the connections between Kavanagh's *The Great Hunger* and "Spraying the Potatoes" and Heaney's poem "At a Potato Digging." The author also mentions the significance of Cecil Woodham-Smith's *The Great Hunger* in terms of Heaney's use of graphic details related to the famine. O'Grady stresses that both Heaney and Kavanagh wanted to challenge the notions of romanticized Irish peasant life in their poems and to present a more realistic depiction of "the rural Irish laborer." More generally, O'Grady distinguishes between the "lyrical" poetry of Kavanagh and the "epical" poetry of Heaney—the Joycean lyrical is more immediate than the more mediated epical.

52 O'LEARY, PHILIP. "Bilingual Contemporary Ireland," *Irish Literary Supplement* 9, 1 (Spring): 24.
Review of *Conlon*, a selection of Heaney's poems translated into Irish by Gabriel Rosenstock, (Coisceim Publishers, 1989). This translation includes selections from Heaney's first seven volumes (up to and including *The Haw Lantern*). The reviewer says that the translations prove that Heaney's "language and rhythms *are* the core of his poetry."

53 O'TOOLE, FINTAN. "Heaney Goes Back to the Roots," *Irish Times* (November 10): Weekend 5.
Heaney's career can be seen as the reluctant acceptance of the idea of the poet as the voice of the tribe. In *The Cure at Troy*, a story of the conflicting demands of individual hurt and collective loyalty, the voice of the tribe is

uppermost. The story of *The Cure at Troy* is used as a metaphor for Northern Ireland, and this story is especially emphasized by the Chorus. The adaptation is the work of a great writer who is not fully attuned to the theatre. Its appeal to both sides in the Northern Ireland conflict is, however, "eloquent, humane and full of the generosity of a very large mind at work."

54 PARINI, JAY. "Poetry filled with the rhythms of life," *USA Today* (December 11): 5D.
    Review of *Selected Poems 1966–1987*. Heaney has pruned the fat from his earlier poetry. He has in the process exposed poems such as "Sloe Gin," "The First Kingdom," "The Haw Lantern," "Clearances," and the powerful sequence called "Station Island," a kind of spiritual autobiography.

56 "Performances fail to match lyric quality of powerful text," *Sunday Business Post* (November 11): B10.
    The review of Heaney's *The Cure at Troy* differentiates between the quality of the text and that of the performance. According to the review, Heaney's text is "rhythmically-lyric, yet deliberately non-literary." Much of the review discusses the actors' inability to handle the colloquialism of Heaney's play, a colloquialism which does not rely upon dialect for its impact.

57 PERKINS, DAVID. "Selected Poems 1966–1987," *Erato/Harvard Book Review* 17–18 (Summer and Fall): 4.
    Review of *Selected Poems 1966–1987* and of James Wright's *Above the River*. Coming from different traditions, they still have some things in common: they are compassionate and elegaic, and they are concerned with a place. Heaney's place is Ireland—rural Ireland and Northern Ireland. He conveys his feelings better than most poets; he is a more precise maker of poetry than Wright or Hardy, and his real genius has not yet been realized.

58 PETER, JOHN. "Triumph at Troy for a modern warrior," *Sunday Times* (London, October 14): Drama 6.
    Review of *The Cure at Troy*. Peter argues that one of the play's central issues is how to achieve "reintegration with dignity." He describes the voice behind and in the play as a "voice of iron grief." Like other great modern Irish plays, Heaney's play is a "purifying" one and ties into the Irish "theatre of guilt."

59 QUINLAN, KIERAN. "[Book Review]," *World Literature Today* 64, 1, (Winter): 115.
    Review of *The Government of the Tongue*. Quinlan argues that the volume emphasizes the political responsibility of the poet and the primacy of the poetic act. The reviewer also admires the quality of the prose itself. The func-

tion of the poet, according to Quinlan's reading of Heaney, is to keep "beauty alive."

60   RATINER, STEVEN. "New Verse Forms Reflect Action," *Christian Science Monitor* (October 5): 11.

Ratiner, writing on the same authors as D'Evelyn (1990.16), observes that Heaney uses the traditional style to explore his native Ireland "and the embattled territory of the human spirit." He is at bottom a poet of nature, which he sees as the primal source. Heaney rigorously examines himself and finds that at times his commitment to art is at odds with his political conscience.

61   REGAN, STEPHEN. "Reviews," *Durham University Journal* 1: 132–33.

Regan reviews *The Government of the Tongue* as concerned with the obligations of art to the world of public events and to itself. There is a recognition by Heaney of poetry's truth and beauty. His preoccupation with the responsibilities of poetry has immediate relevance in the context of Northern Ireland. Speaking of poetry as a redemptive art, Heaney considers the achievements of various poets: Kavanagh, Larkin, Walcott, Milosz, Holub, and Zbigniew Herbert. In part two of the volume, his concern is with the potential of the tongue as a governing rather than a governed force. He upholds the idea of an untrammelled poetry even in an imperfect world. It has to make its way in settings full of prejudice or social discrimination.

62   SACKS, PETER. "Unleashing the Lyric: Seamus Heaney," *Antioch Review* 48, 3 (Summer): 381–89.

Reprint of 1989.45.

63   SCANLAN, ROBERT. "The Cure at Troy," *Erato / Harvard Book Review* 17–18 (Summer and Fall): 3.

Review of *The Cure at Troy*. This is a fine version of Sophocles' play, which links the closing years of the Peloponnesian War with the current turmoil in Northern Ireland in clear, spare verse. In simple language he has given a colloquial rendering of *Philoctetes* which reads as easily as prose. Eminently suitable for the stage in language accessible to Irish, English, and American dialects, this version more than any other emphasizes Edmund Wilson's observation that the play is about "people whose natures have been poisoned by narrow fanatical hatreds. . . . Such people suffer as much as they hate: it is because they suffer that they hate."

64   SEALY, DOUGLAS. "Addition and Selection," *Poetry Ireland Review* 29 (Summer): 95–100.

Sealy reviews Kinsella's *Personal Places* and *Poems from Centre City* as well as Heaney's *New Selected Poems*. Poems about Northern Ireland figure prominently in this selection; however, they probe the poet's own guilt. In *Station Island* he uses Sweeney as his mouthpiece, the artist relieved of responsibility. In *The Haw Lantern* he strikes a new note.

65   SHERIDAN, COLETTE. "Heaney is set to take the Stage," *Sunday Tribune* (London, September 30): 13.
Sheridan's article examines Heaney's upcoming play *The Cure at Troy*. Heaney is quoted as saying that his version is much different from Brendan Keneally's *Medea*. Heaney says that one of the original difficulties with the play is that a god appears at the end; he has attempted to address this problem with the chorus.

66   SLEIGH, TOM. "Grappling with God," *Boston Review* 15, 6 (December): 28–30.
Review of *Selected Poems 1966–1987*. Heaney's Catholicism is adapted to describe feelings about places. After his first three books he left the pastoral for the historical in *North*. In *Field Work* he set poems about married life alongside elegies for assassinated friends. In *Station Island* he uses Joyce's secular, urban intelligence to underline his own anxieties about Irish provincialism. *The Haw Lantern* shows him still using Ireland as his subject but in a more emblematic way. He is an insider who because of his learning is now an outsider. He is a poet who has found new ways to write without turning his back on the old ones.

67   SMYTH, DAMIEN. "Boot on the other foot," *Independent* (October 13): 30.
Smyth reviews the performance of *The Cure at Troy* at the Lyric Theatre, Belfast. He sees Heaney's adaptation of the Greek play as a coded message "for a blind, bitter land." He praises Des MacAleer's powerful performance as carrying the whole play. Heaney's best poetry is reserved for the three-woman chorus. Smyth concludes, "it wouldn't be a Field Day without the politics and Heaney's here are as sad as ever."

68   STEVENSON, ANNE. "A Pen, Snug as a Gun," *New York Times Book Review* 95 (November 11): 11.
Review of *Selected Poems 1966–1987*. Seamus Heaney's topic is Ireland with its divided loyalties and culture. He takes his role seriously and excavates his roots—personal, historical, and mythical. He is essentially a domestic poet, and these are the poems in which he makes his best political statements. When he moves from Ireland to the "Republic of Conscience," he may be doing so to appease his own conscience—the best poems in this section however have to do with absence and emptiness.

69 VANCE, NORMAN. "Contemporary Ireland and the Poetics of Partition: John Hewitt and Seamus Heaney," in *Irish Literature: A Social History; Tradition, Identity and Difference* (Oxford: Blackwell): 209–60.

Vance's chapter on "partition" is prefaced by the author's depiction of the cultural and historical institutions and movements at work during Hewitt's career and in Heaney's world to date. These observations, however, may be too detailed for general readers and too programmatic for others. Vance focuses upon what he sees as the Catholic and sectarian aspects of Heaney's imagination. Vance discusses poems from throughout Heaney's oeuvre. There are substantial sections on *North, Station Island,* and *Sweeney Astray.* Many of Vance's readings emphasize the failure or limitations of the poet's imagination or the poem's performance: "Heaney's voyeuristic excesses in *North* extend to imaginative complicity with endemic violence. . .and metaphorical indulgence of a debased male sexuality." Vance admires Heaney's more abstract poems, such as "Parable Island."

70 WALSH, JOHN. "Bard of Hope and Harp," *Sunday Times* (October 7): 2, 4.

Heaney talks to Walsh about the opening of his play *The Cure at Troy.* In the course of the conversation he also talks of his Catholicism and the poet's role in the community. "Everybody begins alone and ends alone—and the greatest help is to learn that there is *no* help."

71 WARDLE, IRVING. "The other island of Odysseus," *Independent on Sunday* (October 14): 22.

Wardle praises Heaney's treatment of Philoctetes in *The Cure at Troy* production in Belfast. He judges the play to be "superbly written with the directness of a folk ballad."

72 WATERMAN, ANDREW. "Into his proper haunt," *Spectator* 264 (March 24): 33–34.

Review of *New and Selected Poems 1966–1987.* The selection confirms Heaney's stature and allows readers to follow his growth as a poet. While the poet was harsh in selecting from his first two books, readers will find most of his best poetry in this volume. The reviewer could live without the *Station Island* poems. In addition, since Heaney was heavily influenced by Geoffrey Hill's *Mercian Hymns* in the *Stations* prose poems, Waterman also questions Heaney's public display of "parasitism" in the *New and Selected* volume. Heaney's selection also reveals the poet's gaps: "no really good love poems, nor humor beyond fleeting pawkishness, few memorable phrases as distinct from poems."

1991

73 WELCH, DON. "Seamus Heaney: Irish Poet," *Platte Valley Review* 18, 2 (Spring): 83–85.

   Since 1975 Heaney has begun to write in voices other than his own, notably that of the Irish king Sweeney. The image of digging dominates his poems, for it is the life of buried things which spurs his imagination. He is obsessed with words. Poetry is language as it ought to be; it is the artifice, the thing made. He loves and uses the past in his work, yet he can be very contemporary. His is a dark world, complex and labyrinthine. His poetry is pure, strong, and balanced.

74 WOODWORTH, PADDY. "Field Day's men and the re-making of Ireland," *Irish Times* (November 5): 10.

   Woodworth, in the course of his essay on the Field Day organization, talks briefly about Heaney's adaptation of Sophocles' *Philoctetes*, which is about to open at the Abbey Theatre, following its production in Derry by the Field Day Theatre Company.

1991

1 ABAD, PILAR. "Hopkins and the Modern Sonnet Tradition: Dylan Thomas, W. H. Auden, and Seamus Heaney," in *Tradition and Innovation,* edited by P. Bottalla, G. Marra, and F. Marucci (Ravenna: Longo): 223–34.

   Abad considers Hopkins a guide for later sonnet writers and examines some modern poets who have succeeded with the form. To illustrate Heaney's success with the sonnet, he chooses his "Glanmore Sonnets" and "Clearances." He finds coincidences in the four poets: the writing of sonnets belong to significant periods in the poet's life and development; all were interested in the technical aspects of poetry; all used the sonnet as an instrument of self-expression. They all base their sonnet composition on respect for the conventional form as well as on experimentation in what can be called the modern sonnet tradition in English literature.

2 ALLISON, JONATHAN. "[Book Reviews]," *Eire-Ireland* 26, 3 (Fall): 139–42.

   In his review of *Seeing Things*, Allison holds that Heaney is attempting to observe the daily life and imagine the spiritual. The dominant mood of the first part of the book, where many of the poems treat of his father, is elegaic. His diction too is now sparer, but the strength of the poetry is still there. He has not, however, lost his feel for the political and the regional.

3 ATFIELD, JOY ROSEMARY. "Creative tensions in the poetry of Seamus Heaney," *Critical Survey* 3, 1: 80–87.

Heaney in his poetry explores the divisions that loom largely in his life and work, such as realism and artifice, his country's history and its language, and the relationship between the artist and society. His poetic detachment, however, allows him to deal with whatever might constrain or restrain him.

4   BAKER, DAVID. "Framed in Words," *Kenyon Review* 13, 3 (Summer): 169–81.
      Review of *Selected Poems 1966–1987*, together with *Selected Poems* by Louis MacNeice and *Outside History: Selected Poems 1980–1990* by Eavan Boland. Baker states that while Heaney rigorously maintains his Irish identity, he nevertheless tries to distance himself from the naive versions of the Irish pastoral. He documents the past in order to present it in relation to a changed and changing present. In his new selection, his first five books receive the same space as his last two. In this he may be saying that his best work is his new work, yet even in his modest work he shows great control and a clear, intelligent voice.

5   BATTERSBY, EILEEN. "A kindly favourite uncle with the wisdom of a sage," *Irish Times* (June 1): 5.
      Heaney's dilemma is that he is expected to create great poetry while at the same time provide a political agenda for a divided Ireland. The main facts of his life are presented, and certain critics are quoted, notably John Carey, who hails Heaney as the heir to Wordsworth. Heaney's poetry has changed; he is facing new directions. However, he has not entirely pulled out of the political debate, choosing to remain a responsible nationalist.

6   BEDFORD, WILLIAM. "The World Turned Upside Down," *Agenda* 29, 4 (Winter): 57–62.
      Review of *Seeing Things* and of *The Redress of Poetry*. Bedford regards *Seeing Things* as a brilliantly organized transitional work. In it we are given glimpses of the real through the ordinary, yet the poet is straining after an illumination which is not *felt* in the poems. Heaney has some fascinating things to say about George Herbert in *The Redress of Poetry*, which help us to understand the second half of *Seeing Things*. In spite of the wonderful images, the meaning somehow escapes one—this may be due to the power of Heaney's imagination.
      Reprinted 1993.3.

7   BEDFORD, WILLIAM. "Two Irish Poets," *Agenda* 29, 4 (Winter): 57–62.
      Bedford in his review of *Seeing Things* states that it explores the visionary side of life. The imagination is fully at work in this collection, but the illumination for which he searches does not inform the poems.

1991

8 BILLINGTON, MICHAEL. "Agony and the obduracy," *Guardian* (April 6): Arts 18.
Billington concentrates on the political content of Heaney's *The Cure at Troy*. The reviewer particularly likes the treatment of the Chorus and the female Chorus leader; both elements strike "a blow against male obstinacy and sectarian pride." Heaney's verse is described as "compact" and "muscular."

9 "[Book Review]," *Publishers Weekly* 238, 48 (November 1): 65.
The brief review glances at the "visionary intent" of the poetry. This intent (the search for the dead father) informs the volume's "otherworldly" content.

10 "Books of the Month," *Esquire* 116, 6 (December): 61.
This brief review of *Seeing Things* mentions the "visionary" orientation of the poems, which is presented in a kind of "Newtonian aesthetic."

11 BOXER, SARAH. "A New Literary Hero: The Limp, Silent Type," *New York Times Book Review* (June 2): 1, 37.
Discusses the "bog people" and their popularity with writers of the English-speaking world. Seamus Heaney read P. V. Glob's account of the deaths of hundreds of these bog people and composed a series of poems as a result. The poems gave rise to a revival of interest in the bog people, which was further whetted with the discovery of the Lindow Man in 1984. This in turn sparked a whole series of novels and short stories on the bog men.

12 BRANDES, RAND. "The Scale of Things," *Irish Literary Supplement* 10, 2 (Fall): 30–31.
Review of *Selected Poems 1966–1987* and of *Seeing Things*. Brandes comments on how little Heaney's contemporary activities at Harvard, Oxford, and elsewhere are reflected in his poetry. He points out the revisions of parts of the "Station Island" sequence and the incorporation of some prose poems from *Stations*. He finds *Seeing Things* exploiting Heaney's strengths—his childhood experiences, and descriptions of characters. The poet's close relationship with his mother is shown, yet his father assumes a more central role in the work. *Seeing Things* is "about looking through things and also through oneself."
Reprinted 1993.4.

13 BRESLIN, JOHN B. "Seeing Things: John Breslin interviews Seamus Heaney," *Critic* (Winter): 26–35.
Heaney primarily discusses the composition and production of *Seeing Things*. He mentions that the book's working title was *Lightenings,* which

related to death and the uplifting of the soul as described by Shakespeare in *Romeo and Juliet*. Breslin asks several questions related to the twelve-line form in the "Squarings" section of *Seeing Things*. Heaney likes the openness of the form and its ability to reproduce itself. Heaney closes with a few comments upon the importance of Marvell to the style of *Field Work*.

14 BRESLIN, JOHN B. "Vision and Revision: Seamus Heaney's New Poems," *America* 165, 18 (December 7): 438–39.

In his review of *Seeing Things*, Breslin notes Heaney's exploration of new forms to express a vision that may be bitter but nonetheless celebratory. Heaney, as all good poets do, is constantly refining his poetry and experimenting with new forms, and in the second half of the book we see the "Squarings" of 48 poems in four groups of 12. They explore personal memories and display Heaney's great verbal skill. He has found freedom in this new form to work through his own memories.

Reprinted 1993.5.

15 BURRIS, SIDNEY. "An Empire of Poetry," *Southern Review* 27, 3 (Summer): 559–74.

Review of *Selected Poems 1966–1987* and of *Omeros* by Derek Walcott.

Heaney's selection of his poems shows that he is attempting to loosen the "tight gag of place." His early work, particularly *Death of a Naturalist* (1966) and *Door into the Dark* (1969), have suffered most from his rigid selection standards. Much has been spoken about Heaney's political sympathies, especially as shown by *North* and subsequent work. *North* addresses many of the issues that would later engage Heaney in his prose. In this new volume he includes poems from *Field Work, Station Island,* and *The Haw Lantern*, where particularly in the latter, the quiet insistence on hope speaks of a world where people "still speak of redemption and efficacy."

16 CAREY, JOHN. "Touching the Void," *Sunday Times* (London, June 2): Books 1.

In his review of *Seeing Things,* Carey notices that the poems are shaped by "a plea for escape from the tangible" and the theme of "letting go." The review argues that the "loose design of Squarings allows a rich range of subjects" and that that volume's sparse verse marks a significant change in Heaney's mature poetry.

17 CLAMPITT, AMY. "Seamus Heaney and the Matter of Ireland," in her *Predecessors, Et Cetera: Essays* (Ann Arbor: University of Michigan Press): 126–30.

Reprint of 1987.9.

1991

18 CLOUGHERTY, ROBERT JAMES, JR. "The Historiography of Three Irish
Poets: W. B. Yeats, Seamus Heaney and Richard Murphy." Ph.D. dissertation, University of Tulsa.

Ireland's culture and poetry have long held a direct relationship to history as the identity of the Irish race has depended on the popular notion of history. By the same means, Irish historiography has always been subject to the
influence of politics. The result has been a divided history from which Irish
poets have attempted to carve their identity. In the contemporary period,
Seamus Heaney, as a Catholic from Northern Ireland, remains trapped
between the two opposing forces within Irish culture. His work examines the
violence occurring in Northern Ireland and approaches it as a force which has
existed throughout history, regardless of time and place, as seen in the parallels between the bog people of pre-Christian Scandinavia and contemporary
Ireland. His later poetry, since he moved from the North to the Republic of
Ireland, has placed a strong focus on traitors throughout history.

19 CLYDE, TOM. "A game of two halves," *Fortnight* 297 (July/August): 28.

Review of *Seeing Things*. According to Clyde, Heaney is here dealing
with two obsessions—the study of daily life and an opening up of himself to
"visions and spirits." The first section of the book is for Heaney a return to
the familiar themes of his early books. There is nothing new here that the old
ones did not do just as well. The second is the more interesting section, with
Heaney exploring random, subjective insights. Yet there is a sense of dissatis-
faction: we get the feeling that we are dipping into his notebooks. We will
have to see what new direction will come from this. This book, however,
looks like a holding operation. The high points of the work are the translations
from Virgil and Dante which open and close the book.

20 CORKE, HILARY. "A Slight Case of Zenophilia?" *Spectator* 266 (June 8):
36–37.

Review of *Seeing Things*. Heaney is an important poet, yet his work can
be obscure, reminding one of Wallace Stevens. His childhood memories are
colorful yet have little to say to him or to the reader.

21 COSTA, PETER. "A Conversation with Seamus Heaney," *Harvard Gazette*
(April 26): 5–6.

Costa talks with Heaney about his play *The Cure at Troy*. Heaney comments on its performance by Field Day. He relates the play to the Northern
Ireland situation, to the Berlin Wall, and the events of 1989. He speaks of his
apprehension in dealing with dialogue and the problems of being a poet: "It's
easy to be a poet. . .when you're writing. The test is in the in-between times."
He concludes with reflections on parallel lives and on imagined things.

22 COUGHLAN, PATRICIA. "'Bog Queens': The representation of women in the poetry of John Montague and Seamus Heaney," in *Gender in Irish Writing*, edited by Toni O'Brien Johnson and David Cairns (Milton Keynes; Philadelphia: Open University Press, 1991): 88–111.

Coughlan sets out to investigate the role of feminine figures in the poetry of Seamus Heaney and John Montague, both of whom have women play a major role in their poetry. In Heaney's "Bog Poems" he personifies the landscape as feminine and equates it with death. The feminine is seen as Other but not equal. Other poems in *North* give a gender-historical view of the English Conquest of Ireland: "politics is seen in terms of sexuality, but not the reverse." Coughlin concludes that the poetry of both Heaney and Montague "is insistently and damagingly gendered."

23 DEANE, SEAMUS. "Oranges and Lemons," *New Statesman & Society* 4, 125 (April 5): 18–19.

A review of the production of *The Cure at Troy* at the Tricycle Theatre, London, April 2–27. The play concentrates on a dual debate, between betrayal and justice and between isolation/death and fate/history. The Field Day dramatists are preoccupied with freedom which is achieved by facing the historical experience. Heaney's poetry, as with *The Cure at Troy*, "is a turn from place to time, from a past. . .to a mobile future that refuses localism and risks another language."

24 DENMAN, PETER. "[Book Review]," *Irish University Review* 21, 1 (Spring/Summer): 154–56.

Brief review of *New Selected Poems 1966–1987* and three other works. The changes from *Selected Poems 1965–1975* are noted, especially the more generous representation of poems from *Field Work* to *The Haw Lantern*: "An excellent introduction for anyone wishing to catch up on Seamus Heaney's achievement so far."

25 DONOVAN, KATIE. "Why many Irish poets are taking the stage," *Irish Times* (January 22): 10.

Donovan talks to Sebastian Barry, Tom McIntyre, Seamus Heaney, Dermot Bolger, Aidan Carl Matthews, Anne Hartigan, and Brendan Kennelly about their decision to enter the theatre world. For Heaney, the move to playwriting is using his poetic gift in a new way. After his translation of *The Cure at Troy*, and after being forced to take into consideration the visual and aural dimensions of theatre, he has "a notion" to write an original play.

26 DRIVER, PAUL. "Janus Faced Verses of Shifting Brilliance," *Weekend Financial Times* (June 1–2): XI.

Driver argues in his review of *Seeing Things* that the poems are simultaneously backwards and forwards looking. The reviewer questions whether

Heaney is playing with "Heaneyism" or bound by it. Driver discusses the many literary poems and the translations in the book. The reviewer also wonders if Heaney has become an international poet in the wrong sense because of what he perceives to be echoes of Walcott or Ashbery. This is a transitional volume according to Driver.

27 DUNN, DOUGLAS. "Real presences," *Irish Times* (June 1): Weekend 5.
Review of *Seeing Things*. The well-known poets of today have to be aware of the pressures to be socially responsible. Heaney acknowledges this pressure on someone such as Pasternak in "The Sounds of Rain." In the "Squarings" sequence, we see his infatuation with everyday objects, which is spiritual, sensuous, and still intellectual. This is a new path for Heaney, which shows a more mature and assured lyric voice. The local pieties are explored and contested in well constructed poetry.

28 EYRES, HARRY. "Deny yourself and speak plain for Sophocles," *Times* (London, April 2): 16.
In his conversation with Eyres on *The Cure at Troy*, Heaney speaks of his fascination with Philoctetes. He was first drawn to him through the realism of the rotting foot; the possible allegorical and political connections followed. The plot follows Sophocles' text closely, but Ireland is always present in the play. Heaney sees Philoctetes himself as an image of the writer who "must bear witness to the integrity of refusal."

29 FENNELL, DESMOND. "The Heaney Phenomenon: 'A disparity between the work and the reputation,'" *Irish Times* (March 30): Weekend 5.
The "Heaney phenomenon" has inhibited serious critical discourse about Irish poetry because it intimidates Irish critics. Heaney is not a major poet because his poetry is "poor in word and meaning" and is not "in the ordinary sense of the word musical." In spite of these limitations he ranks as a major poet because of the consensus of the London critics and the American East Coast academic establishment. Heaney himself also takes his own career seriously and responds to "market forces."

30 FENNELL, DESMOND. "Whatever You Say, Say Nothing," *Stand* 32, 4 (Autumn): 38–65.
Reprint of 1991.1; reprinted 1993.13.

31 FENNELL, DESMOND. *Whatever You Say, Say Nothing: Why Seamus Heaney Is No. 1* (Dublin: ELO Publications).
Fennell notes Heaney's success and grants that he is a genuinely good poet. He also asserts that Heaney has more than talent on his side: the influence of Philip Hobsbaum, the publicity attending the Northern troubles, and Heaney's own caution and circumspection. He also argues that the real archi-

tects of Heaney's reputation have been the members of the academic literary establishment, particularly the American academics.

Reprinted 1991.30; 1993.13.

Reviewed by Brian Fallon in *Irish Times*, June 22, 1991; by Mary Campbell in *Books Ireland*, September, 1991. The book was also the subject of a series of letters to the Editor of the *Irish Times* under the heading "The Heaney Phenomenon," as follows: John Quinn, April 4; Eilis Dillon, April 8; Desmond Fennell, April 8; Eugene O'Brien, April 13; Sean Healy, April 16; Robert Welch, April 16; Paul Durcan, April 17; Ciaran Cosgrove, April 19; Margaretta D'Arcy/John Arden, April 20; Ciaran Holahan, April 20; Julian Girdham, April 24; Dorothy Walker, May 2; Desmond Fennell, May 23; Theo Dorgan, May 31; Bert Wright, June 3; Sean Healy, June 8; and Desmond Fennell, June 12.

32 FOSTER, JOHN WILSON. "Heaney's Redress," in *Colonial Consequences: Essays in Irish Literature and Culture* (Arbour Hill, Dublin: Lilliput Press): 168–205.

In this lengthy essay Foster examines the entire Heaney corpus. He finds Heaney's concern is with the place of poetry and its relation to political reality. Each volume of his poetry has a cumulative value effect and constitutes a poet's manifesto. Together with his essays, they verify "the reality of poetry in the world." Foster sees the political as "the most revealing metaphor" in Heaney's poetry. His mission is to constitute poetry's self-determination. This is inseparable from his own status in a divided province and country.

33 FOSTER, JOHN WILSON. "The Poetry of Seamus Heaney," in *Colonial Consequences: Essays in Irish Literature and Culture* (Mullingar: Lilliput Press): 81–96.

Reprint of 1974.3; reprinted 1976.11; 1993.14.

34 GROSS, JOHN. "When the Past turns up on the Doorstep," *Sunday Telegraph* (London, April 7): XIII.

In this brief review of *The Cure at Troy*, Gross concentrates on the play's "colloquial" language.

35 HARGREAVES, IAN. "Ulster Dog Gnaws at Ireland's Shadows," *Weekend Financial Times* (June 1): XXII.

In this interview with Heaney, the poet discusses the dangers of giving too many interviews and sees his ironic position with humor: "so it's a condition of complete self-destruction." The poet discusses Milosz, Yeats, Dylan Thomas, and others. Heaney declares that "there's a formalist in me that will never die." After talking about postmodernism and *Seeing Things*, he says of religion: "there's no heaven, no afterlife of the sort we were promised and no personal god." "Suspicion" and "distrust" are key terms in the interview.

1991

36   HART, HENRY. "Seamus Heaney and the Pastoral Tradition," *Southern Review* 27, 2 (Spring): 475–78.

A review of *The Poetry of Resistance: Seamus Heaney and the Pastoral Tradition* by Sidney Burris (1990.5). Burris is aware of the problematic status of the the pastoral in contemporary culture. Heaney is attracted to the pastoral because of its ability to convey political messages in a palatable form. It is more potent in his early work, but he still returns to Northern Ireland's religious and political problems because the pastoral can concentrate attention on them.

37   HOFMANN, MICHAEL. "Dazzling Philosophy," *London Review of Books* 13, 15 (August 15): 14–15.

Review of *Seeing Things*. The poet's greatest difficulty is how to go on being one, and Heaney knows of the need to move on. This is his most auto-biographical and plain-spoken book; it is also his most Irish book since *North*. As the *Haw Lantern* had the hollow round or sphere as a single physical or geometrical schema, so does *Seeing Things* have the straight line or pattern of straight lines as its schema. The human content is taken from the poet's own life. In Part II of the book, called "Squarings," he shows his new form—the twelve-line poem made up of four tercets. This book is full of poetic positions the exact opposite of those in his early poetry.

Reprinted 1993.17.

38   KELLAWAY, KATE. "Curse of a Fallen Archer," *Observer Review* (April 7): 59.

Kellaway's review of *The Cure at Troy* comments upon the "classical" elements of the Field Day production. Although the language (comprised of conventional and contemporary idioms) occasionally subsumes the action, the reviewer concludes that it is a play well worth "hearing."

39   KIBERD, DECLAN. "Heaney's Magic," *Colour Tribune* (Dublin, June 9): 21.

In this finely written and insightful article on the occasion of the publication of *Seeing Things*, Kiberd examines Heaney's talent and success in the context of contemporary cultural politics and in relation to modern Irish literary figures. The lengthy text considers several aspects of Heaney's critical reception: his complex interaction with British critics, Irish begrudgers, and the general reading public. Kiberd attributes Heaney's popularity to both the performance of the poems and of the poet: "Heaney is arguably the finest reader of poetry on the circuit today." The root of Heaney's appeal is his "not caring" in the Kavanagh sense. This attitude allows him "to improvise, to experiment, to try something different." Kiberd, therefore, finds the most rewarding poems of *Seeing Things* to be those of the "occasional, impromptu, unfussy" sort. One comment worth noting is Kiberd's assertion that Heaney had been "forced to move south and leave his lectureship at Queen's University Belfast, following loyalist threats after he appeared on TV."

40 LANE, ANTHONY. "The roll[sic] of the poet in a material world," *Independent* (June 15): 29.

Lane, in his review of *Seeing Things,* says, "The gerund seems the ideal grammatical form for Heaney." The poet takes a simple object or activity and looks at it from an unfamiliar angle. Sometimes his seeing is woolly and dramatically lacking. Compared with *North*, which Lane regards as Heaney's best work, there seems to be a new freedom here. *Seeing Things* begins and ends with translations from Virgil and Dante, both dealing with crossings. There are some great moments in this book which can lead us across the threshold into poetry.

41 LEVI, PETER. "Scythe, Pitchfork and Biretta," *Poetry Review* 81, 2 (Summer): 12–14.

Levi in his review of *Seeing Things* notes that the poems remind one of Heaney's previous poetry for their resonance. Heaney writes as an outsider to life. The easiest poetry is in the first half. The language and rhythm are combined as few other poets can do. The second half of the book contains some of his best lines. The range of precision in meaning, the intellectual strength are beyond a brief review. This "is the poetry we have been looking for in English for so long."

42 LOGAN WILLIAM. "A Letter from Britain," *Poetry* 157, 4 (January): 222–38.

In this survey of the state of poetry in the British Isles, Logan states that since Larkin's death "the appreciations of the British have fallen to Seamus Heaney, Geoffrey Hill, and Ted Hughes." He goes on to comment briefly on Heaney, noting that the tensions in his work have been more intimate than "the affectations of Hill or Hughes." He suspects that in the 1980s Heaney has not written continually to his strengths and argues that his *Sweeney Astray* was remarkably clumsy. Heaney's criticism, however, has spoken more of the art within the art than any prose since that of Eliot.

43 LUCAS, JOHN. "Father Figures," *New Statesman & Society* 4, 157 (June 28): 37–38.

Review of *Seeing Things.* The celebratory tribute to the poet's father takes up much of the first part of this book. The work is also full of the presence of other poets: Eliot, Hardy, Wordsworth, Virgil, Dante, and Keats. Heaney is a master who "occasionally lifts a poem clean of the humdrum." It is not the best work by Heaney; however, "no one but Heaney could have written the best of it."

1991

44 McGUINNESS, ARTHUR E. "Seamus Heaney: The Forging Pilgrim," *Essays in Literature* 18, 1 (Spring): 46–67.

McGuinness traces the thematic shift from the poet as "feminine incubator" to "masculine forger" in *Field Work* and *Station Island*. In the latter work Heaney has adopted the mode of the forger: assertive, controlled, master, and maker. The author applies "forger" particularly to the elegies and "Glanmore Sonnets" of *Field Work*. McGuinness examines the sense of alienation and loss of feminine security which inform the Sonnets. There is a lengthy discussion of the poet's depiction of his marriage in the volume—depictions which foreground experiences of "defamiliarization." The fact that the ghosts of "Station Island" are male appears significant to McGuinness. Of the ghosts, the author notes that Joyce is not nurturing but ironic. The essay concludes that Heaney now seems to be seeking "mysteries" instead of securities and that he has become a more independent poet.

45 MACKINNON, LACHLAN. "A Responsibility to Self," *Times Literary Supplement* 4601 (June 7): 28.

Review of *Seeing Things*. MacKinnon sees in Heaney's work an attempt to escape his "Irishness," which has resulted in the poet's being "lamed by the extra-poetic authority of civic and largely externally imposed responsibility." After commenting upon the validity of attacks on Heaney's work because of its "teachability," which is the result of the poems' "little imaginative surplus," the reviewer finds *Seeing Things* as a positive development because "Heaney has learnt not to sound like himself" and has escaped the "burden of being Seamus Heaney."

46 MANGAN, MICHAEL. "Radio," *Plays International* (October): 37.

In this review of the BBC Radio 3 broadcast on January 1, 1994 of Heaney's *The Cure at Troy*, Mangan says that although contemporary poets do not always make good playwrights, Heaney taps the "force of tradition" and through his vernacular "translates the Greek experience vividly into the present day." The "Chorus" did not work well on radio.

47 MASON, DAVID. "Poetry Chronicle," *Hudson Review* 44, 3 (Autumn): 509–18.

Heaney's *Selected Poems 1966–1987* is one of several volumes mentioned in this review essay on political poets. The reviewer admires Heaney's editing for the selection. Mason, who confesses to coming from a small town, also likes Heaney's "verbal density" and pastoral images. The "Station Island" sequence is the reviewer's favorite because of the poet's unsentimental approach to life. This tough stance Morgan deems "politically responsible."

48 MOLONEY, KAREN M. "Heaney's Love to Ireland," *Twentieth Century Literature* 37, 3 (Fall): 273–88.

Moloney provides a word-by-word reading of Heaney's poem "Ocean's Love to Ireland." In addition to her concentration on the prosody, Moloney approaches the subject matter from the perspective of the Celtic tradition of the "goddess of sovereignty," Eriu. The author also provides extensive historical information and uses Sir Walter Raleigh's poem "Ocean's Love to Cynthia" as a poetic and political reference point. Moloney concludes that Heaney adopts the perspective of the raped maid not only to show sympathy with the victim (Ireland), but also to demonstrate the maid's "invincibility."

49 MONTENEGRO, DAVID. "Seamus Heaney," in *Points of Departure: International Writers on Writing and Politics: Interviews by David Montenegro* (Ann Arbor: University of Michigan Press): 180–97.

In this interview conducted at Harvard in 1987, Heaney and Montenegro discuss Irish politics and writing; the poet and the public event; violence and poetry; action and aesthetics; the poetry of the ear and the poetry of the eye; individual Irish and American poets; and the Vietnam War. Throughout he talks of his own poetry, particularly *The Haw Lantern,* and the writing of poetry—"The world is irrigated by the imagination."

50 MORRISON, BLAKE. "Seamus Famous: Time to be dazzled," *Independent on Sunday* (May 19): 26–27.

Review of *Seeing Things.* The review relies heavily upon material taken from Morrison's interview with Heaney regarding *Seeing Things.* Morrison finds Heaney too predisposed to say the right thing in the right post-structuralist language. He quotes Heaney as saying that holding the chairs at Harvard and Oxford is "like having two bishoprics." Heaney describes the twelve-line form of "Squarings" as embodying the "music of the arbitrary"; he enjoys the spontaneity of the form. *Seeing Things,* according to Heaney, is the book that most resembles *Death of a Naturalist.* Asked if he believed in an afterlife, Heaney says that he believes in the "atheist position, or the Wordsworthian one."

51 MURATORI, FRED. "[Book Review]," *Library Journal* 116 (November 15): 86.

Brief review of *Seeing Things.* The poet is engaged "on a midlife journey into the interior." He makes the reader feel as well as see the sights. His language is tactile and anchors the poet's aspirations as well as his past—a language that elevates and transcends. He is one of the few who can do this.

1991

52   MURPHY, JAMES J. "On Living in a Dark Time: A Reading of Seamus Heaney's *The Cure at Troy*," *Chautauqua* 2, 4 (March): 15–16.

 Murphy categorizes the play as about history: how the past can be a festering sore and how memory can breed hatred. Heaney sees in the Greek play an analogy for Ulster's problems. The poet can remind us of the past and help us to see beyond the present and so escape the terrible hatred.

53   NIGHTINGALE, BENEDICT. "Crimes that Cross Centuries," *Times* (April 6): Arts 17.

 Nightingale, in his review of *The Cure at Troy*, stresses the lucidity of the language, the faithfulness of the play to the original, and the political implications of the play (justice and forgiveness).

54   NOBLE, TIM. "Seamus Heaney: The Deep Grammar of the Human Condition,"*Month* 24 (June): 266–68.

 A successful poem, Noble asserts, must draw us into the poet's experience while at the same time pushing us out to reflect on our own. Noble shows how three of Heaney's poems—"Follower," "Station Island," and "From the Frontiers of Writing"—do just that while they also illustrate some of his major themes. The themes are the role of the poet; the place of the poet in society; the nature of love and hate; and loyalty, pain, and incomprehension. The main subject of "Follower" is role reversal and dependence. Dependency is also among the themes of "Station Island." Here he shows how we must face our own ghosts and do our penance. In "From the Frontier of Writing" we are shown that in a hostile atmosphere, writing must be justified and explained. To stand still is to move backwards.

55   O'CONNELL, SHAUN. "Erin go ugh!" *Boston Phoenix Literary Section* (August): 7–8.

 Defending Heaney against Desmond Fennell's *Whatever You Say, Say Nothing: Why Seamus Heaney Is No. 1* (1991.29), O'Connell concludes that Fennell "denigrates" the poet's achievement and "slurs" his character. O'Connell responds point by point to the pamphlet's accusations, covering issues from the apolitical aspects of Heaney's poetry to what Fennell calls Heaney's attraction to "the puritan lyric."

56   O'TOOLE, FINTAN. "Dr. Fennell's Confusion: The Hidden Agenda in the criticism of Seamus Heaney," *Irish Times* (April 6): 5.

 Reading between the lines, O'Toole claims that Fennell's true reason for criticizing Heaney in *Whatever You Say, Say Nothing* (1991.29) is that Fennell thinks that the poet has not used "his standing to stand up for 'our side' in the Northern conflict."

57   PARKER, MICHAEL. "Full of Unroofed Scope," *Honest Ulsterman* 92 (December): 68–72.

Parker, in his review of *Seeing Things,* sees a Heaney more at ease with himself. His father, who was a prominent figure in his first book, has a large place also here, as a figure not of awe but of affectionate acceptance. The matters of his youth are still fresh in his memory, and we can expect him to return to them again.

58   PENNA, CHRISTOPHER. "Knowing Place, Keeping Place: Approaches to Place in the Poetry of Seamus Heaney." Ph.D. dissertation, University of Delaware.

From *Death of a Naturalist* to *Seeing Things,* a sense of place as something more fundamental than simply landscape or scenery is central to Seamus Heaney's poetry. Though his writing, especially in his earlier books, is characterized by vividly realized images of the landscapes of his native Ulster, his use of these images reveals his alertness to the cultural, personal, and kinesthetic dimensions of his environment. Informed by this sensibility, Heaney's poetry is a complementary expression of place rather than mere scenic description. Frequently his writing alternates between proximate and distant relationships to place. His movement between these two stances parallels the struggle between alienation from, and identity with, place that is likewise evident in his work.

59   "Poetry: A Soul on the Washing Line," *Economist* 319 (June 22): 98–102.

Interview upon the publication of *Seeing Things.* Heaney talks about his father's influence on the volume, who he says was "completely wordless." He also mentions that he wanted his poems to manifest a type of "free fall," and to make the language "do something akin to beaming it up, like in 'Star Trek.'" He concludes by going over his conception of "eternal life" as it relates to the poems and language in *Seeing Things.*

60   PORTER, PETER. "Private world of a poetic celebrity," *Sunday Telegraph* (London, June 2): X.

Porter begins his view of *Seeing Things* by asserting that Heaney is the only heir to Yeats's title in terms of audience. While Yeats works on the grand, and often rhetorical, public scale, Heaney is more like an "embroiderer." Porter sees the twelve-line poems in the "Squarings" section as an "ordnance survey of the poetic mind." Porter concludes that the work may be "over-insured by its very lapidary skill."

61   QUINLAN, KIERAN. "[Book Review],"*World Literature Today* 65, 1 (Winter): 118.

Review of *The Place of Writing.* One of the few reviews of Heaney's third collection of prose. Although Heaney touches upon some of the same

1991

themes in this volume which appear in *The Government of the Tongue*, there are also a few differences. Heaney discusses not only contemporary poets, but also poets such as Yeats and MacNeice. Quinlan notes that not only does place affect a poet's writing or that poets often create their own places, but also that writing is itself a place. Place, however, is not always present or positive; it can appear even when absent and inhibit when present. Quinlan sees Heaney's observations of Yeats in the essays as revisionist.

62 QUINLAN, KIERAN. "Under Northern Lights: Re-Visioning Yeats and the Revival," in *Yeats and Postmodernism*, edited by Leonard Orr (Syracuse: Syracuse University Press): 64–79.

Quinlan concentrates on Yeats as seen by the *Field Day* group of Irish Writers—Heaney, Deane and others, who write "from the actual political urgencies of the day in the world outside." They questioned Yeats's selective image of Ireland's past. Heaney argued in 1979 that the alternative tradition of Carleton, Joyce, and Kavanagh has to be affirmed because it is much more in touch with the realities of Irish life.

63 RAINE, CRAIG. "Famous Seamus," *Vanity Fair* 54, 12 (December): 244–47, 266, 268.

In his exposé, Craig Raine, British poet and one-time poetry editor of Faber and Faber, takes us behind the scenes and into Heaney's "personal" world. Raine's article includes everything from a description of Heaney's study to raw psychological readings of Heaney and his family and friends. Raine provides witty, self-conscious sketches of Heaney. Farrar, Straus and Giroux, Raine emphasizes, rejected Heaney's first three books. Heaney's reputation is the subject of much of the article.

64 REYNOLDS, OLIVER. "Irishmen," *London Magazine* 31, 5/6 (August/September): 108–10.

Review of *Seeing Things* and of works by Ciaran Carson and Paul Durcan. The physical world is here informed by the spirit, as Heaney applies poetry to ordinary things. Reynolds concludes that the book "is as heartening a book as any of its predecessors."

65 RICHMAN, ROBERT. "At a tangent," *New Criterion* 9, 8 (April): 65–71.

In his review of *Selected Poems 1966–1987*, Richman argues that Heaney has produced a decidedly anti-Hughesian and apolitical selection. The reviewer sees Heaney as a "rootless modernist," whose main theme is alienation. Richman discusses several poems at length in this review essay, and he concludes by mentioning the importance of the "Clearances" sequence in the poet's more recent volume *The Haw Lantern*.

66 SCHRICKER, GALE C. "'Deliberately at the Centre': The Triptych Structure of Seamus Heaney's *Field Work*," *Eire-Ireland* 26, 3 (Fall): 107–20.

Heaney's interest in the triptych, shown in *Station Island* and in *The Haw Lantern*, is most clearly illustrated in *Field Work*. The "Glanmore Sonnets" sequence divides the volume into three sections of 21, 10 and 21 pages. Schriker discusses both pictorial and verbal triptychs. In *Field Work* she argues that Heaney sees himself in the context of past, present, and future. We see him evolving from wanting to heal and be healed, to being healed and instructed in the "Glanmore Sonnets," and to being prepared to help heal others in the final section of the work. The triptych form of *Field Work* allows the reader to follow the poet sequentially through his experiences.

67 SMITH, STAN. "Seamus Heaney," in *Contemporary Poets*, 5th ed. (Chicago: St. James Press): 400–402.

Smith's entry for Heaney includes biographical details and a bibliography, followed by a comprehensive essay on the major works up to and including *The Haw Lantern*. Smith speaks of Heaney's awareness of the violence of Irish history, his description of rural life, his treatment of the larger world, and the "new and clarified thoughtfulness" of the recent work.

Revision of 1980.37; 1985.77.

68 TAYLOR, PAUL. "A hit and a myth," *Independent* (April 8): 13.

Taylor frames his review of two plays, one of which is Heaney's *The Cure at Troy*, in terms of Larkin's "myth-kitty." Taylor writes that one early proposed title for the play was "Ulcer Says No." Taylor approves of the "movingly modest conclusion" of the play in contrast to the original's *deus ex machina*.

69 THORPE, ADAM. "A Sense of the Sublime," *Observer* (June 2): 55.

Thorpe's review of *Seeing Things* mentions the Catholic and liturgical dimensions of the book. The reviewer appreciates Heaney's move into the light while retaining his eye for exacting details. He prefers Heaney's questioning of the boyhood self in *Seeing Things* to that of the poet questioning the blown-up victim of *Field Work*.

70 TOBIN, DANIEL EUGENE. "Passage to the Center: Imagination and the Sacred in the Poetry of Seamus Heaney." Ph.D. dissertation, University of Virginia.

Many critics have observed that Seamus Heaney's poetry finds inspiration in Romantic theories of imagination, theories some think naively privilege identity over indeterminacy, the ordering claims of art over the disordering powers of nature and the world. As such they see in his work an

incipient pastoralism, an avoidance of the challenges of historical consciousness and the skeptical view of language, identity, and meaning. For such critics his poems are pre-modern: even his treatment of Ulster's political conflict
betrays a naive myth of return to tribal origins. Rather than propelling his
work to new creative possibilities, his quest for self-definition is nostalgic.
But these commentators fail to recognize that Heaney's quest is fueled by the
need for greater self-consciousness in his art, a need that places his work at
the center of our culture's own search for meaning beyond the claims of radical doubt.

71   TRACY, ROBERT. "When Hope and History Rhyme," *Irish Literary
Supplement* 10, 2 (Fall): 31–32.
        Tracy in his review of *The Cure at Troy* sees it as an oblique commen-
tary on contemporary Ulster. Since *Sweeney Astray,* Heaney has been preoccupied with the artist's freedom from politics and the isolation of that
freedom. In this adaptation of Sophocles' *Philoctetes,* Heaney does not pre-
scribe a cure, but reminds us that a cure is possible.
        Reprinted 1993.30.

72   VENDLER, HELEN. "Choices," *New Yorker* 67 (April 15): 99–103.
        In her review of *Selected Poems 1966–1987,* Vendler looks at Heaney's
evolution as a poet. His early rich vocabulary has been replaced by short lines,
and bare statements. The certainties of philosophy and religion have been left
behind. However, his aesthetic inquiry remains strong.

73   WEST, DAVID. "How it works? Enjoying a piece of poetry," *Times Saturday
Review* (Dublin, June 1): 21.
        West takes part of Heaney's poem in *Seeing Things* ("Lightenings" I, ii)
and comments on the apparent subject of the poem, building a house, in
which he also speaks of making a poem. West assigns to the poem the title
"The Bastion of Sensation."

74   WHEELER, EDWARD T. "With roots in the bog," *Commonweal* 118, 8
(April 19): 262–64.
        Review of *Selected Poems 1966–1987.* There is little to be amused with
in these poems, though there is much affirmation there. What makes Heaney
so good a poet is his vision, sense of place, and origins. His work with language and its sounds stems from an appreciation of the mix of Irish/English in
Ireland. He is overwhelmed by the landscape and by nature, and his close
observation becomes transformation. He shows us a world before the fall of
Adam which still is conscious of what has since happened.

75   WILLS, CLAIR. "Language Politics, Narrative, Political Violence," *Oxford
Literary Review* 13, 1–2: 20–60.

Wills's highly theoretical essay uses brief references to Heaney and other contemporary Irish poets to discuss the "placing [of] Ireland" in relation to the politics of language and issues of postcolonial identity. The author foregrounds Heaney in the section "Mother Tongues: Femininity, History and the Irish Nation," in which Wills quotes from "Act of Union" in her examination of the "metaphor of woman as topography, the motherland, and the idea of a mother-tongue." Wills continues this analysis by referring to the place-names of *Wintering Out* and their extended connection to the *dinnseanchas* tradition. As exemplified in Toome, however, Heaney's etymological constructs (in contrast with Muldoon) simply become "museum pieces, mere curiosities to be visited and contemplated in isolation."

76 WOOD, JAMES. "Looking for a Place Where Things Matter," *Review Guardian* (May 30): 24.
     Wood asserts that unlike earlier titles of Heaney's books, which are descriptive, *Seeing Things* is "prescriptive." In his review, Wood asserts that many of the poems are almost indistinguishable from his earlier work. The language of the poems, according to Wood, is often uninspired and prosaic. However, the "Squarings" section of the book "redeems" the first selection of poems. He particularly likes the poem about the latch.

1992

1 ALLEN, MICHAEL. "'Holding Course': *The Haw Lantern* and Its Place in Heaney's Development," in *Seamus Heaney: A Collection of Critical Essays*, edited by Elmer Andrews (London: Macmillan): 193–207.
     Reprint of 1988.1.

2 ALLISON, JONATHAN. "Acts of Union: Seamus Heaney's Tropes of Sex and Marriage," *Eire-Ireland* 27, 4 (Winter): 106–121.
     Heaney has been fascinated with sex and marriage. At first it signified male strength joined with female tenderness. Later it ceased to represent harmony, becoming instead a metaphor for forced, unstable union, imprisonment, and self-destruction, which suggests the destruction of order in Northern Ireland.

3 ALLISON, JONATHAN. "Imagining the Community: Seamus Heaney in 1966," *Notes on Modern Irish Literature* 4: 27–34.
     The political and the private are two themes which find expression in Heaney's writing in the 1960s. In the political sphere he shows a sympathy with and membership in the political minority of Northern Ireland. This communal identity and his artistic solitude are the poles within which much of his later work is concerned.

1992

4   ANDERSON, MARY. "Seamus Heaney: Incertus, the Fretting Poet," *Études Irlandaises* 17, 2: 79–82.

Anderson's essay focuses on Heaney's interpretation of the dynamic relationship between the masculine and feminine in poetry and language as it relates to his poetic and political stance.

5   ANDREWS, ELMER. "Introduction," in *Seamus Heaney: A Collection of Critical Essays*, edited by Elmer Andrews (London: Macmillan): 1–10.

From the beginning the accessibility of Heaney's poetry was its great advantage. He, like Kavanagh, emphasized the rural roots. Having established himself, he was expected to comment on the political violence in Northern Ireland. In *North* Heaney showed "the anguish of uncertainty." Opposing and critical views to Heaney's explorations were voiced by Carson, Simmons, Fennell, Lloyd, and Edna Longley. Other critics defended Heaney. The central problem "is the way in which Heaney seeks to resolve the tension between his sense of a historical situation and the demands of his own imagination." Andrews states his intention in this book to offer an assessment of Heaney's work from a variety of standpoints "and to relate it to its social, political and artistic contexts."

6   ANDREWS, ELMER. "The Spirit's Protest," in *Seamus Heaney: A Collection of Critical Essays*, edited by Elmer Andrews (London: Macmillan): 208–32.

In Heaney's poetry one finds the benign, gravitational pull of home, family, and landscape. Nevertheless, in the early poetry there is the feeling of flight of being pulled away. This tension between going away and being rooted underlies all of the poet's work. The greater part of Andrews's essay deals with *Seeing Things,* which he sees as a going away, a breaking out of old patterns in the hope of a better future.

7   BAYLEY, JOHN. "Irishness," *New York Review of Books* 39, 12 (June 25): 14–16.

Review of *Seeing Things* together with books by Montague and Longley. The ghost of the Irish language still remains in the poetry written by Irishmen. Heaney mixes fantasy and daily life so effortlessly in his poetry. Most of the review is devoted to Montague's poetry.

8   BROWN, RICHARD. "Bog Poems and Book Poems: Doubleness, Self-Translation and Pun in Seamus Heaney and Paul Muldoon," in *The Chosen Ground: Essays on the Contemporary Poetry of Northern Ireland*, edited by Neil Corcoran (Bridgend: Poetry Wales Press; Chester Springs: Dufour Editions, 1992): 153–67.

Heaney is obsessed by origins, especially in *North*. Words are special examples for they possess both ancient and modern meanings, (e.g., *bog* is the

Irish word for *soft*, in modern Danish it is the word for *book*). Both nature and literacy contend with one another in his work. A strong influence on the doubleness in Heaney's poetry is the pun. Modern readers have strong prejudices against the pun, and at first sight the main loser is the poet himself. The master of the pun, James Joyce, is brought together with Heaney in "Leaving the Island" and its revision in *Station Island*. Heaney has made his own "the self-generating, self-consuming postmodern Switzerland of the pun."

9   BROWN, TERENCE. "The Witnessing Eye and the Speaking Tongue," in *Seamus Heaney: A Collection of Critical Essays*, edited by Elmer Andrews (London: Macmillan): 182–92.
     Brown states that we often find in Heaney's poetry a questioning of the efficacy of the poetic art itself. When the Northern crisis erupted in 1969 Heaney was forced to confront that crisis. His dilemma was that of the conflict between beauty and political violence. His guilt feelings are brought to the fore in *Station Island*. In *The Haw Lantern* he speaks freely, and "the kind of assured utterance. . .gets direct, ample expression, in verse of full-throated ease, an earnest of what we may now hope for from this most gifted of poets in his maturity."

10   BURNETT, DAVID. "The Fire i' the Flint and the Gum which Oozes: Two Modes of Poetry," *Durham University Journal* (January): 119–22.
     Review of *English Poets: British Academy Chatterton Lectures*, edited by Helen Gardner. The review draws heavily upon, and explores at length, Heaney's conception of poetic production as represented in the review's title.

11   BUTTEL, ROBERT. "Seamus Heaney (13 April 1939–   )," in *Concise Dictionary of British Literary Biography, Vol. 8, Contemporary Writers, 1960 to the Present* (Detroit: Gale): 142–65.
     Reprint (updated) of 1985.10.

12   C. N. "Poetry," *Times Literary Supplement* 4653 (June 5): 28.
     Review of *Sweeney's Flight*. This book sets some stanzas from Sweeney Astray opposite photographs by Rachel Giese. Places are important to Heaney. The photographs add to the interpretation of this "topographical" work.

13   CHANG, KUO-CHING. "Self-empowering Revisions: History, Politics, and Literary Practice." Ph.D. dissertation, University of Rochester.
     Explores the interactions among history, socio-political actuality, and literary writing. It centers around the thematics of social dialaectics and historical consciousness in the works of six contemporary writers—Jean Rhys, E. L. Doctorow, Seamus Heaney, Gerald Vizenor, Thomas Pynchon, and Adrienne

1992

Rich—examining how the writers revision the relations of politics to cultural history and how they recenter marginalized subjects in Western culture.

14   COBB, ANN. "[Book Review]," *Harvard Review* 1 (Spring): 138–41.
    Cobb, in her review of *Seeing Things,* states that in these poems Heaney goes into new, hitherto unexplored places. There are encounters with the dead here, but the dead are not accusing as in *Station Island.* His wit is freer here than before. In "Squarings," the final sequence, the sensuous grip, the meaning rooted in the landscape and the texture of the earth, are loosened and instead we see a trust in the unknown. The imagination is free and is seeking a new direction.

15   CROTTY, PATRICK. "Fathers and Sons," *New Welsh Review* 5, 1 (Summer): 12 -23.
    Crotty explores the themes of tradition and identity in modern Anglo-Irish poetry. Identity becomes significant only when the demand for it has been frustrated. The work of Irish poets has been motivated by the desire to assert the authentic Irish experience and to affirm the presence of the past. The destruction of the Irish language broke the link with the precolonial past. Yeats tried to establish a continuity between the Ireland of the sagas and modern Ireland. Some of the contemporary writers feel that though Irish is not their mother tongue, English is not the proper substitute. For them Joyce is the great figure in Irish writing because of his fostering an un-British personality and because his art is rooted in the middle class. The northern poets come from a variety of social and religious backgrounds with their attending diversity of attitudes towards the British connection. After the neatly constructed poems of his first two books Heaney adopted a short unrhymed line as he began to deal with the matter of Ireland. The future will decide if his recent work "amounts to any more than an attempt to escape history."

16   CROTTY, PATRICK. "Lyric Waters," *Irish Review* 11 (Winter 1991/92): 114–20.
    Review of Michael Longley's *Gorse Fires* and *Poems 1963–1983*, and of Heaney's *The Cure at Troy* and *Seeing Things*. The translation from the *Aeneid* which opens *Seeing Things* introduces the motifs which follow—thresholds, boats, rivers, roofs, and the weather. The best part of the book is the sequence of 12-line poems titled "Squarings," which is very much informed by the spirit of Wordsworth. While it contains some of Heaney's best poetry, it has few successful individual poems. The book as a whole is his "most exciting and least satisfying volume. . .its metaphysical vigour sitting oddly beside its formal lassitude." In *The Cure at Troy*, Philoctetes reminds us of Sweeney. Neoptolemus, however, is very much a Heaney figure worrying over that which was done and that which should be done. Predictably, Philoctetes gets all the good lines—poets are sympathetic to complainers.

17 DESMOND, JOHN F. "Allegories of Dual Citizenship: Seamus Heaney's *The Haw Lantern,*" *Eire-Ireland* 27, 2 (Summer): 60–75.

Desmond discusses certain poems from *The Haw Lantern* in which the poet travels to imagined places. In these places the poet confronts appearances and tests which underline the poet's dilemma in contemporary history—the allegiance to history and art, to truth and beauty. What emerges is a vision constructed out of the tensions of modern life, the redemptive power of poetry.

18 DOOLEY, DAVID. "Poetry Chronicle," *Hudson Review* 45, 3 (Autumn): 509–17.

Review of *Seeing Things* and of works by Czeslaw Milosz, Cesare Pascarella, Les Murray, Howard Nemerov, Mary Stewart Hammond, and Andrew Hudgins. Heaney's book is a well-crafted collection of short lyrics, some of which are inspired by simple objects. He also writes of memories of the past and of reconciliation with his father. His ear is better than ever, and his sense of rhythm is masterful.

19 DUERDEN, SARAH JANE. "Ungoverning the Lyric Tongue: The Public Poetry of Seamus Heaney." Ph.D. dissertation, Arizona State University.

Recent criticism of the poetry of Seamus Heaney suggests a lack of consensus as to whether he writes public poetry. He has been accused of being both apolitical and reticent and nationalist and outspoken. These antithetical judgments arise from equating public poetry with what Heaney describes as crisis poetry: poetry couched in topical terms that verges on becoming propaganda or poster poetry. Although in his public poetry Heaney adopts the covert strategies employed by post-colonial and Eastern European poets, he continues also the autobiographical tradition of Wordsworth's public poetry. In both his prose and his poetry, Heaney struggles and succeeds in producing public rather than crisis poetry.

20 GREELEY, ANDREW. "Lenten Books," *Commonweal* 119, 5 (March 13): 27.

Greeley suggests Heaney's *Seeing Things* for Lenten reading. This new collection means two things, seeing the hard realities and also seeing their meaning, their mystery. Heaney has the propensity to find grace everywhere. He sees the world through Catholic eyes, and he may well be the most Catholic writer since Joyce.

21 HAMILTON, IAN. "Excusez-moi," *London Review of Books* (October 1): 10–11.

Hamilton states that at first Heaney's poetry did not seem to offer much of a challenge. Since 1969, with the eruption of violence in Northern Ireland his poetry "has been a moving drama of discomfiture." In *The Haw Lantern*

1992

there are poems of professionalism for Harvard, for William Golding, etc. He is also learning from the poets of Eastern Europe. The "Clearances" sequence registers silence and emptiness. He has been subject to examination both by himself and by others' expectations of him.

22 HARMON, MAURICE. "'We pine for ceremony': Ritual and Reality in the Poetry of Seamus Heaney, 1965–75," in *Seamus Heaney: A Collection of Critical Essays*, edited by Elmer Andrews (London: Macmillan): 67–86.
Reprint of 1987.25.

23 HARRIS, T. J. G. "Subtlety & Paradox," *PN Review* 18, 3 (January/February): 61–62.
Harris reviews *Seeing Things*, along with Bernard O'Donoghue's *The Weakness*. Harris commends the book's style and restraint. No one poem stands out over the others because the book is meant to be read as an integrated whole. *The Haw Lantern* showed Heaney moving towards a more pure style and ready for a newer kind of poetry, which we now find in *Seeing Things*. Here we have a strong, direct style from "one of the subtlest of our poets." It may puzzle some readers—Harris advises those readers to stay with it to discover the book's many riches.

24 HART, HENRY. *Seamus Heaney: Poet of Contrary Progressions* (Syracuse: Syracuse University Press): xii, 219 pp.
An exploration of Heaney's work from the beginning through *The Haw Lantern* (1987), arranged chronologically. Hart offers a discussion of the poems, Heaney's personal situations, and his assimilation of contemporary literary theory. Hart charts the development of Heaney's poetry, tracing his intellectual and spiritual growth as well as his response to the various political and other movements of his time. The best way into Heaney's poetry is to understand the man in terms of oppositions and conflicts.

25 HAWLIN, STEFAN. "Seamus Heaney's 'Station Island': The Shaping of a Modern Purgatory," *English Studies* 73, 1: 35–50.
Hawlin takes the "Station Island" sequence of *Station Island* and shows how it imitates the religious pattern of the pilgrimage. For Heaney the spiritual renewal results in a re-dedication to his vocation as a poet. Dante is his model, through which he presents meetings with people he has loved. There are two other influences within the sequence: Joyce's *A Portrait of the Artist* (1916) and Heaney's own version of Sweeney, a medieval Irish king. Hawlin takes us through the sequence in order ending with the encounter with James Joyce.

26 HERINGTON, JOHN. "The song of the bow," *The New Criterion* (October): 73–75.

Review of *The Cure at Troy.* Herington sees Sophocles' Philoctetes as a study of utter loneliness. It also presents a kind of heroism which in our time can move us. Seamus Heaney's version of the play, while following the original closely, has certain insertions at the beginning and end which in effect substitute for a critical apparatus. It is a triumphant version. It is hard to imagine it being better done.

27 HIRSCH, EDWARD. "Home Is Where the Heart Breaks," *New York Times Book Review* 97 (May 17): 7.
Reviews of *Provinces* by Czeslaw Milosz, *Selected Poems* by Derek Mahon, and Heaney's *Seeing Things.* Heaney's question "Where does spirit live?" is given special urgency by the death of his father, whose spirit permeates this volume. The first part of the book is mostly elegaic, as the poet recalls dead friends. The second half consists of the long poem "Squarings"— a sequence of 78 12-line poems—a "visionary poem of memory and supposition."

28 HOSMER, ROBERT. "What We See and Feel and Are," *Southern Review* 28, 2 (April): 431–41.
Review of six collections of poetry including *Seeing Things.* Within the frame of lines from Virgil's *Aeneid* and Dante's *Inferno* Heaney starts on a journey of memory both inward and outward, haunted by his desire to see his father. The three-part title poem deals with seeing what is invisible. The "Squarings" sequence takes the poet to underworlds and other worlds. "Here his voice has the greater depth and resonance of a more assured and mature lyric poet."

29 KERRIGAN, JOHN. "Ulster Ovids," in *The Chosen Ground: Essays on the Contemporary Poetry of Northern Ireland,* edited by Neil Corcoran (Bridgend: Seren Books): 237–69.
Kerrigan described Ovid as a poet of two parts: the Ovid of the sophisticated, pleasure-seeking Roman years; and the Ovid who was banished for a period of exile at Tomis—the poet becoming a victim of his art. The Ovidian strain is apparent in such modernist poets as Eliot, Pound, Williams, Stevens, Yeats, and others. It is also to be found in Northern Ireland writers such as Hewitt, Mahon, Muldoon, Montague, Paulin, Heaney, and Longley. The writers with a Catholic background—Muldoon, Montague, Heaney—know their Latin, and to them Ovid is a familiar figure. For them, too, there is a history of internal and foreign exile because of faith and politics. For the others the concerns are the imperial decline and the seeking of peace from a legacy of war. Heaney, in leaving Northern Ireland for Wicklow, sees himself in *North* as an "inner emigré." The hero of *Sweeney Astray* is an exile in his own country.

30 KIRCHDORFER, ULF. "Animals and Animal Imagery in the Poetry of Elizabeth Bishop and Seamus Heaney." Ph.D.dissertation, Texas Christian University.

    The study shows that animals and animal imagery comprise a significant part of the work of Bishop and Heaney. An examination of the animal aspect of their poetry illuminates the poets' themes, techniques, and achievements as well as limits.

31 LIVINGSTON, JAMES. "Seamus Heaney," in *Critical Survey of Poetry: English Language Series, vol. 3*, revised edition (Pasadena; Englewood Cliffs: Salem Press): 1440–52.

    Livingston surveys Heaney's life and work under various headings. The thrust of the essay is under the "Analysis," in which Livingston discusses each volume of poetry up to and including *The Haw Lantern* (1987). He sees Heaney as being at once parochial and universal. He finds his metres, figures, and textures relatively straightforward, which makes for understandable, approachable poetry. He is, moreover, a master technician who produces a varied music "with echoes of modulated phrase and evocative sound patterns."

    Revised reprint of 1982.11.

32 LLOYD, DAVID. "'Pap for the dispossed': Seamus Heaney and the Poetics of Identity," in *Seamus Heaney: A Collection of Critical Essays*, edited by Elmer Andrews (London: Macmillan): 87–116.

    Reprint of 1985.46.

33 LOGAN, WILLIAM. "Inner Translations," *Poetry* 160, 3 (June): 170–74.

    In his review of *Seeing Things*, Logan finds the volume too self-conscious and lacking the "instinctive or marked or passionate" quality of his pre-*Field Work* writing. In particular, Logan argues that Heaney "is drawn to narrative, but he cannot shape a story with the rude tempo or inevitability of Frost." Consequently, the reviewer describes the poems of "Squarings" as "offhanded and a little desperate."

34 LONGLEY, EDNA. "The Aesthetic and the Territorial," in *Contemporary Irish Poetry: A Collection of Critical Essays*, edited by Elmer Andrews (London: Macmillan): 63–85.

    Longley discusses Heaney's work in relation to that of Michael Longley, Mahon, Muldoon, and Carson, among others. She cites Heaney's "Chekhov on Sakhalin" and refers to *The Government of the Tongue*. She also examines Heaney's construction of place and the limits of some Marxist readings of Irish poetry. In addition, she alludes to the work of MacNeice and Hewitt. There is an interesting aside in which Longley discusses literary magazines at Queen's University Belfast and Trinity College Dublin and "The Group."

35 LUCAS, JOHN. "Seamus Heaney and the Possibilities of Poetry," in *Seamus Heaney: A Collection of Critical Essays*, edited by Elmer Andrews (London: Macmillan): 117–38.

Lucas in this essay—which includes also discussion of Wordsworth, Hewitt, Yeats, Kavanagh, and Paulin—speaks of Heaney's concept of "dwelling." This concept is shaped by a dream of "annealment"—between city and countryside, Protestant and Catholic, male and female, North and South. When Heaney embarked on his writing career, the possibility of such an annealment seemed possible. However, the history of the past twenty years has diminished that optimism. Heaney's poetry is an effort to affirm the dream in the face of the historical reality.

36 McELROY, JAMES. "Poetry," *Los Angeles Times Book Review* (December 27): 6.

Brief review of *Sweeney's Flight*. This is a marriage between image and text in which once more Heaney reminds his readers that the Irish language can still serve to present the natural world.

37 MALLOY, CATHARINE. "Seamus Heaney and His Reader: Orchestrating the Discourses." Ph.D. dissertation, Marquette University.

The various discourses in Seamus Heaney's poetry resonate with the personal, social, ideological, and cultural issues of a specific historical time. Because there is a continuous intrusion of dialogues orchestrated by the speaker, a polyphony of discourses is created. Using Bakhtin's concept of dialogism is one way to interpret Seamus Heaney's poetry. It offers a post-structuralist approach to it that neither confines nor restricts reader or poet.

38 MALLOY, CATHARINE. "Seamus Heaney's 'Station Island': Questioning Orthodoxy and Commitment," *Notes on Modern Irish Literature* 4: 22–26.

Malloy argues that *Station Island,* like much of Heaney's poetry, questions the responsibility of the artist to his art. It is a continuation of his debate with himself. The shades with whom he talks inspire him to question his own artistic consciousness. His last encounter is with the shade of Joyce, who urges him to keep his faith in art and in his poetry to probe "the divine the Dark Mystery."

39 MATTHIAS, JOHN. "Inside History and Outside History: Seamus Heaney, Eavan Boland, and Contemporary Irish Poetry," in *Reading Old Friends: Essays, Reviews, and Poems on Poetics 1975–1990* (Albany: State University of New York Press): 281–94.

Reprint of 1990.43.

1992

40   MURRAY, LES. "A Music of Indirection," in *The Paperback Tree: Selected Prose* (Manchester: Carcanet): 270–73.
        Reprint of 1987.50.

41   NOBLE, TIM. "Prophetic Insights," *The Month* 25 (January): 34.
        In his review of *The Cure at Troy* and of *Seeing Things*, Noble remarks the fact that *Seeing Things* follows so closely on *The Cure at Troy*. Both remind us of Heaney's facility with language, and some of the play's themes reappear in the poems. The change of the play's title from *Philoctetes* to *The Cure at Troy* seems important. Healing involves letting go, and this is what Heaney sets out to do in *Seeing Things*. He discovers the ability to see the child's world with the wonder of the child and the maturity of the adult. The translations from the *Aeneid* and the *Inferno* are re-expression in the same way. Heaney chooses events and re-expresses them in the language of poetry. Going into the past is not difficult; creating a present which looks forward from these memories is a greater challenge.

42   O'BRIEN, PEGGY. "Lough Derg, Europe and Seamus Heaney," *Irish Review* (Winter 92/93): 122–30.
        O'Brien traces Lough Derg's history and significance beyond Irish religious and cultural reference points to its Medieval European counterparts and pagan affinities. The essay discusses the Irish literary treatment of Lough Derg by examining the related works of William Carleton, Sean O'Faolain, Denis Devlin, Patrick Kavanagh, and Seamus Heaney. The author argues that Heaney uses Lough Derg's European heritage as a way of escaping "cultural essentialism." O'Brien, in her reading of "Station Island," asserts that Heaney writes out of his sense of "difference" and separation from the conventional constructions of Lough Derg. Instead of seeing the place as a religious and cultural (that is, pure Irish) center, Heaney imagines "Station Island" as a place of "many identities, none of them fixed." "Station Island" can be read as Heaney's exploration of historical and cultural discontinuity.

43   O'CONNOR, JOHN J. "An Irish Poet Takes a Longer View, Much Longer," *New York Times* (March 17): B1.
        Article on Heaney's TV appearance on "The South Bank Show" (London/Bravo [US]) during which he talked about *Seeing Things* and read from the book.

44   PEACOCK, ALAN. "Mediations: Poet as Translator, Poet as Seer," in *Seamus Heaney: A Collection of Critical Essays*, edited by Elmer Andrews (London: Macmillan): 233–55.
        Peacock argues that *The Cure at Troy* generally was not treated by reviewers in relation to the rest of his work. He further states that the

play is part of Heaney's continuous examination of the situation in Northern Ireland and should be understood as a "coherent development in Heaney's career as a writer." *Seeing Things* is also concerned with the voice of the past. In both works however there is the attempt to find a way to deal with issues arising from loyalties to family and to country.

45 PINSKY, ROBERT. "Poetry in Review," *Yale Review* 80, 1/2 (April): 236–54.
      Heaney's *Seeing Things* is one of four books reviewed in this essay. Pinsky comments upon the familiar "mighty roots" of *Seeing Things*: Heaney's ability to infuse any object with "talismanic force" and the poet's "reverent memory." Heaney's genius, according to Pinsky, lies in his adeptness at involving the heroic in the here and now. He refers to Heaney as a *European* poet.

46 RATINER, STEVEN. "Seamus Heaney: The Words Worth Saying," *Christian Science Monitor* (October 7): 16–17.
      In this interview, Ratiner talks with Heaney primarily about *Seeing Things*. Heaney discovers still new ways of talking about verse, this time in terms of the "justified" line. Heaney also discusses the puzzling relationship between the social and writing self. The poet refers to one his familiar touchstones, T. S. Eliot's concept of the "auditory imagination." Heaney gives a lengthy response regarding the "twelve-liners" in *Seeing Things*. He also talks about his return to Glanmore, the death of his parents, and his new attraction to "sky-place," which "is a kind of mind-place."

47 ROHSLER, CARON. "Features. . . ," *Alternative*, Magdalen College (January 23): 6.
      In this student interview Heaney is asked to respond to a comment by Craig Raine. Some poems by Heaney had been selected for discussion in students' examination papers. Raine had observed that as a result of this Heaney had become "a pig in a bacon factory." Heaney talks about the imaginative and writing processes in terms of "levers." He also talks about how he sees his role as Professor of Poetry at Oxford.

48 RUANE, MICHAEL E. "Seamus Heaney: Poetic Injustice," *Philadelphia Inquirer Magazine* (November 29): 12–14, 30, 32.
      This is a general essay based on conversations with the poet and attendance at a reading at Harvard. Ruane discusses Heaney's early life, his popularity, his physical appearance, his teaching style, his religion, and the Northern Ireland conflict. Ruane describes the poet's life in Ireland and at Harvard and his meetings with Robert Lowell and Helen Vendler.

1992

49 SCHIRMER, GREGORY A. "Seamus Heaney (1939–)," in *British Writers, Supplement II: Kingsley Amis to J. R. R. Tolkien* (New York: Scribner): 267–82.

Schirmer's essay gives the biographical data in some detail. He then proceeds to assess the poetry book by book, ending with *The Haw Lantern*. Throughout he discusses the poet's struggle to come to terms with political reality without compromising his own artistic integrity. Schirmer concludes that at the heart of Heaney's poetry is a faith in his art together with the need to constantly reexamine that faith.

50 *Seamus Heaney: A Collection of Critical Essays*, edited by Elmer Andrews (London: Macmillan; New York: St. Martin's Press). 273 pp.

An anthology of twelve essays which deal with Heaney's entire work. The writers examine a wide variety of aspects of his work. There is an analysis of the poetry as well as the values embodied in his language.

Contents: "Introduction" by Elmer Andrews. "The best way out is always through" by Andrew Waterman. "The Trouble with Seamus" by James Simmons. "'We pine for ceremony': Ritual and Reality in the Poetry of Seamus Heaney, 1965–75" by Maurice Harmon. "'Pap for the dispossessed': Seamus Heaney and the Poetics of Identity" by David Lloyd. "Seamus Heaney and the Possibilities of Poetry" by John Lucas. "Irish Ghosts: 'Station Island'" by Louis Simpson. "'A rich young man leaving everything he had': Poetic Freedom in Seamus Heaney" by Robert Welch. "The Witnessing Eye and the Speaking Tongue" by Terence Brown. "'Holding course': *The Haw Lantern* and Its Place in Heaney's Development" by Michael Allen. "The Spirit's Protest" by Elmer Andrews. "Mediations: Poet as Translator, Poet as Seer" by Alan Peacock.

51 SIMMONS, JAMES. "The Trouble with Seamus," in *Seamus Heaney: A Collection of Critical Essays*, edited by Elmer Andrews (London: Macmillan): 39–66.

Simmons admits to being ill at ease in seeking to understand the great welcome for Heaney's first book *Death of a Naturalist*. Compared with Derek Mahon's first book, *Night Crossing*, it is at a disadvantage. *Door into the Dark* is an improvement, with two successful poems, "Thatcher," and "Requiem for the Croppies." *Wintering Out* has fresh images and an air of maturity; however, his treatment of drama and people "always gets bogged down in descriptions of landscape." In *North,* Heaney does not give "any very profound account of the present Troubles in Northern Ireland." In *Field Work* Simmons finds a good measure of humanity and humour, though Heaney is still "dominated by his tribal pieties." *Station Island* "compounds the early faults." Flann O'Brien does better on Sweeney in his *At Swim Two Birds*. *The Haw Lantern* is a tepid return to old themes. Heaney is a skillful poet, according to Simmons, but he is not to be compared to Yeats or Kavanagh.

52 SIMPSON, LOUIS. "Irish Ghosts: 'Station Island,'" in *Seamus Heaney: A Collection of Critical Essays*, edited by Elmer Andrews (London: Macmillan): 139–49.

Simpson asserts that *Station Island* is about being a poet. The guide is Dante. Simpson deals with the "Station Island" sequence of twelve poems. He poses the question, "Can you only be concerned with poetry when the people around you are engaged in political action?" He finds Heaney defending his stance and refusing to allow politics to take over and make up his mind for him.

53 SMITH, STAN. "The Distance Between: Seamus Heaney," in *The Chosen Ground: Essays on the Contemporary Poetry of Northern Ireland*, edited by Neil Corcoran (Bridgend: Poetry Wales Press; Chester Springs: Dufour Editions, 1992): 35–61.

This essay explores Heaney's *Haw Lantern,* often in terms of issues discussed in *The Government of the Tongue*. The author focuses upon the "middle state" and the "middle voice" of Heaney's spoken and unspoken communications. This study relies upon Donald Davie's *Purity of Diction in English Verse* and upon post-structuralist theories of language.

54 TAYLOR, HENRY. "Heaney 'Seeing Things' as few other poets do," *Washington Times* (March 1): 17.

Taylor finds in *Seeing Things* much of what he has liked in Heaney's work thus far, especially the poet's language, which effectively combines "conversational tone and chiseled inevitability." This could have been a better book, according to Taylor, who finds some of the "Squarings" poems written out of "convenience" and not "necessity."

55 THWAITE, ANTHONY. "The Poet and the Uses of History," *Washington Post Book World* (January 5): 1, 14.

In his review of *Seeing Things,* Thwaite obliquely compares Heaney to Tennyson when describing the Irish poet's collection as "Parnassian"—that is, uninspired. Thwaite wonders if Heaney has come to be a "nine-to-five" poet. He concludes: "I hesitate to call the book a marvel. It is not Heaney writing at the top of his bent."

56 TRIGGS, JEFFERY ALAN. "Hurt into Poetry: The Political Verses of Seamus Heaney and Robert Bly," *New Orleans Review* 19, 3–4 (Fall-Winter): 162–73.

Triggs examines the poetry of Bly and Heaney, and notes their different approaches to the political and social problems of the poet. Both began their

1993

careers writing personal and pastoral poetry, but eventually turned to "poetry of overtly political significance." Though they both remain devoted to the craft of poetry, they write from different traditions. In Heaney's case, unlike that of Bly, the tradition welcomes public stances. While Heaney speaks as a representative of his culture he "has never allowed public utterance sayings to become the *raison d'etre* of his work."

57 WATERMAN, ANDREW. "'The best way out is always through,'" in *Seamus Heaney: A Collection of Critical Essays*, edited by Elmer Andrews (London: Macmillan): 11–38.
    When Heaney was writing his early naturalistic poems, he was unaware of the political upheaval which would challenge his digging. This would take him deeper into and ultimately beyond his rural domain. The transitional collection was *Wintering Out*, an uneven collection in which he is trying out new directions. *North* extended this enterprise, and Heaney shows a vision of Irish history of greater scope than anything in his previous work. In *Field Work,* the tone is elegiac yet celebratory—there is a stepping back from the Northern Ireland problem. Waterman is disappointed in *Station Island,* which he calls "portentous rumination on his role." He finds that while *The Haw Lantern* includes failures in imagination and language, it is an exciting collection: "The poet is entitled to the failures innovation risks."

58 WELCH, ROBERT. "'A rich young man leaving everything he had': Poetic freedom in Seamus Heaney," in *Seamus Heaney: A Collection of Critical Essays*, edited by Elmer Andrews (London: Macmillan): 150–81.
    Welch argues that Heaney is concerned that his poetry should spring from a strong source. From the beginning he is concerned with getting access to tradition, language, self, etc. In the end, he comes to his own place not by the conventional, beaten path but rather by a tortuous and risky journey. He is always ready for, and accepting of, change and challenge.
    Reprinted 1993.35 under title "Seamus Heaney: 'Leaving Everything.'"

1993

1 BATTERSBY, EILEEN. "Live poets' society," *Irish Times* (April 6): 10.
    The article describes the events at the Galway International Poetry and Literature Festival (Cuirt). There is a photo of Heaney and an account of his reading at the festival.

2 BAYLEY, JOHN. "Living in and Living Out," *Contemporary Literary Criticism* 74: 186–88.
    Reprint of 1989.4.

3   BEDFORD, WILLIAM. "The World Turned Upside Down," *Contemporary Literary Criticism*, 74: 188–89.
    Reprint of 1991.6.

4   BRANDES, RAND. "The Scale of Things," *Contemporary Literary Criticism* 74: 1921–95.
    Reprint of 1991.12.

5   BRESLIN, JOHN B. "Vision & Revision: Seamus Heaney's New Poems," *Contemporary Literary Criticism* 74: 197–98.
    Reprint of 1991.14.

6   BYRON, CATHERINE. *Out of Step: Pursuing Seamus Heaney to Purgatory* (Bristol: Loxwood Stoneleigh). 260 pp.
    This book arises from a dissatisfaction with Seamus Heaney and with *Station Island*. Byron makes the pilgrimage to Patrick's Purgatory—Lough Derg—to find out what she missed in Heaney. She offers a strong feminist reading of *Station Island*. She becomes aware of other voices besides Heaney's speaking on religion and politics. The book is part criticism, part autobiography, and part social analysis.

7   COLLINS, FLOYD. "Seamus Heaney: The Crisis of Identity," *Gettysburg Review* 6, 1 (Winter): 140–59.
    In his review of *Selected Poems 1966–1987*, Collins maintains that a certain crisis of identity persists throughout Heaney's career. In his first two works, he draws on images from his childhood connecting literature with the earth. In the following three works, his search for identity is grounded within a cultural and historic framework. In *Field Work, Sweeney Astray, Station Island*, and *The Haw Lantern*, he forges a bond of kinship with the living while he confronts death, at first in *Station Island* and on an intensely personal level in *The Haw Lantern*.

8   CORCORAN, NEIL. "The Poetry of Northern Ireland: Seamus Heaney, Michael Longley, Derek Mahon," in *English Poetry Since 1940* (London: Longman): 180–92.
    In his discussion of the three poets, Corcoran asserts that the publication of Heaney's *Death of a Naturalist* in 1966 ushers in an immense change in the relationship between Irish and English poetry. His poetry and that of Longley and Mahon has to make a case for itself in the face of the violence in Northern Ireland. Heaney's strength lies in the intelligence and energy of the symbols and metaphors which instill his poetry. His work uses a small number of images and symbols to show his own sensibility, as well as the history of Ireland and its people. He also confronts his Northern Ireland experience, not directly but "by refracting it through some exterior or alien material." His

major impact on British and Irish poetry lies in his working a tradition so that it addresses contemporary needs.

9   CORCORAN, NEIL. "From the Frontier of Writing," *Contemporary Literary Criticism* 74: 160–68.
        Reprint of 1987.11.

10   CRAIG, PATRICIA. "Green Spirit of the Hedges," *Honest Ulsterman* 95: 125–27.
        Review of *Sweeney's Flight*. The main section of the book consists of selected poems accompanied by photographs by Rachel Giese. The revised version of *Sweeney Astray* is also here as an appendix. Craig sees the Giese photographs as achieving "a very striking balance between breadth and minuteness of vision, between intricacy and suggestiveness." The photographs are not illustrations to the text; they are, rather, an enhancement of it.

11   DEANE, SEAMUS. "Seamus Heaney: The Timorous & the Bold," *Contemporary Literary Criticism* 74: 156–60.
        Reprint of 1985.22.

12   DOAN, JAMES E. "Recollecting Sweeney," *Irish Literary Supplement* 12, 1 (Spring): 29.
        Doan in his review of *Sweeney's Flight* briefly traces the history of the work, which he sees as reflecting the opposition between the old Irish order and the new Christianity. He comments on the photographs by Rachel Giese, which accompany the text and add subtlety to the work.

13   FENNELL, DESMOND. "Whatever You Say, Say Nothing," in *Heresy: The Battle of Ideas in Modern Ireland* (Belfast: Blackstaff Press): 130–77.
        Reprint of 1991.31; reprinted 1991.30.

14   FOSTER, JOHN WILSON. "The Poetry of Seamus Heaney," in *Colonial Consequences: Essays in Irish Literature and Culture* (Syracuse: Syracuse University Press): 81–96.
        Reprint of 1974.3; reprinted 1976.11; 1985.73; 1991.33.

15   HAMILTON, IAN. "Excusez-moi," *Contemporary Literary Criticism* 74: 170–72.
        Reprint of 1987.24.

16   HILDEBIDLE, JOHN. "A Decade of Seamus Heaney's Poetry," *Contemporary Literary Criticism* 74: 162–70.
        Reprint of 1987.29.

17   HOFMANN, MICHAEL. "Dazzling Philosophy," *Contemporary Literary Criticism* 74: 189–92.
     Reprint of 1991.37.

18   KEARNEY, RICHARD. "Seamus Heaney: Between North and South: Poetic Detours," in *Visions of Europe: Conversations on the Legacy and Future of Europe* (Dublin: Wolfhound Press): 82–89.
     In this interview by Kearney, Heaney comments upon his empathy with the disjointed lives of Eastern European writers. He also talks about the complexities of the European heritage in relation to Ireland, which was in some ways culturally isolated. Holub is discussed at length, as well as some differences between European and American approaches to history and language. Heaney closes with an allusion to Orpheus.

19   KEEN, SUZANNE. "When perfection is openhanded," *Commonweal* 120, 4 (February 26): 26–28.
     Review of *Seeing Things* and of works by Andrew Hudgins and Alan Shapiro. Keen sees the work as carrying the reader on a voyage to investigate the metaphors and purposes of journeying. Heaney's elegies examine the gap between the living and the dead and the difficult return. The second part of the book contrasts things seen with visions discovered.

20   KINZIE, MARY. "Deeper than Declared: On Seamus Heaney," in her *The Cure of Poetry in an Age of Prose* (Chicago: University of Chicago Press): 200–229.
     Reprint of 1988.36.

21   McCLATCHY, J. D. "The Exile's Song," *Contemporary Literary Criticism* 74: 172–75.
     Reprint of 1987.42.

22   MAC DUBHGHAILL, UINSIONN. "Heaney stresses Merriman's place in world literature," *Irish Times* (August 23): 6.
     This is an account of Heaney's address before the Merriman School in Lisdoonvarna, Co. Clare, on August 22, 1993. He deals with the changing interpretations of Merriman's work *Cúirt an Mheán Oiche* (*The Midnight Court*) two hundred years after it was written. These changes reflect the wider changes in Irish society over the past hundred years. Heaney maintains that more attention has been paid to the "sociological freight" of the poem than to its merit as a work of literature. A poet has to give free utterance to the creative vision—a poem is not the kind of message on which political systems are founded.

1993

23   MALLOY, CATHARINE. "Silence as Liberator in Seamus Heaney's 'The
     Underground,'" *Notes on Modern Irish Literature* 5: 19–22.
         Malloy notes that silence in poetic texts can join people and things; it
     can enrich meditation and say more than words can. Hansel and Gretel
     retrace their way home by means of the silently placed stones. The
     Underground shows that silence uncovers other discourses between husband
     and wife.

24   MOLINO, MICHAEL. "Flying by the Nets of Language and Nationality:
     Seamus Heaney, the 'English' Language, and Ulster's Troubles," *Modern
     Philology* 91, 2 (November): 180–201.
         Molino argues that Heaney in his attempt to address the continuing
     problem of violence and repression in Northern Ireland used a vernacular
     poetry. He developed this innovative voice in his poetry between 1968 and
     1972. Molino examines this poetry and assesses some of the poems Heaney
     excluded from *Wintering Out*. He also examines those poems that were
     revised for their appearance in *Wintering Out*. His use of the diversity of Irish-
     English language in *Wintering Out* "explores one method of reinscribing
     Ireland's politics, literature and languages."

25   O'CONNOR, LAURA. "The Circularity of the Autobiographical Form: A
     Study of Seamus Heaney's 'Station Island,'" in *Biography and
     Autobiography: Essays on Irish and Canadian History and Literature*, edited
     by James Noonan (Ottawa: Carleton University Press): 179–86.
         O'Connor argues that Heaney's poetry is predominantly autobiographi-
     cal and inherently circular. *Station Island*, in which confessional poetry is
     emphasized, presents "the circular form of autobiography and the persistent
     recurrence of the circularity motif in Heaney's poetics."

26   PARKER, MICHAEL. "Heaney at Queen's," *Honest Ulsterman* 94
     (January): 99–102.
         Extracts from *Seamus Heaney: The Making of a Poet*, which concern
     Heaney's experiences at Queens University from 1957 to 1961. These
     extracts capture the poet in his "Parnassian" phase. They also include refer-
     ences to Heaney's earliest publications in Queen's literary magazines *Q* and
     Gorgon.

27   PARKER, MICHAEL. *Seamus Heaney: The Making of the Poet*
     (Basingstoke: Macmillan; Iowa City: University of Iowa Press; Dublin:
     Gill and Macmillan). 294 pp.
         In *The Making of the Poet*, Parker reads Heaney's poetry in light of
     extensive biographical information. Parker provides new information drawn
     from several interviews with Heaney's family and friends. Although the book
     examines all of Heaney's volumes up to and including *Seeing Things*,

Parker's most helpful research informs the initial chapters on Heaney's early poetry. There is a substantial section on Heaney at St. Columb's and at Queen's University Belfast. In addition to biographical readings, Parker relies upon psychoanalytic analyses to explore Heaney's work. Unlike other studies of Heaney's work which quote uncritically from *Preoccupations* or *The Government of the Tongue*, Parker draws upon less well-known, often uncollected poems and critical writings to help illuminate the poems and the life.

28 SANDYS, STEPHEN. "Seeing Things: The Visionary Ardor of Seamus Heaney," *Salmagundi* 100 (Fall): 207–25.
    Sandys considers *Seeing Things* in the light of Heaney's twenty-five years as a poet. For Sandys, every theme of Heaney's poetry is worked into this collection. Lyrics of rural memories fill the first half of the volume. In "Squarings," the second half, which Sandys regards as the capstone of the work, the poet faces "perspectives of becoming." Sandys notes three themes in the book as a whole: Heaney's obsession with language; knowing the world of the poet; and the poet's vocation in a disturbed world.

29 SINKLER, REBECCA PEPPER. "Hell Night at the 92d Street Y," *New York Times Book Review* (May 9): 31.
    Sinkler discusses the publication of *The Inferno* (ed. Helper and Merrill), which includes translations by Heaney. She also describes the accompanying reading that took place at the Y.

30 TRACY, ROBERT. "When Hope and History Rhyme," *Contemporary Literary Criticism* 74: 195–96.
    Reprint of 1991.70.

31 VENDLER, HELEN. "A Wounded Man Falling Towards Me," *Contemporary Literary Criticism* 74: 183–86.
    Reprint of 1990.53.

32 VENDLER, HELEN. "On Three Poems by Seamus Heaney," *Contemporary Literary Criticism* 74: 175–77.
    Reprint of 1988.75.

33 WADE, STEPHEN. *More on the Word Hoard: The Work of Seamus Heaney* (Nottingham: Pauper's Press). 132 pp.
    Wade's admittedly subjective readings of Heaney's work, from *Death of a Naturalist* to *The Cure at Troy* and *Seeing Things,* discusses both formal issues, such as Heaney's images, lexicon, and "masks," and issues related to the more abstract and universal components of Heaney's work, such as themes (sacrificial, purgatorial), aesthetic orientations, and philosophical beliefs. Wade's readings of Heaney often discuss the poet in terms of the Romantic

1993

tradition and rely upon early reviews of Heaney's books as reference points for Wade's own evaluations. Wade argues that Heaney's "true achievement. . .is mainly in his concern for equal insight into moral responsibility and a proper relation to society, in both life and art."

Included is a reprint of 1989.54, which is published under title "Self-Knowledge and Pastures New: The 'Station Island' Sequence."

34   WATSON, GEORGE. "A dandy strut disturbed by sudden pistol shots," *Independent* (July 31): 29.

In the course of an essay on writers inspired by the conflict in Northern Ireland, Watson remarks that Heaney, while rejecting the role of "spokesman for the tribe," yet senses that the writer should bear witness. Heaney's insistence on the reality of tradition and identity has set him at odds with those of the Irish critics who "espouse pluralism and fluidity."

35   WELCH, ROBERT. "Seamus Heaney: 'Leaving Everything,'" *Changing States: Transformations in Modern Irish Writing* (London: Routledge): 241–69.

Reprint of 1992.58.

Index